Data Architecture

Data Architecture
From Zen to Reality

Charles D. Tupper

AMSTERDAM • BOSTON • HEIDELBERG • LONDON
NEW YORK • OXFORD • PARIS • SAN DIEGO
SAN FRANCISCO SINGAPORE • SYDNEY • TOKYO
Morgan Kaufmann Publishers is an imprint of Elsevier

Acquiring Editor: Jenifer Niles
Development Editor: David Bevans
Project Manager: Danielle S. Miller
Designer: Alisa Andreola

Morgan Kaufmann is an imprint of Elsevier
30 Corporate Drive, Suite 400, Burlington, MA 01803, USA

Library of Congress Cataloging-in-Publication Data
Tupper, Charles.
 Data architecture : from zen to reality / Charles Tupper.
    p. cm.
 Includes bibliographical references and index.
 ISBN 978-0-12-385126-0 (pbk.)
 1. Data structures (Computer science) 2. Software architecture. I. Title.
 QA76.9.D35T85 2011
 005.1'2—dc22   2010049600

British Library Cataloguing-in-Publication Data
A catalogue record for this book is available from the British Library.

ISBN: 978-0-12-385126-0

For information on all MK publications visit our website at www.mkp.com

Dedications

I dedicate this book to Carol Ann Dawes, for her profound friendship and endless belief in me; to my wife, who has unwaveringly supported me in this endeavor; and most of all, to my friend and mentor, Richard Yevich (may you rest in peace), for without his trust and faith in me, this would never have happened.

Wherever you are, Richard, I hope you are smiling because, yes, it's finally done.

CONTENTS

Chapter 3   Enterprise-Level Data Architecture Practices **57**

Chapter 4   Understanding Development Methodologies **75**

SECTION 2   THE PROBLEM

Chapter 5   Business Evolution **95**

Chapter 6   Business Organizations **117**

SECTION 3   THE PROCESS

SECTION 4   THE PRODUCT

Chapter 13   Concepts of Clustering, Indexing, and Structures 241

SECTION 5   SPECIALIZED DATABASES

Chapter 17   Data Warehouses I **309**

PREFACE

First, note that I have used *Zen* in the title of this book. I have been asked many times why I used such an esoteric term. After all, what is the meaning of Zen? To clarify the meaning of Zen, we must examine the philosophical environment that gave rise to Zen: Indian and Chinese philosophies. In India, Buddhism arose out of a Hindu environment, and later one form called Mahayana evolved. Taoism, a philosophy that also contributed much to Zen, was developed in China.

It was in China where imported Mahayana Buddhist ideas fused with existing Taoist ideas to form what was later called Zen. Concepts that are typically attributed to Mahayana Buddhism and Taoism are integral parts of Zen thought. These concepts helped me in my choice for the title.

Zen is a philosophy, a religion, a psychology, and a way of life, but these are interpretations of Zen. It is said that Zen is complex and contradictory but remarkably simple; that Zen is empty and void but remarkably full and delightful. Simply put, Zen is a way of being. It also is a state of mind. Zen involves dropping illusion and seeing things without distortion created by your own perceptions.

Words and concepts can be useful, but mistaking them for reality can cause many problems. Concepts about reality are not reality. The menu is not the food. In order to experience Zen, one needs to dissolve all preconceptions, beliefs, concepts, and judgments about the self and the universe and see the *now*.

So what is Zen? Zen simply *is*. Often it seems that the search for Zen's meaning reveals nothing but contradictions. Any realization of truth seems impossible. Yet, Zen has a unique way of pointing at the "thatness" of everything. Zen brings us face to face with the true original nature of things, undefiled by cultural conditioning and neurotic tendencies.

When this is applied to data, it simply means that data *is*. It exists in its own state, without our perspectives and views of it. It has a now and a whatness of existence. So it is this "presence or oneness" of data that we begin with and move toward discrete interpretations of how it can be shaped, molded, viewed, illustrated, structured, and understood. It is with this in mind that the book is titled *Data Architecture: From Zen to Perceived Reality*.

I wrote this book because something has been fundamentally lost in the last decade in the information technology world. We are no longer developing information stores that address the present and future needs; we are merely generating information stores that meet the current needs.

Like everything else over the last 15 to 20 years, new products are being designed from a tactical point of view with built-in obsolescence. There is no long-term view, no strategy, without which it is impossible to develop data stores that are built to last. It is time to revisit the basic principles from which we deviated to get to this point.

Instead of the evolution that was prophesied in the 1970s and early 1980s, what happened instead was a revolution where many good things were lost and destroyed at the expense of developing things rapidly and at low cost. This is not a polemic against what has occurred in the last 10 to 15 years but merely a commentary and observational review of some of the basic principles that were the basis of the initial evolution.

It is time to revisit those principles and try to rescue and reinstate some of those values to validate our course in building proper data architectures that will stand the test of time. It is also time to review many of the principles posited by Peter Drucker concerning the knowledge workers that interact with those data architectures.

You see, the evolution started with a basic principle that knowledge is created from data by people for people to use for the greater good of all people. Modern business has somehow drifted away from people and quality and is now focused on money and speed. On a more specific note, this book's goal is to raise the awareness of the single most ignored component of the original evolution in the IT world: architecture.

Architecture—the method of design and planning things before they are constructed—is being overlooked or bypassed in the haste to develop and deliver the product. The focus has shifted from the *process* to the *product*. The quality, and even the quantity, doesn't appear to matter anymore as long as the product gets out and the delivery time is short. This short delivery time, dovetailed with built-in obsolescence, is leading the inroads to the explosion of consumerism. With the advent of the rampant consumerism comes the downfall of the principles of building things to last.

The focus in recent times has been on how fast "it" can be done without defining what "it" is. A plan is nothing without an architecture or strategy behind it. Would you hire 37 carpenters to build a house with no blueprints? You would probably end up with a house with ten bedrooms, three kitchens, and no bathrooms.

Without architecture, there is chaos. To quote John Zachman in the preface to his newest E-book:

If you get really honest and search all of history, seven thousand years of known history of humankind, to find out how humanity has learned to cope with two things, complexity and change, there is one game in town: ARCHITECTURE.

If it (whatever it is) gets so complex you can't remember everything all at one time, you have to write it down … ARCHITECTURE. Then if you want to change it (whatever it is), you go to what you wrote down … ARCHITECTURE.

How do you think they build hundred-story buildings or Boeing 747's, or IBM supercomputers … or even simple things like a one-bedroom house or a Piper Cub or the PC on your desk? Somebody had to write it down … at excruciating levels of detail … ARCHITECTURE. Now, if you want to change any of those things (with minimum time, disruption, and cost), how do you change them? You go to what you wrote down … ARCHITECTURE. The key to complexity and change is ARCHITECTURE.

The understanding of the overall structure is necessary if the goal is to be achieved. Too often we are trying to deliver the product and we set up metrics to find out why things are too slow. And too often the metrics involved become more important than the progress they are intended to measure.

More often the goal actually gets lost in the frenzy to ensure accurate metrics. In order to ensure a lasting artifact or construct, a methodology must be followed. It doesn't matter what the methodology is as long as it begins with the conceptual or strategic, moves downward and broadens to the design level, goes through a preconstruction assessment process, and then broadens again at the construction or implementation level.

At each level, the work products need to be mapped against the matrix or the environment in which it will function. This is done in order to ensure that there will be no disjoints as the effort is expanded with each level of development. With the utilization of a methodology comes the delivery of the artifacts that are so desperately needed.

These are the policies, plans, guidelines, metrics, and structures that allow the design to be modeled and evaluated to some degree before construction. Along with these artifacts are the organizational structures and separation of responsibilities that ensure balanced and efficient products to the software development process. When the software process develops efficient and extensible mechanisms that guide and control the business process, the result is a smoother-running organization that creates its product more cost effectively. Moreover, the organization is in a better position to deal with market pressures and changes.

The book itself is divided into four sections, with a fifth section that covers specialty databases. The first four sections are The Principles, The Problems, The Process, and The Product. Each section consists of four chapters that cover associated problems within that subject area.

The Principles section covers the data architecture and data design principles that are necessary to reintroduce architecture into the business and software development process. The Problems section deals with the business and organizational issues of modern businesses and how structured and architected approaches may help them remain flexible and responsive. The Process section deals with the software application development process and defines some tools, techniques, and methods that ensure repeatable results in software development. The Product section deals with the artifact results of the process and how and what can be done with the output products to make them more efficient in the real-world environments. The fifth section, which covers specialty databases, deals with different database issues that have arisen in the business data processing environment. These include data warehousing, objects and objects relational databases, and distributed databases.

The book was written at a conceptual level and can also serve as an index to other works that would provide more detail. It was designed to educate those in business management who are involved with corporate data issues and information technology decisions. It is also structured enough to serve as a text to those in a higher-level education process who will be involved in data or information technology management.

I hope this book helps to channel the chaotic and sometimes frenetic activity in modern business today. Using architected and methodological approaches will produce better business organizations. Better business organizations will retain and leverage their data while producing better applications more cost effectively. Cost-effective businesses produce better products more efficiently, thereby increasing their profit margin. If done properly, there will be more profit, less waste, and a happier workforce. I hope you enjoy reading this book and finding growth in the process.

1

THE PRINCIPLES

1

UNDERSTANDING ARCHITECTURAL PRINCIPLES

Defining Architecture

ar·chi·tect (är'ki-tekt') n. (Abbr. arch., archt.)

1. One who designs and supervises the construction of buildings or other large structures.
2. One who plans or devises: The United States is considered to be the chief architect of the economic recovery of the Middle East.

The word "architect" is of Greek origin and is composed of two roots: arch and tect. Arch means "primary," "primitive," or "coming before," and tect means "make" or "come into being." Thus, when the two roots are combined to form the word "architectos," it can mean "coming before" + "come into being." Using these multiple meanings, we can figure out the definitions of architect and architecture. A good working definition of architecture would be "a primitive plan" or "a plan before construction." This definition captures the essence of it: Architecture is an analytical effort that is created prior to the occurrence of any real construction activity. It is the abstracted framework or outline that provides guidelines for the construction from the beginning to the end.

The discussion of architecture is interesting both from the point of its expansive concepts to its detailed specificity at the point of physical implementation. The following is an excerpt from an Information Architecture course (that ultimately never came to fruition) that speaks to the concept requirements:

> The object of this course is to lead to an understanding and application of the principles of design—particularly architectural design. The fundamental purpose of architectural design is illuminated by the logic of the process of design: target, options, concepts, actions, and completion. Exploring the design process integrates both the physical and nonphysical requirements and influences; the measure of human processes and the collective

events of many processes; the social and cultural influences operating in such processes; and the meaning of information extensions, directions, order, and closure.

The importance of the relationship between human processes and the information environment is introduced with an emphasis upon construction of information models. Composition, especially the theory of wholes and parts, is examined in the light of structural reusability, continuity, and change—principles and conditions applicable either to a single business process or, in a much wider context, to the task of capturing an entire enterprise into its business environment.

Architecture is an ancient skill that has been practiced by visionaries since the prehominids decided to create and build shelters to cope (interface) with the chaotic life patterns of their natural world. A primitive designer probably had the same level of respect in his tribe as the shaman (if they were not one in the same). As humanity evolved, these special individuals carried forward the inherent principles or patterns that had proven successful in their evolution. Knowledge of structures and the patterns and mechanisms of building was accumulated and passed on—and on and on. This process of handing down skills and patterns hastened the development of communication.

What would happen if a primitive hut builder created a very radical design? Most likely, no one would accept the structure unless the designer communicated the advantages of the new design to the tribe. Additionally, when the primitive designer/builder started his effort, he just had to create a few huts. As tribal growth occurred, there was much more work to design and lay out the groundwork for many huts and meeting places in addition to creating the huts.

These habitation structures had to be made to interface with and take advantage of the natural background and environment. The designer/builder's input to the site selection of camping grounds became critical. He became an integral asset to the tribe's survival. Just as the designer/builder had to keep learning to construct and maintain the structures out of local materials, he had to accumulate and retain the knowledge he had gained to be passed on to future primitive architects.

All along the way there was a continual implementation of what knowledge had been accumulated up to that point, and, more important, that knowledge was made public. It would not be kept private or restricted because the tribe's livelihood rested on the designer/builder's integrity. The design had to be understood and accepted by the entire tribe and had to be depended on for the tribe's survival. At each level appropriate knowledge was imparted to those concerned.

The individuals in the tribe were educated in the best techniques. This skill sharing allowed more growth and stability. Implementation had provided a new plateau to build on. As the tribes were educated, all of the members learned the skills necessary to build and keep the structure intact. Adaptations had to be made for the differences in environment. Some of the designs had to be ultimately flexible, while others had to be extremely stable and less flexible. Evolution of designs became more complex and more important to the survival of the whole tribe. The adaptability of the designs became an important feature of the designs and was therefore included in the saved information. These codes of construction and site selection became, after a millennium, building codes. This body of principles and logic used in designing for those codes would ultimately be called "architecture."

These individuals were astute at recognizing patterns in the real world around them. The strength of a wood and grass wattle hut wasn't as great as a cave's, but it served the same purpose: it kept them safe from the elements. After all, caves wouldn't be available everywhere they went, so such natural shelters were at a premium and often had to be competed for. Primitive hut designers realized that a hut could be built in the same design as a cave—tall in the middle and low at the sides for storage room and sleeping. Fire could be put at the mouth of the hut or outside with the heat reflected in, or, better yet, heated stones from the fire could be rolled into the hut to radiate warmth.

Situating the construction on a higher foundation isolated it from the ravages of heavy rains. Building it on the sheltered side of a hill kept cold winter blasts from chilling the inhabitants and also protected the fire. They also learned to build these shelters close to water and plentiful sources of game. In essence they adapted the housing to the environment, being respectful of it and integrating the structure with as many natural principles as possible.

Pattern recognition and pattern use are embedded in the principles of early humankind's existence, so the use of architectural principles is quite ancient. While it may have had different names through the ages, and its practitioners had different labels, the principles are the same: Plan before you build, and design with the user in mind. Integrate the plan into the environment where it will be situated.

These are the same principles that prompted the first individual of vision to step out of the cave and find a way to bring it along with him as he moved around to follow food. He had the responsibility of defining a working structure and method, showing and convincing others that the structure and method were feasible, and, finally, ensuring that the structure and method would be reusable in spite of the local environmental conditions. All of these concepts and his ability to perceive the patterns where they could best be implemented led to humankind's success and adaptation.

Obviously, we no longer have to worry about building safe habitats for cave dwellers. They already did that themselves. But we learned things along the way. And the primitive art and science of architecture evolved from simple tribal housing to providing a place for the very essence of cultures. Architecture and its principles have burgeoned and expanded to include all parts of the fabric of today's society.

Design Problems

The design process is unique, and it is easy to see that the goal of the design process is a solution. So this all seems very simple, but unfortunately, this is not the case. As we have already discussed, the real crux of design is defining the problem in the context in which it must be resolved. The contextual analysis is the hard part. In a true design process, the work area must first be defined and delineated from the context it is in. Whether it is a problem or opportunity, it needs to be separated from the matrix in which it exists. If the matrix or context is dynamic, however, the problem area is dynamic as well.

The design solution ends up being a balancing of the solution to the forces defining the problem's boundaries. It becomes an integral fit and, if constructed properly, will adjust to the context in which it exists. Take a simple problem like building a mechanical device. The forces in play are economy (or the cost of the components), performance (both of the product itself and of the ability to create the product), simplicity (the more components involved, the more complex the building process), and interfit (assembling the components to create the product).

Material handling studies indicate that the fewer the types of material used, the faster assembly will be, so simplicity is important. This will conflict with the performance force because we know that using the best material for each part will make the product last longer. The performance may affect the interfit force vector, since the materials chosen for the best performance may require more effort to assemble than simpler, less functional materials. All of these force vectors affect economy because they all impact the price of the item in some way. It is the balancing of

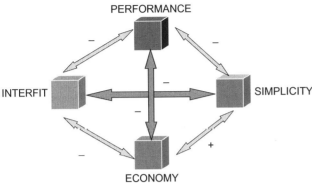

PERFORMANCE

INTERFIT

SIMPLICITY

ECONOMY

Assign a value based on interaction and it will provide
the quadrant for best delivery

Figure 1.1 Forces on a design problem.

these forces that determines the solution. Figure 1.1 shows how the resolution can be reached. By assigning a positive or negative quality to the interaction among these forces, we can come up with a simple solution depending on the product's purpose.

We have chosen economy as our driving force, so we can see that a positive relationship exists between simplicity and economy. Based on this, we can apply whatever performance and complexity choices we want as long as they remain in that quadrant. If assembly was primary and simplicity was secondary, then balancing would be in that quadrant, with the resulting solution not being as economical as might be desired.

While this is an extremely simple visual display of a complex set of interactions, in the end it is the balancing of those dynamic forces at work in the context of the problem/solution area that will provide the optimum solution. Simply put, the problem area cannot be removed from its context because it is a part of the context of the whole and is defined by the dynamic forces working on it in that context. How, then, are problems addressed in an architectural manner? The answer is, by using patterns and pattern interactions.

Patterns and Pattern Usage

What is a pattern? Christopher Alexander (1979) is an architect who processes at a high level of abstraction. He has revolutionized many spheres of thought by his presentation of intuited principles. These principles unify many efforts and disciplines through art, architecture, and science. Included in these are "scientific art" or "artistic science of information architecture and design." He embodied these principles in a philosophy of architecture, which involves patterns and pattern usage. In his book *The Timeless Way of Building,* he described the characteristics of architectural patterns as follows:

> *Each pattern is a three-part rule, which expresses a relation between a certain context, a problem, and a solution. As an element in the world, each pattern is a relationship between a certain context, a certain system of forces that occurs repeatedly in that context, and a certain spatial configuration, which allows these forces to resolve themselves. As an element of language, a pattern is an instruction, which shows how this spatial configuration can be used, over and over again, to resolve the given system of forces, wherever the context makes it relevant. The pattern is, in short, at the same time: a thing, which happens in the world, and the rule which tells us how to create that thing, and when we must create it. It is both a process and a thing—both a description of a thing which is alive and a description of the process which will generate that thing.*

Concepts for Pattern Usage

While the concepts behind the Alexander principles may seem mystical and far removed from information structures, they work for precisely that reason. They are so abstracted as to be general enough to define the common truths and rules of interaction about anything, including data and information. They reflect the essence of the inherent patterns of the data. The paradigm that Alexander propounds is that anything built or constructed is based on three concepts that he calls The Quality, The Gate, and The Timeless Way. We'll look at each briefly.

The Quality

The Quality is created when the attributes in the design make that design "live"—that is, designs that are flexible, extensible, adaptable, and reusable and have other qualities of living things, except, of course, self-reproduction and metabolism. What Alexander is saying is that the characteristics of some designs make them more responsive to change than other designs. By being in harmony with their environment, they become responsive to the changes in that environment.

The Gate

The Gate is the common pattern language (CPL), which is the universal network of patterns and pattern relationships contained within the planner, the builder, the user, and the environment in which the building will take place. It is a multi-dimensional model that involves all of the forces shaping the architectural structure in the area where it will be built.

A pattern language for a specific architectural structure is chosen by the designer from the overall CPL. Whether the target architectural structure is simple or complex, it is critical that the chosen language be functionally complete (it must address the needs of all involved). The value of simple patterns cannot be underestimated; without them, integrated common pattern languages would not exist. The Gate is a mechanism, a door if you will, by which Alexander's quality is achieved. It simply means that the set of chosen interactions within an individual design have been defined and formalized specifically for that design.

The Way

According to Alexander, pattern languages are applied using The Way. That is, they are applied one pattern at a time to successively evolve an initial architecture and unfold it into a "live design," or said in Alexander's words, a design with "The Quality." This is simply stated as serially building up the master pattern and common pattern language over time by the integration of the individual patterns and their individual pattern languages. The initial way of doing this is to focus on the generic centers with the problem areas, developing clusters and defining their interactions and relationships. Subsequent to this, each pattern that is integrated makes more explicit, or "flowers," the previous design by amplification and extension. With each cycle of integration, more and more definition is reached until the problem areas coalesce out of the seeming chaos. In data architecture, the parallel would be the integration of business views to understand and compile the use cases and process paths for a model.

Alexander also added some additional complementary concepts to this paradigm to ensure that architectures are created with The Quality. These are universal recursive properties, centers, and structure preserving transformations. I will endeavor to simplify these somewhat.

Universal Recursive Properties

Alexander describes these properties as "measurable" properties of living things that also have an aesthetic appeal. He identified these "universal" recursive properties in the structures of buildings over the last 10-plus years. The recursive aspect is unique in that it encourages the self-referencing feedback that allows further definitional evolution to occur. This is the way the amplification and extension of the pattern languages and designs occur.

While this may seem highly abstracted, it is merely stating that a feedback mechanism within a design is necessary to ensure that the design stays alive and responsive to changes that may occur in its environment.

Centers

As we have seen, centers are the loci of the preceding recursive properties. Without these loci, the integration of the patterns and designs is not possible. They act as reference points and overlay points during the integration process. Alexander found that structures that have the characteristics of living things have centers. In data architecture, we would call these entity cluster areas within a business "subject areas."

Structure-Preserving Transformations

Alexander describes these transformations as those that preserve the preceding universal properties. As such, we may recursively differentiate a "whole" preserving these properties and generating "centers" surrounded by the recursive properties. This allows us to extract a specific design as a copy of the whole and then customize it for the specifics needed. It also allows the existence of the whole to live alongside or nested above it. By preserving the essential nature of the structure, it can share this essence as a child or a clone of the original.

In data architecture this is represented by the subject area mapping within and the enterprise architecture that can allow specific models to be generated from and reconciled back to the enterprise model. Every entity in creation has an architectural template whether or not it is seen or acknowledged. This is the pattern by which it was developed and is maintained. In living things it is DNA sequences, and in other creations it is composed of other building blocks. It is the same in data processing, although it might not seem so.

Principle

An architecture is the response to the integrated collections of models and views within the problem area being examined.

Sometimes the underlying architecture appears to depend on the chaos theory and produces a chaotic environment and system. As a result, sometimes the application gets built, and sometimes it is abandoned.

Over the last 30 years of information systems design and implementation, the author observed that you can build information systems without architectures. You will also build the same system again and again and again, improving it each time until in effect you have created the correct architecture over time. However, it is more cost-effective and efficient to build quality systems using an architectural approach from the beginning.

Information Architecture

in·for·ma·tion (in'fər-ma'shən) n. (Abbr. inf.)
Knowledge derived from study, experience, or instruction. Knowledge of a specific event or situation; intelligence. See synonyms at knowledge. A collection of facts or data; statistical information. The act of informing or the condition of being informed; communication of knowledge. Example: Safety instructions are provided for the information of our passengers.

Therefore, if we combine the definitions of architecture and information, we get "one who designs and supervises the construction of knowledge derived from study, experience, or instruction, or knowledge of a specific event or situation, or a collection of facts or data." The information architect's job is to define the nature and scope of an information service before the first line of code is put into place. Information architecture is the plan for the data, much like an architect's drawing.

Today, people in the business world are mired in data—data that is collected, saved, split, spliced, spindled, folded, and mutilated to create useful information. When the data are read, they supply the information the reader is seeking. Once this information is gathered and controlled, however, the user must retain it as he or she gathers more information. And to complicate things even further, the user must be taught how to use the information. That is the real challenge!

How can we structure not only the data but also the gleaned information so that it will make a difference? It is imperative for us to structure and keep the data because it may be needed later to derive a different set of information. The user needs to understand what is being saved and why.

Knowledge workers want to find the necessary information, understand it, use it to solve their problems, and get on with the rest of their daily business. They interact with information daily.

In order to complete their tasks, they need to find answers to questions, complete forms, access data, find specific numbers, and learn about products and services. All of this requires some form of data structure to allow them to complete their tasks.

Organizations are always seeking ways to improve productivity and quality. It is easy to apply metrics to a structure that is known and understood. They don't want to waste resources on poorly architected structures and processes that are difficult to maintain. Not only does it waste resources, but the solutions created are often obsolete before they are completed. Interested parties in the data processing industry estimate that 80 percent of the cost of an application process is the cost of maintenance. Changes to poorly architected structures and processes take longer, and often changes that are implemented to these structures feel arbitrary and haphazard. Structures and processes without solid, extendable information architecture require and entail more levels of decisions, approvals, and political battles. Simply put, it is easier and cheaper in the long run to do it correctly. The correct way is to analyze and then implement, not the other way around.

Structure Works!

Information architecture gives meaning to the mass of unrelated needs, words, and pictures and fits them together so it can be used. The skill is in the knowledge of framing and structuring the data. Organizations need people who can extract information from those who have it, put this information in a structured form, and maintain or refine it over time. The people who are able to do this are the architects of that business's information. Modern business strategists believe that organizations that can manage layers of knowledge (processes, procedures, technologies, messages, figures, experience) in a "living design" mode as defined by Alexander can maintain a competitive edge.

As just mentioned, today's corporations seek to employ architecture as a way of organizing their current business solution complexities and chaotic technology environments. Most corporations have had a track record of failed and unintegrated efforts that have resulted in their inability to produce business solutions in a rapid, cost-effective manner. So they try to enforce architecture as a blanket over the problem areas. This leads to further chaos, as increasing manpower and money are expended on integrating the disintegrated environment.

This is kind of like trying to drain a swamp while fighting off the alligators that have taken up residence. Trying to change

Principle

Analyzing and defining an area must be done prior to doing any activity within that area. Without understanding all that must be done, incorrect assumptions can be reached. Short-term vision may handicap future development. Inappropriate scoping may produce artificial boundaries where there should be none.

things in the middle of a process is seldom successful. It is far better to understand what management plans to use the swampland for, survey and chart it, drain the swamp (making it uninhabitable for alligators), and prepare a map of the newly revealed obstacles.

Architecture is the embodiment of the philosophy that requires the analysis of the area of focus prior to any activity within that area. This ensures that the expense is minimized and the project can be scrapped if it is deemed impossible, too expensive, or a little of both. Architectures require that everyone concerned in the analysis, design, and construction must utilize the same set of reference materials and frameworks for making decisions. These reference materials and decision frameworks are generally specified in principles, guidelines, policies, or standards.

Many feel that once the principles, policies, guidelines, and standards have been defined for a given architecture, some level of inflexibility has been introduced. In truth, some standards are somewhat rigid. More flexibility is gained by using principles, policies, and guidelines that allow for the specification of exceptions or limits of acceptability. (Ambiguity is less acceptable when building an organizational infrastructure than when describing approaches to creating architectures.) When a proper architecture with its attending reference structure of policies, principles, guidelines, and standards is in place, development takes place in an environment that is free of impediments. In addition, the resulting applications will integrate and coordinate more efficiently. The architecture itself becomes at this point extensible, allowing further definition and design to take place.

Architectures evolve through this process of refinement and extension. In many cases general rules are made specific as needed to resolve business problems. Therefore, even if the initial architecture is flexible, over time it may acquire many of the characteristics of a rulebook if not kept viable by constant vigilance and maintenance.

Alternatives to the architecture approach are constantly being sought because of the evolution in both software and hardware that is accelerating with time. In this rapidly changing

Principle

Using architecture leads to foundational stability, not rigidity. As long as the appropriate characteristics are in place to ensure positive architectural evolution, the architecture will remain a living construct.

Principle

Well-developed architectures are frameworks that evolve as the business evolves.

environment, architecture may appear to be a roadblock to rapid business decisions and solutions, but this is not the case. Architecture provides guidelines and frameworks by which these decisions can be made more easily, since an "inventory" of what already exists is available. It is also true, however, that architecture precludes trial-and-error processes and experimental discovery. This is no more evident than in the object-oriented paradigm. However, we must learn a lesson here: just as trial and error and experimentation belong in the lab for discovery purposes, a plan must exist for development outside the laboratory to allow common understanding and coordinated development to take place.

This is where Alexander's principles can be applied. By retaining the essence of the initial pattern and framework, the whole may be retained while it is allowed to evolve to solve a business problem. The technique that each corporation must learn is that its architectures must remain living organisms that evolve with the business need. Neglecting this, the architecture will grow old and inflexible and eventually die.

Problems in Architecture

If architectures are the solution to the common design and construction problems that currently exist, why aren't they more prevalent? In some cases, the question is, why didn't they work? If there are problems or pitfalls with the architect approach, what can be done to remedy the problems or avoid the failings?

As we see it, there are three basic problems that must be addressed with today's architectures:

1. In most corporations, a poor correlation exists between architectures and the day-to-day business of information system development. This is common in newly implemented

architectures because most developers cannot adapt to changes midstream, but this flaw can also be observed in established architectures when the architecture itself is not supported by management and therefore is bypassed and avoided by the developers. When the architecture is implemented, the feasibility and utility of the architecture will be determined after it has been in use for a while. Much like sailing a boat across a lake on a windy day, many tacks must be made to get to the other side. A problem arises, however, if the architecture continues to remain unlearned and unused. Then it will become an alien rigid mechanism that will require massive amounts of pressure from management to force the use of it.

In the second instance, the established architecture is viewed as too "ambiguous" or "pie-in-the-sky" and therefore is of no use in the day-to-day effort at the detail level. Often the developer realizes much too late that the success of the project is most often achieved on the planning table and the construction and implementation work is merely the execution of the plan.

2. The architectures today are both top-down in nature and nondistributive in focus. Too often "analysis paralysis" takes place, and the concept of requirements collection is overemphasized to the detriment of the project. It is a fact that the more time spent in analysis, the shorter the time spent in development. However, one can get caught in an analysis trap and go beyond the scope or boundary that had been established. Care must be taken not to do this. Additionally, there is the problem of the moving framework. Architecture must have some fluidity to remain viable. The top-down approach to architecture best accomplishes this, but time and over-analysis can produce a rigid structure that cannot adjust easily to change. When we define a target structure in any level of specification or detail, we limit the options that can be used to implement it. In most cases these are constructive boundaries, but they still limit the possible solutions to the implementation. As policies are interpreted to standards and procedures and the resulting structures become embedded in applications, the cost of changing a standard or policy increases. Because of the cost of changing the standards and policies, the architecture can become stiff and unused. In the long term, if not watched carefully, the atrophied, prematurely aged architecture is often defended as the status quo, even though its viability has expired. The result is that radical solutions must be taken to reenergize the development process. Again, by following Alexander's principles, organizations can

deal with these problems by allowing and promoting shared centers and clusters. The principles, policies, and standards associated with these can develop and unfold just as the design does as it evolves.

3. Some of the problems today have a great deal to do with the architects themselves. In addition to the overanalysis previously mentioned, in many cases the architect did not scope the business problem appropriately, and the result is the "investigative" architecture that grows as each extended data and process path is followed to its conclusion. The result of this is an overall architecture that is doomed to fail, primarily because the time and effort expended captured an out-of-scope requirement at a time when it was ill defined. This also leads to the elimination of the possibility of adding purchased packages to the software inventory by measuring and assessing the packages using inappropriate and poorly defined requirements. When out-of-scope requirements are used to select software packages, the packages don't meet the business needs. Also, the effort often ends up with a new definition for the enterprise universe, which should not happen.

All of these problems can be ameliorated by having a strong enterprise architecture and a model-driven development methodology (which we will cover later in the book). Enterprise architectures must follow a different set of rules and remain at a higher level of abstraction in order to provide the seeding necessary for other lower-level models. Alexander's principles apply here, too. By following the approaches that encourage the definition of the centers and clusters of the business, the enterprise architecture becomes almost a by-product of the process. Using this enterprise architecture allows the essence of the enterprise's business to be captured, and yet development can flourish to unfold and blossom the overall architecture with each successive individual implementation.

Architectural Solutions

Individual development architectures are intended to limit choices. By doing this, they can be used to guide manpower and

Practice

Make architecture work by placing the responsibility for the solution in the hands of the key stakeholders. They are responsible for making the architecture live.

development efforts down planned pathways to achieve target goals. In this manner they also achieve repeatable results.

The key to making an individual architecture work is placing the responsibility for the solution in the hands of the key stakeholders. The architect in this scenario is the technical assistant to the decision-making process. The resulting solutions should be reviewed and reassessed over time. The architect must continue to understand the implementation, provide technical knowledge, and facilitate data conflicts.

Such a pivotal person, however, can face many pitfalls. Architects by nature have the ability to see the concept or abstraction by distancing themselves from the details. At the same time, good architects can discuss a detail's impact on the whole because they have a clear understanding of the whole as well as an ability to descend to the level of detail necessary to understand the problem. If they are too distant from the work, they will alienate the business community and miss the real requirements. If they are too close, they will misinterpret some requirements and miss others completely. The best option to pursue is to ensure that the individual architecture deliverables are specific, well understood, and treated as milestones in the development process rather than documentation requirements. A well-husbanded architecture will make the design live.

Architectures must be viewed as living, breathing mechanisms that are dynamic in their growth based on the changes in the environment. They should be utilized more as frameworks to build within rather than a strict code of adherence during construction, and the output should be viewed more as an artifact of the process than a fixed set of documentation that must be produced. They must wed the information and process requirements together in a structure that facilitates the business function. One school of thought emphasizes this premise.

The "Form Follows Function" Concept

Nobody knows for sure who first proclaimed, "Form follows function." Most historians believe it was Horatio Greenough, and all agree that Louis Sullivan, the master architect of the American skyscraper of the late nineteenth and early twentieth centuries, made it his slogan, though not entirely his guideline. In any event, "form follows function," or functionalism, became the prime tenet of the modern movement of architecture from its inception.

Form follows function is a good idea—the belief that practicality and common sense engender good design principles. But this must be examined in a little more detail because it can be misconstrued if taken at the simplest, highest level. Unfortunately, too many people in the world of architecture, including data architecture, have tried to make the form fit the function rather than just design by the inherent characteristics of the form and let the functions be captured as they evolve.

The form, or the coalesced inherent characteristics of something, allows it to perform some functions well and others poorly. A brick makes excellent building material, yet when used as a hammer, it leaves something to be desired. (Conversely, building a house out of hammers is a ludicrous thought.) But the use of a brick for a lightweight structure to be built on a platform is contraindicated where another building material would be fine. Using a hammer of any kind, be it sledge, claw, or ball-peen, is preferable to using a brick to pound in a nail.

Therefore, a family or collection of like things might have more interchangeability when needed. Also, in order to classify a thing and group or level it in a grouping hierarchy properly, one must know the complete characteristics about the thing. To design a form for a collected set of characteristics of data, one has to understand all of its possible uses. When the form is designed properly, it is operable in many different functions and therefore becomes reusable. When all the functions are defined that can reuse the form, then the collected function/form also becomes reusable.

The question then becomes, how do we create architectural patterns with data that will serve the immediate need and the future need of the businesses as they evolve? At the same time, how do we make the components reusable so we do not have to custom-make things each time? Some of these questions can be answered with standardized languages and specified roles and responsibilities, but these are only part of the solution. There must be an understanding of the business need and the business environment in which we are addressing the problem. Also, there must be an understanding of what the business environment is evolving to and how the architectural structure will solve the business user's problem.

The principles involved in information architecture are as follows:

- Understand the object of construction in terms of its composition and the environment in which it exists. Is there harmony or discord?
- Understand the object of construction in terms of its own evolution. Is it extensible?
- Understand the use of the object of construction in a current and future way. Can it be used for another purpose later?

- If the function is to be agile, is the form dynamic and flexible in order to respond to the quickly changing pressures within its environment?

Guideline: Composition and Environment

Always design with an understanding of what the environment will be for the information structure. If it is in harmony with the current environment, training and knowledge transfer will be simplified. If the composition is similar, then current infrastructure methods and personnel can be used to achieve the goal. For example, building a relational database is independent of a platform or DBMS manufacturer. Always leverage the composition and environment you have.

Guideline: Evolution

Always design without time as a boundary. Structures that have a characteristic of being extensible and flexible survive longer because they require less effort to implement change. Entropy is at work in the universe, so don't implement tightly bound, rigid structures. Corner cases and exceptions will destroy rigid structures in minimal time. Change is inevitable and must be allowed for and even encouraged. The only type of conservatism that should be entertained is that the structure should only be as big as it has to be. No excess need should be put in it.

Guideline: Current and Future

Always design structures that are unbiased to the current usage. If it is built with the first two principles, it will always be used until there are no more reasons to use it. Unbiased structures tend to keep room for growth and change while allowing corner cases and exceptions to be handled outside the structure. For example, schools designed for the baby boom became community centers and finally senior centers before some actually were taken over for local government offices as the population grew and aged. They are still in use 40-plus years after being designed and built. It is important to keep it as close to the original concept and understanding as possible. In the case of schools, they were places where groups could gather as a whole or be divided into smaller groups. It was a place where many activities could be conducted at the same time.

These are basic patterns that have evolved with iteration, and they are all basic precursor tenets to the use of architecture in the information world that also embrace the basic principles of Alexander. In the next chapter we will discuss frameworks, which also follow Alexander's principles. We conclude with a brief parable about architecture.

A Parable

In England there is a wall that is several thousand years old. It has existed from a time where there was little sense of ownership, throughout the rolling years, down to modern times where everything is owned and has a price tag. It has served as a barrier for keeping warlike attackers out, and as times became more civilized, it became part of fortification for towns. Eventually, as the towns disappeared, it became a pasture wall. This wall is amazing for two reasons:

1. It has existed for these thousands of our measured years. Through the thousands of seasonal changes, countless wars, fires, storms, and earthquakes, it has stood steady, still serving the purpose for which it was built: separating the people or things on one side from those on the other. It forms, protects, and defines a boundary.

2. It is also amazing for its structure. One would think that to survive these thousands of years, it had to be massive and rigid, but it is not. In fact, it is the opposite of solid, massive, and rigid. It has many chinks, gaps, and holes in it, and it looks as if it could fall down at any moment. As it turns out, its structure is the very reason for its survival. Wind blows through the holes, rain drains through the gaps and chinks to the earth, and snow fills the holes. If the snow turns to ice, the ice has room to expand without causing further damage to the wall. Even in the hottest scorching sun, there was room for the rocks to expand without cracking other rocks. Through thousands of seasons the structure of the wall proved its survival.

The lesson we should learn from this is that massive rigid structures do not stand the pressures of time. Lighter, more open structures allow changes to be made without tearing down and building a new structure. The open structure provides flexibility to the forces brought about by the pressures of time.

The principle illustrated by this parable (which, by the way, is true) is that a structure need not be massive to stand the tests of time. It merely needs to be architected with the primary forces that will act on it in mind and that it must still serve the necessary purpose.

Data Policies (Governance), the Foundation Building Codes

To properly come into an age where architected development produces repeatable results, a modal shift is required by the enterprise as to how the investment object that we know as data is perceived. In most cases, companies have not achieved this modal shift. Data are perceived as just a necessary part of doing business. They have not learned to leverage that data and therefore end up being left behind in the marketplace by their competitors.

Why go through the effort of educating the staff and changing the enterprise culture's perception of data? Many reasons exist, but the first and foremost is that the marketplace today is data driven. He or she with the best data (including speed, data integrity, and applicability) can service clients faster and respond to market forces more rapidly with less impact than his or her competitor.

Those who have made the modal shift have integrated certain operating concepts into the culture of their companies. The most fundamental of these are generally embodied in the data policies and principles that are espoused and committed to by all levels of management. This is more commonly known as data governance.

The implementation of data policies, functions, and roles is examined in more detail in later chapters. At the architectural level, it is important to understand that these principles exist to ensure the integrity and protection of hard-earned assets that the company can leverage for multiple purposes. The data policy principles defined following represent the foundation of data governance and should be accepted and acknowledged by all data owners, data stewards, data captains, data custodians, and dedicated resource knowledge workers.

Data Policy Principles

1. Data must be assembled and maintained in an integrated manner to support the evolving business needs and to ensure customer service of the highest quality.
2. Data, and the structures and constructs used to develop and house it, are renewable and reuseable assets of the enterprise and as such need to be secured in the most prudent manner possible.
3. Data must be of the highest quality and integrity possible to ensure that the business decisions made based on it are

responsive to the company's needs in a dynamic and competitive business environment.

4. Data must be stored or placed in the structures and locations most appropriate to its optimal utilization and safekeeping by using the best options available in the technology forum.

5. Data ownership policies and custodial responsibilities must be defined in order to ensure the accountability of the needed quality and integrity within the organization.

6. Data must be captured, validated, scrubbed, and utilized according to industry-wide standards and methods, using accepted tools and techniques that ensure consistency.

7. Data must be captured, validated, and scrubbed at the earliest point in the enterprise process to ensure that all subsequent dependent processes have minimal impact to data quality issues.

8. Data sharing must be encouraged and fostered to ensure that the business decisions that are being made are consistent between different business areas within the enterprise

Without commitment to the data policy at all levels, the data-driven engine that maintains the competitive edge will fail to move the company forward and eventually will lead to noncompetitive strategies and operations.

References

Alexander, C. (1979). *The timeless way of building.* New York: Oxford University Press.

Alexander C. (October 24, 1964) *Notes on the synthesis of form.* Cambridge, MA: Harvard University Press.

2

ENTERPRISE ARCHITECTURE FRAMEWORKS AND METHODOLOGIES

Architecture Frameworks

In Chapter One, we saw how side products of the process by which people formalize patterns are inherent in their psyche. This resulting product is an attempt to provide an ordered communication interface between the inherent patterns in an individual's psyche and his or her external world. These can also be called interpretive layers, platform specifications, level definitions, or concept aggregations. All of these definitions focus on the interpretive layer between an individual and his or her external world.

As we saw, architect Christopher Alexander first introduced the concept of patterns as a tool to encode the knowledge of the design and construction of communities and buildings. Alexander's patterns describe recurring elements and rules for how and when to create the patterns. Some designers of data processing software have begun to embrace this concept of patterns and use it as a language for planning, discussing, and documenting designs.

In his seminal and far-reaching works on pattern analysis, Christopher Alexander provided a far better definition of the interface between man and reality than any specific group of scientists or think tank wizards. This is because he abstracted rather than focused by exclusion. Alexander is a prime example of his own principles; an architect by profession, his insights and general observations provide deep and far-reaching meaning to all parts of life, including how we process data for commercial information purposes. It is in this frame of thought that we can approach how we can use patterns for the processing of data, extract information from that data, and discover how that information can be used in today's world.

Principle

An architecture represents combined perspectives in a structured format that is easily viewable and explains the context of the area being analyzed to all those viewing it.

When creating architecture of a very high level, such as the architecture of the software development process, it is necessary to have a framework to identify and specify the components of the architecture. The artifact structure of this framework in both document and word form is the methodology specification.

We are not talking pie in the sky here. While we may be addressing something very abstracted, we also need to realize it has an impact in the real world. We will discuss these in more detail, but the world of architecture—particularly information architecture—can have a significant effect on your bottom line. The importance of architecture can be determined by answering a few simple questions:

- Is your organization spending too much money building IT systems that deliver inadequate business value?
- Is IT seen as improving or hampering your business agility?
- Is there a growing divide between your business and IT personnel?
- Finally, and perhaps most important of all, is your organization truly committed to solving all of these problems, and does that commitment come from the highest levels of the organization?

If the answer to all of these questions is yes, then enterprise architecture is the program you should embrace. It is up to the management of the organization to take up the standard and lead. Today, four enterprise architectures dominate the field: the Zachman framework for enterprise architecture, The Open Group Architecture Framework (TOGAF), the Federal Enterprise Architecture (FEA), and a Gartner Framework. The first problem was managing the increasing complexity of information technology systems. The second problem was the increasing difficulty in delivering real business value Windows systems.

All of these problems are related. The more complicated a system is, the less likely it is to deliver maximum business value. The better you manage complexity, the more you improve the likelihood that you will deliver real business value.

So should you care about enterprise architecture? That depends on how you feel about positively affecting your organization's bottom line. If managing system complexity and delivering business value are priorities for you, you care about enterprise architecture methodologies. If you are focused on maintaining or rebuilding IT credibility in your organization or if you strive to promote the use of IT to maintain a competitive position in your industry, you should continue to read this chapter. If these issues don't concern you, then these methodologies have little to offer.

The relationship between complexity and planning for buildings is similar for information systems: If you are building a simple single-user system, you might not need architects at all. If you are building an enterprise-wide, mission-critical, highly distributed system, you might need a database architect, a solutions architect, an infrastructure architect, a business architect, and an enterprise architect. This chapter discusses possible methodologies that could be utilized to develop the overall architectural vision for an organization. This is the responsibility of the enterprise architect, who specialized in the broadest possible view of architecture within the enterprise. This is the architect's architect—the architect who is responsible for coordinating the work of all of the other architects.

Building a large, complex, enterprise-wide information system without an enterprise architect is like trying to build a jet plane without a master aeronautical engineer. Can you build a jet without using a master aeronautical engineer? Probably. Would you want to fly it? Probably not.

Here are some of the terms you will see in this chapter:

- *Architect*—one whose responsibility is the design of an architecture and the creation of an architectural description.
- *Architectural artifact*—a specific document, report, analysis, model, or other tangible asset that contributes to an architectural description.
- *Architectural description*—a collection of products (artifacts) to document an architecture.
- *Architectural framework*—a skeletal structure that defines suggested architectural artifacts, describes how those artifacts are related to one another, and provides generic definitions for what those artifacts might look like.
- *Architectural methodology*—a generic term that can be described in a structured approach to solving some or all of the problems related to architecture.
- *Architectural process*—a defined series of actions directed to the goal of producing either an architecture or an architectural description.
- *Architecture*—the fundamental organization of a system embodied in its components and their relationships to one another, the environment, and the principles guiding its design and evolution.

- *Enterprise architecture*—an architecture in which the system in question is the whole enterprise, especially the business processes, technologies, and information systems on the enterprise.

We will use these key terms to discuss enterprise architecture methodologies, the problems these methodologies are trying to solve, and their approaches and relationships to one another.

Brief History of Enterprise Architecture

The field of enterprise architecture essentially began in 1987 with J. A. Zachman's (1987) article "A Framework for Information Systems Architecture." Zachman laid out the challenge and the vision of enterprise architectures that would guide the field from that point through the present. The challenge was to manage the complexity of increasingly distributed systems. It is said that the costs involved and the success of a business depend on its information systems. Zachman's vision was that business value and agility could best be realized by a holistic approach to overall systems architecture that explicitly looks at every important issue from every important perspective. His multiple-viewpoint approach to architecting systems is what he originally described as an information systems architectural framework, which was later renamed as an "enterprise architecture framework."

The Zachman Framework for Enterprise Architecture

The Zachman framework is a template for organizing architectural artifacts (in other words, design documents, specifications, and models) that takes into account both the artifact targets (for example, business owners and system builders) and the particular issue that is being addressed (for example, data and functionality).

Zachman originally explained his IT template using the building industry as an analogy. In that industry, architectural artifacts are implicitly organized using a two-dimensional organization. One dimension is "the various players in the game." For a physical building, some of these players are the owner (who is paying for the project), the builder (who is coordinating the overall structure), and a zoning board (which ensures that construction follows local building regulations).

The building architect prepares different architectures for each of these players. Every player demands complete information, but what constitutes completeness is different for each of the players. The owner is interested in a complete description of the functionality and aesthetics of the building. The builder is interested in a complete description of the materials and the construction process. The owner doesn't care about placement of studs in the walls or what nails are used or what shingles are used. The builder doesn't care how the bedroom windows are aligned with the morning sun.

The second dimension for a particular artifact organization is the descriptive focus of the artifact: the *what, how, where, who, when,* and *why* of the project. This dimension is independent of the first. Both the builder and the owner need to know *what,* but the owner's *what* is different from the builder's *what.* The answer to *what* depends on who is asking the question.

In his first papers and in a subsequent elaboration in 1992, Zachman proposed that there are six descriptive areas of focus—data, function, network, people, time, and motivation—and six player perspectives—planner, owner, designer, builder, subcontractor, and enterprise. These dimensions can be arranged in a grid, as shown in Figure 2.1.

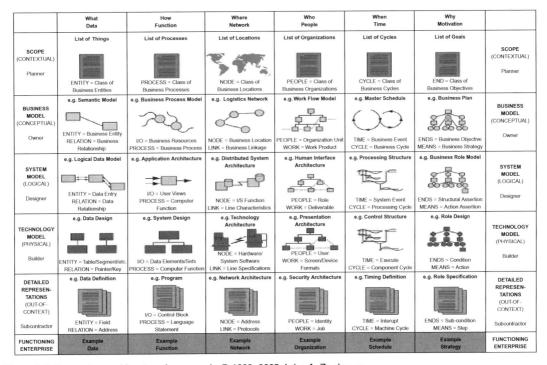

Figure 2.1 Enterprise architecture framework. © 1986–2005 John A. Zachman, Zachman International.

From the business owner's perspective, "data" means business entities. This can include information about the entities themselves, such as customers and products, or information about relationships between those strategies, such as demographic groups and inventories. If you are talking to a business owner about data, this is the language you should use. From the perspective of the person implementing the database, "data" does not mean business entities but refers to rows and columns organized into tables and linked together by mathematical joins and projections. If you are talking to a database designer about data, don't talk about customer demographic groups; talk about normal form relational tables.

It is not that one of these perspectives is any better than the other or more detailed than any other or is of higher priority than the other. These perspectives on data are critical to a holistic understanding of the systems architecture. It is the architect who integrates these into a cohesive whole.

As mentioned earlier, Zachman's framework consists of six functional focuses, each considered from the perspective of a major player. Figure 2.1 shows the 36 intersecting cells in a Zachman template—one for each meeting point between a player's perspective (for example, business owner) and a descriptive focus (for example, data). As we move from left to right in the grid, we see different descriptions of the system, all from the same player's perspective. As we move from top to bottom, we see a single focus, but the change is the player who is viewing that focus.

Zachman's framework first suggests that every architectural artifact should live in one and only one cell. There should be no ambiguity about where a particular artifact lives. If it is not clear in which cell a particular artifact lives, the problem most likely lies with the artifact itself.

Second, Zachman's framework suggests that an architecture can be considered a complete architecture only when every cell in an architecture is complete. A cell is complete when it contains sufficient artifacts to fully define the system for one specific player looking at one specific descriptive focus. When every cell is populated with appropriate artifacts, there is a sufficient amount of data to fully describe the system from the perspective of every player (stakeholder) looking at the system from every possible angle.

Third, the framework suggests that the cells in a column should be related to one another. Consider the data column (the first column) in the template. From the business owner's perspective, the data are information about the business. From the database administrator's perspective, however, the data are rows and columns in the database.

Although the business owner thinks about data quite differently from the database administrator, some relationship between these perspectives should exist. Someone should be able to follow an owner's business requirements and show that the database design is, in fact, being driven by those requirements. If the business owner has requirements that are not traceable down to the database design, it must be asked if the business needs will be met by this architecture. On the other hand, if there are database design elements that do not trace back to the business requirements, we might ask if we have included unnecessary data at the database level.

The Open Group Architecture Framework

The Open Group Architecture Framework is best known by its acronym: TOGAF. TOGAF is owned by the Open Group (www. opengroup.org). The TOGAF view of an enterprise architecture is shown in Figure 2.2. As shown, TOGAF divides an enterprise architecture into four categories:

Business architecture describes the processes that the business uses to meet its goals.

Application architecture describes how specific applications are designed and how they interact with one another.

Data architecture describes how the enterprise data stores are organized and accessed.

Technical architecture describes the hardware and software infrastructures that support the applications and their interactions.

TOGAF describes itself as a "framework," but the most important part is the architecture development method, better known as ADM. ADM is a process for creating architecture. Given that ADM is the most visible part, it can be categorized as an architectural process instead of either an architectural framework or a methodology.

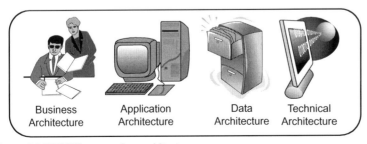

Business   Application   Data   Technical
Architecture   Architecture   Architecture Architecture

Figure 2.2 TOGAF's enterprise architecture.

As an architectural process, it is complementary to the Zachman framework. Zachman relates how to categorize your architect artifacts, and TOGAF gives you a process for creating them. TOGAF defines the world of enterprise architecture as a continuum of architectures, called the enterprise continuum, which defines the process of creating a specific enterprise architecture as moving from the generic to the specific. TOGAF ADM provides a process for driving this movement from the generic to the specific:

1. The most generic architectures are called Foundation architectures.
2. The next level of specificity is referred to as Common Systems architectures. These are principles that one would expect to see in many, but not all, types of enterprises.
3. The level of specificity after that is called Industry architectures. These are principles that are specific across many enterprises that are part of the same business domain, such as pharmaceutical enterprises.
4. Finally, the most specific level is called Organizational architectures. These are architectures that are specific to a given enterprise.

Figure 2.3 shows the relationship between the enterprise continuum and the enterprise architecture development method (ADM).

TOGAF defines the various knowledge bases that live in the foundation architecture. Today you might run into the technical reference model (TRM) and the standards information base (SIB). The TRM is a suggested description of the generic IT architecture, and the SIB is a collection of standards and pseudo-standards that the Open Group recommends you consider in building an IT

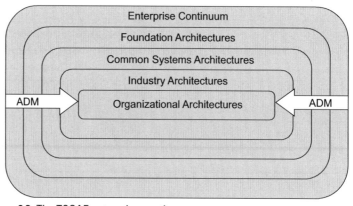

Figure 2.3 The TOGAF enterprise continuum.

architecture. TOGAF presents both the TRL and the SIB but suggests that neither is required.

For any organization, the day-to-day experience of creating an enterprise architecture will be driven by the ADM, a high-level view that is shown in Figure 2.4. TOGAF ADM consists of eight phases that are cycled through after an initial "priming of the pump."

In some organizations, achieving buy-in for an enterprise architecture can be difficult. This is especially true if the effort is driven from the IT organization and even more so when there is a history of distrust between the business and the technical side of an organization. This often necessitates the use of an external consultant.

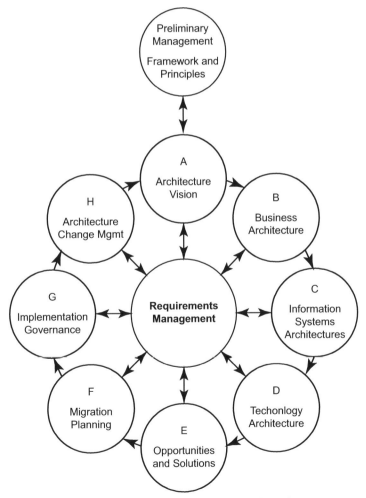

Figure 2.4 The TOGAF architecture development method (ADM).

As soon as a request has been received, an external consultant who is skilled in TOGAF principles can ensure that the project has the necessary support within the company to define the scope of the project, identify constraints, document business requirements, and establish high-level definitions for both the current architecture and the future architecture. The current and future definitions of technology architecture (category D in Figure 2.4) will include high-level definitions for all four of the EEA subarchitectures shown in Figure 2.2: business, technology, data, and application architectures.

The culmination of the effort will be a statement of architecture work, which must be approved by the various stakeholders before the next phase of the ADM begins. The point of this phase is to create an architecture vision for the first pass through the ADM cycle. The TOGAF consultants will guide the company toward choosing the pilot project, vetting the project against the architectural principles established in the preliminary phase, and ensuring that the appropriate stakeholders have been notified.

In Figure 2.4, the architectural vision created in circle A (architecture vision) will be the main input into circle B (business architecture). The TOGAF consultants' goal in circle B is to create a detailed base and target business architecture, as well as perform a gap analysis between them. A successful phase B requires input from many stakeholders. The major outputs will be detailed descriptions of the base and target business objectives and the gap descriptions of the business architecture.

Circle C (information systems architecture) does for the information systems architecture what phase B does for the business architecture. TOGAF defines nine specific steps for this phase, each with multiple substeps:

- Develop a base data architecture description.
- Review and validate principles, reference models, viewpoints, and tools.
- Create architecture models, including logical data models, data management process models, and relationship models that map business functions to CRUD data operations.
- Select data architecture building blocks.
- Conduct formal checkpoint reviews of the architecture models and building blocks with stakeholders.
- Review critical criteria (performance, reliability, security, integrity).
- Complete the data architecture.
- Conduct a checkpoint/impact analysis.
- Perform a gap analysis.

The most important deliverable from this phase will be the target information and applications architecture.

Technology architecture (circle D) completes the technical architecture and the information technology infrastructure necessary to support the target architecture. Technology architecture assesses the various implementation possibilities, identifies the major implementation projects that must be undertaken, and evaluates the business opportunity associated with each.

The standard recommends that the TOGAF consultant's first pass at technology architecture should focus on projects that will deliver short-term payoffs and create an impetus for proceeding with longer-term projects. This is good advice in any architectural methodology. Therefore, the TOGAF consultant should be looking for projects that can be completed as cheaply as possible while still delivering the highest perceived value.

Circle F (migration planning) is closely related to technology architecture. In this phase of the TOGAF, the consultant works with the company's data governance body to sort the projects identified in phases into priority orders that include not only the costs and benefits (listed in D) but also the risk factors.

In circle G (implementation governance), the TOGAF consultant takes a prior list of projects and creates architectural specifications for the implementation projects. These specifications include acceptance criteria and lists of risks and issues.

In the final phase, H (architecture change), the consultant modifies the architectural change management process with any new artifacts created in this last iteration and with new information that becomes available. The consultant is then ready to start the cycle again. One of the goals in the first cycle is the transfer of information, so the consultant's services are required less and less as more and more iterations of the cycle are completed.

Much of the results of the process can be determined as much by the consultant's/company's relationship as it will be by the TOGAF specification itself. TOGAF is a very adaptable methodology, and specifics for the various architectural artifacts are sparse. TOGAF allows phases to be done in random order, skipped, combined, reordered, or reshaped to fit the needs of the situation. Therefore, two different TOGAF-certified consultants may use two very different processes, even when they are both working with the same organization.

The Federal Enterprise Architecture

The Federal Enterprise Architecture (FEA) (CIO, 2001) was implemented by the U.S. federal government in an effort to unite its myriad agencies and functions under a common enterprise architecture. The Federal Enterprise Architecture effort is still in its infancy, since most of the major pieces have been available only since 2006. FEA is the most complete of all the methodologies discussed in this chapter. It has both a comprehensive template, like Zachman, and an architectural process, like TOGAF.

FEA can be viewed as either a methodology for creating an enterprise architecture or the architectural result of executing that process for a particular enterprise. In this chapter, the FEA is reviewed from the methodology perspective as to how it can be applied to businesses in the private sector.

FEA can be described as consisting of five reference models, one for each area of activity: business, service, components, technical, and data. But there is much more to FEA than just the reference models. A full recap of FEA must include the following:

- A perspective on how enterprise architectures should be viewed
- A set of reference models for describing different perspectives of the enterprise architecture
- A process for creating an enterprise architecture
- A transitional process for migrating from a pre-EA to a post-EA paradigm
- A taxonomy for cataloging assets that fall within the purview of the enterprise architecture
- An approach to measuring the success of using the enterprise architecture to drive business value

Some examinations of FEA's benefits follow.

The FEA View on Enterprise Architecture

The FEA view on EA is that an enterprise is made up of *segments*. A segment is a major business functionality, such as human resources. Within FEA, segments are divided into *core mission area* segments and *business services* segments. A core mission area segment is one that is central to the purpose of a particular agency within the enterprise. For example, in the Health and Human Services (HHS) agency of the federal government, health is a core mission area segment. A business services segment is one that is foundational to most organizations. For example, financial management is a business services segment that is required by all federal agencies.

Another type of enterprise architecture asset is an *enterprise service*, which is a well-defined function that spans agency boundaries. An example of an enterprise service is security management. Security management is a service that works in a unified manner across the whole breadth of the enterprise.

The difference between enterprise services and segments is confusing. Although both are shared across the entire enterprise, business services segments affect only a single part of the organization, whereas enterprise services affect the entire enterprise. For example, in the federal government, both the HHS and the Environmental Protection Agency (EPA) use the human resources business services segment. However, the people who are managed by human resources are different in HHS than those in the EPA.

Both the HHS and the EPA also use the security management enterprise service. But the security credentials controlled by the security management service are not specific to either of those agencies. The fact that segments are defined globally facilitates reuse across agency boundaries. One can define the usage segments across the enterprise and then use a defined set to locate opportunities for architectural reuse.

Figure 2.5, for example, shows a segment map of the federal government from the FEA *Practice Guide* (OMB, 2006a). As shown, many segments (the vertical columns) are used in multiple agencies, and any or all of these are good candidates for sharing.

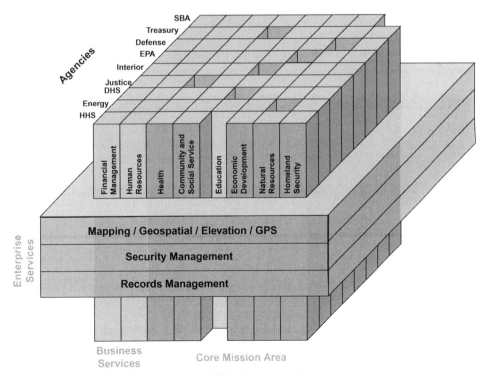

Figure 2.5 Segment map of the federal government FEA reference models.

The five FEA reference models are focused on establishing a common business language. The goal is to facilitate communication, cooperation, and collaboration across agency boundaries. According to the FEAPMO (OMB, 2006b):

The FEA consists of a set of interrelated "reference models" designed to facilitate cross-agency analysis and the identification of duplicative investments, gaps, and opportunities for collaboration within and across agencies. Collectively, the reference models [compose] a framework for describing important elements of the FEA in a common and consistent way.

Another example would be if the Internal Revenue Service (IRS) decided it needed a population *demographics* system to track taxpayer data. After a lengthy search for a system with these characteristics, they proceed to build one. Unknown to the IRS, the Government Printing Office (GPO) has a population demographics system that is almost exactly what the IRS needs. They just happen to call it a *customer-information* system. So the IRS goes out and builds its system from scratch instead of adapting or expanding the one already built by the GPO. If they continue to do so, the IRS will waste considerable money.

This, then, is the goal of the five FEA reference models: to give standard terms and definitions for the domains of enterprise architecture and to facilitate collaboration and reuse across the federal government. The five reference models are as follows:

- The *business reference model (BRM)* gives a business view of the various functions of the federal government. For example, the BRM defines a standard business capability called *water resource management* that is a subordinate function of natural resources that is considered a line-of-business of the broader services for citizens' business areas (2007).
- The *components reference model (CRM)* gives an IT view of systems that can support business functionality. For example, the CRM defines a *customer-analytics system* that was described earlier in the hypothetical interchange between the IRS and the GPO (2007).
- The *technical reference model (TRM)* categorizes the various technologies and standards that can be used in building IT systems. For example, the TRM defines *HTTP* as a protocol that is a subset of a service transport that is a subset of service access and delivery (2007).
- The *data reference model (DRM)* defines standard ways of describing data. For example, the DRM defines an *entity* as something that contains attributes and participates in relationships (OMB, 2007).

- The *performance reference model (PRM)* defines standard ways of describing the value delivered by enterprise architectures. For example, the PRM describes *quality* as a technology measurement area that is defined as "the extent to which technology satisfies functionality or capability requirements" (2006c).

The FEA Process

The FEA process concentrates on developing a segment architecture for a subset of the overall enterprise (in FEA's case, the enterprise is the federal government and the subset is a governmental agency) and is described in FEA Practice Guidance (OMB, 2006d). The overall segment-architecture development process is as follows:

- *Step 1:* Architectural analysis—defines a simple but concise vision for the segment and relates it to the organizational plan.
- *Step 2:* Architectural definition—defines the target architecture of the segment, defines the performance goals, develops design alternatives, and develops an enterprise architecture for the segment, including business, data, services, and technology architectures.
- *Step 3:* Investment and funding strategy—justifies the program funding; defines ROI.
- *Step 4:* Define the program management plan and execute projects—create a plan for managing and executing the project, including milestones and performance measures that will assess project success.

The Gartner Process

So far, we have seen three different methodologies that come together under the banner of enterprise architectures. This last methodology is a little different. It isn't a taxonomy (like Zachman), a process (like TOGAF), or a complete methodology (like FEA). Instead, it can be defined as a *practice*. It is the enterprise architecture practice of a large IT research and consulting organization: Gartner.

How do you choose a physician? Do you interview candidates on how well they know the medicine? Do you sit candidates down and ask for a detailed description of the methodology each follows for a diagnosis? You might ask your friends, but they probably only know a limited pool of candidates. One approach to choosing a physician is to go to a well-known institution (a hospital or medical school) and choose from among their staff. In this approach, you are counting on the institution to have chosen highly qualified physicians. Does that institution insist on rigid standards for its physicians to follow? Even if it does, it is not your primary concern. Your initial concern is only the reputation of the institution.

This is very similar to the Gartner approach to enterprise architecture. You invite Gartner consulting because they do or don't use TOGAF. You don't use Gartner because they do or don't follow Zachman's taxonomy. You use Gartner because they are well known in their field. You assume that they hire well-qualified specialists and encourage collaboration and best practice.

If you are a Gartner customer and you check the Gartner library for research notes describing their enterprise architecture practice, you can find many such documents—for example, *Gartner Enterprise Architecture Process: Evolution 2005* and *Gartner Enterprise Architecture Framework: Evolution 2005* (Greta James et al., 2005). However, these documents contain little descriptive information and, in any case, were published in late 2005. Gartner contends that these best practices are timeless, and they continue to update them as appropriate. To summarize the Gartner practice: *Architecture is a verb, not a noun.* What exactly does that mean? It means that the ongoing process of creating, maintaining, and leveraging an enterprise architecture gives that enterprise architecture its vitality. An architecture that is just a bunch of by-product artifacts that sit gathering dust is useless.

Gartner believes that enterprise architecture is about partnering together three constituents: business owners, information specialists, and the technology implementers. If you can integrate these three groups and unify them behind a common vision that drives business value, you have succeeded. If not, you have failed. Success is measured in pragmatic metrics, such as driving profitability.

Gartner believes that the enterprise architectures must start with a target architecture, not with the current state. If you are cleaning your garage, you don't exhaustively document everything being thrown out. Gartner focuses on what and where the end goal is. Gartner recommends that an organization begin by defining where its strategic direction is and what business drivers it is responding to. Gartner will want this story in plain business language. The only goal is making sure that everybody understands and shares a single vision.

Most organizations are facing major changes in their business processes. The process of creating an enterprise architecture vision is the organization's opportunity to collaborate and ensure that everyone understands the nature, scope, and impact of the upcoming changes in their business process.

When the organization has this single vision of the future, the impact of the vision will force changes in the business, technical, information, and application architectures of the enterprise. The shared vision of the future will require modifications to all of these architectures. To Gartner, enterprise architecture is about strategy, not about engineering. It is focused on the target. The two things that are most important to Gartner are *where an organization is going* and *how it will get there.*

Let's say the company management likes what it hears. How will the Gartner engagement proceed? With FEA, TOGAF, or Zachman, management needs to start by finding a qualified consultant who understands the methodology. With Gartner, this step is much the same. Gartner sends an EA consultant. The first thing the consultant wants to do is make sure the architecture is driven from the highest levels of the corporation. Exactly how the consultant will proceed is difficult to predict because Gartner does not have a firm, step-by-step process. However, it is likely that the consultant will start by focusing on management's strategic vision for the company. He will want to specify vision in business terms and reject any discussion of technology. Here are some possible business vision statements the consultant might elicit:

- The company will have stores in at least ten states, spread out over eight geographic regions by the year 2013. It will accomplish this mainly through acquisition of regional pharmacies.
- The company will be able to assimilate new regional systems within 180 days of finalization of purchase.
- The company will reduce its purchasing costs by 10 percent by centralizing regional purchasing into a central system.
- The company's central office will be able to view consolidated sales and inventory reports from all stores that include data up to and including the previous day.
- The company will be able to reduce its inventory to no more than a ten-day supply.
- Patients will be able to transfer prescriptions from any of the company's pharmacies to any other.
- Patients will be able to request prescription refills though a Web interface and receive e-mail notification of their availability for pickup.

None of these visionary statements mentions technology (except as a delivery mechanism in the last statement). The consultant keeps these early discussions focused on business strategy.

Part of the consultant's job will be to prioritize the bulleted items. Let's say management decides that the highest priority is consolidating purchasing, because this will improve profitability in the near term. The consultant will soon work to turn management's idea about consolidated purchasing into a common requirements vision (CRV). The CRV is where we will see some of the changes that will be required to drive management's vision for the company. The consultant will work with the business to develop a target business architecture that supports consolidated purchasing. As soon as they have defined the future system, they will review their current architecture to see what can be reused.

The consultant will work with the CIO to develop a target information architecture that allows regional inventories tracking and procurement consolidation. They will also work on the technical architecture for the IT systems that will support the new business architecture. After they understand the future, they will look at current architectures for opportunities to reuse existing assets.

After the consultant has completed the high-level architecture for their strategic vision, they will step back from the picture until the consolidated purchasing system has been implemented. As soon as the implementation of consolidated purchasing has been completed, the consultant will step back in to help with the next iteration. His approach will be to keep the architecture at a high level and business-focused, and hone in on details only when and where necessary.

Conclusions

This chapter covered a broad introduction to the field of enterprise architecture. Two of the four major methodologies (Gartner and FEA) have undergone major changes in the last two years alone. As this review has shown, these methodologies are quite different from each other, both in goals and in approach. This is good news and bad. It is bad news because it increases the complexity for many organizations if they are choosing a single enterprise architecture methodology. The good news, however, is that these methodologies complement each other. For many organizations, the best choice is all of these methodologies, blended together in a way that works well within that organization's constraints. Whatever route is chosen, it is important to understand enterprise architecture as a path, not a destination. It is not a project but a program. An enterprise architecture has no value unless it delivers real business value as quickly as possible. One of the most important goals of any enterprise architecture is to bring the business and technology sides together so both are working effectively toward the same goals.

Principle

The enterprise architecture delineates the data according to the inherent structure within the organization rather than by organizational function or use. In this manner it makes the data dependent on business objects but independent of business processes.

In many organizations, there is a culture of distrust between the technology and business folks. No enterprise architecture methodology can bridge this divide unless there is a genuine commitment to change. *That commitment must come from the highest level of the organization.* Methodologies cannot solve people issues, but they can provide a framework in which those problems can be solved.

As soon as you have that commitment to change, an enterprise architecture methodology can be a valuable tool for guiding that change. This change can manifest itself in many ways. Some of the predicted benefits from a successfully implemented architectural enterprise include the following:

- Improvements in using IT to drive business adaptability
- Closer partnership between business and IT groups
- Improved focus on organizational goals
- Improved morale, as more individuals see a direct correlation between their work and the organization's success
- Reduced numbers of failed IT systems
- Reduced complexity of existing IT systems
- Improved agility of new IT systems
- Closer alignment between IT deliverables and business requirements

It is obvious that an organization that does well in these key areas will be more successful than one that doesn't. This is true regardless of whether success is measured with tangible results, such as profitability and return on investment, or intangible results, such as customer satisfaction and lower employee turnover.

Enterprise Data Architectures

These artifacts of the framework process represent the inherent relatedness of data components in current usage structures. Enterprise data architectures are the transcription of the

Principle

Processes that use data change far more frequently than the data structures themselves.

information owner's product requirements from the owner's perspective. Current data architectures are dependent on the premise that data resides at the center of modern data processing. Data must be approached from the highest level of perspective, since it is perceived as the real-world objects it represents and exists as a function of normal business operation.

Architectures, particularly the enterprise data architectures, insulate a business from unnecessary data change and provide an immediate means of assessing impending change. When architectures are fully specified, they provide explicitness and specification of the composition of the product without the creative effort and investment of building a prototype or the need for detailed analysis. We can assess the impact of change with minimal expense.

Therefore, the enterprise data architecture is essentially a strategic design model that becomes the environmental foundation for the multiple development activities that ensue on owner approval of the enterprise development plan. The fundamental benefits of an enterprise data architecture are as follows:

- Enterprise data architectures provide global understanding of the business data needs while still representing the corporate policies.
- Enterprise data architectures allow strategic development of flexible modular designs by encapsulating the data with the business while insulating it from the technology process.
- Enterprise data architectures provide a framework for communication between the customer and developer/service agent so the customer understands the scope, options, and price of the product/service.
- Without an enterprise data architecture, decentralization, distribution of information, or reallocation of control would be impossible and would in fact create chaos.

Enterprise Models

The typical organization has a vastly diversified collection of organizations, policies, processes, systems, values, and beliefs.

Within that organization, information technology in most companies has a large collection of diversified applications, networks, organizations, processes, projects, systems, and technologies. An enterprise model is constructed most properly by mapping the components of an organization, its IT organization, and its system architecture all together.

By applying the Alexander model of design to the pattern-based architecture, we can see how it affects these enterprise states. The "quality" is created when the characteristics in the enterprise design make that design "live." That is, the enterprise design will contain the captured characteristics that ensure the flexion, extension, adaptation, and reuse and have other qualities of living things.

"The Gate" is whatever common pattern language embodies the universal network of patterns and pattern relationships dedicated to the enterprise domain being modeled. When designing a specific application within this enterprise domain, a pattern language for a specific design should be chosen by the designer from the common pattern language in use at the organization.

As stated before, pattern languages are applied using "The Way"—in this case, whatever integration method has been advocated for the enterprise. That is, we apply one pattern at a time, successively evolving an initial architecture into an unfolded "live design," or in Alexander's terms, a design with "The Quality." This, simply put, is the iterative reconciliation of a completed architectural area into the whole of the enterprise data architecture.

The most important task at hand is to capture and define those patterns within the enterprise that will allow a common pattern language to be defined for that enterprise. It is a time-consuming yet rewarding task in that it optimizes the benefits of a structured approach such as Zachman's framework merged with the abstractive qualities of an object framework mechanism.

Because of its simplicity and sympathetic nature to both the traditional/Zachman and the OO movement, the pattern architecture movement as a whole is growing in the industry, and the most common CPLs will be defined for all common industries at some point in the form of templates.

The Enterprise Data Model

The enterprise data model is of particular importance in understanding the data architecture because it is at this level that all diversified applications, networks, organizations, processes, projects, systems, and technologies come together. It is, and always will be, about the data. For the purposes of this book, the enterprise data architecture is the focal point, while the enterprise activity model and all the other associated encapsulations are excluded. It is not that they are any less critical, but because they are best handled in a book dedicated to the subject.

The Importance of the Enterprise Data Model

In the typical organization, the components of the enterprise data model assets do not necessarily form a coherent whole. In fact, most of the corporate environments don't keep current enterprise data models, and the ones that do do not enforce a systematic control over its evolution or maintenance. In many companies, multiple, nonintegrated models are created by the accountants, business analysts, and software developers. They are not strategic planners. The reason it is so important to know how the enterprise operates today is because it most likely will be changed rapidly and incrementally. Keeping an ongoing model for the enterprise's data is essential to managing environmental risk and change. In fact, this model can and should be used as a configuration management tool for the entire enterprise.

The enterprise no longer can be managed solely by using the leadership of its executives, nor can it just manage by financial numbers, the revenue produced by the marketers, or the production of its operations. It must look at all of its processes and data and define a way to manage them collectively. However, it is also true that one cannot dwell into every detail of every process. A unique balance for the enterprise must be found in order for the model to be simultaneously useful and manageable.

A *pattern* has been defined as "an idea that has been useful in one practical context and will probably be useful in others." Patterns offer the promise of helping the architect to identify combinations of architecture and solutions that have been proven to deliver effective solutions in the past and may provide the basis for effective future solutions.

Pattern techniques are generally acknowledged to have been established as a valuable architectural design technique by Christopher Alexander (1979), who described this approach in his book *The Timeless Way of Building*. This book provides an introduction to the ideas behind the use of patterns, and Alexander followed it with two further books—*A Pattern Language* and *The Oregon Experiment*—in which he expanded on his description of the features and benefits of a patterns approach to architecture.

Software and buildings architects have many similar issues to address, and so it was natural for software architects to take an interest in patterns as an architectural tool. Many papers and books have been published on them since Alexander's book, perhaps the most renowned being *Design Patterns: Elements of Reusable Object-Oriented Software* (Gamma et al., 1995). This book describes simple and elegant solutions to specific problems in object-oriented software design.

Object Concepts: Types and Structures Within Databases

Every object within the database has a type, and each type has an internal and an external definition. The external definition, also called the *specification*, consists of the operations, properties or attributes, and exceptions that users of the object can access. The internal definition, also called the *implementation*, consists of all the details of the operation and any other requirements that are not visible to the user of the object.

- A *class* is a *specification* that defines the abstract behavior and abstract state of an object type.
- Literal *specifications* only define the abstract state of the object.
- An *operation* is the abstracted behavior of an object.
- A *property* is the abstracted state of an object.
- A *representation* is the implementation of that *property*.

Inheritance

This characteristic has been referred to or called many names. It is called most commonly the super type–subtype relationship or generalization specification relationship. The concept is to express the relationship between types as a specialization of the type. Each subtype *inherits* the operations and properties of its super type and adds more operations and properties to its own definition. For example, coffee, beer, and soda are all beverages and *inherit* the general operations and properties of beverages, yet they have their own unique operations and properties. *Persistency*, or the ability to persist or remain intact after an operation is completed, is often defined as being inherited from a higher level of persistency class.

Object Life Cycles

Each object has a unique identifier or object ID (OID). As it goes through its life cycle from creation, to locking, through comparison with other objects, to copying to create new objects with the same property values, and finally to deletion, it retains the OID. An object may be *transient* (that is, managed by the program language run-time system) or *persistent* (that is, sustained and managed in storage by the ODBMS). Rules state that the object lifetime is independent of its type.

Relationships and Collections

Relationships map objects to other objects. Relationships can be classified as one to one, one to many, and many to many. Actions on relationships occur through standard relationship operations. This translates into operations that form or drop relations, or to add or remove a single object from the relationship. The "to" side of the relationship corresponds to one of the following standard collection classes:

Set – an unordered collection of objects or literals with no duplicates allowed

Bag – an unordered collection of objects or literals that may contain duplicates

List – an ordered collection of objects or literals

Array – a sized, ordered collection of objects that is accessible by position

Dictionary – an unordered sequence of associated value pairs with no duplicates.

This should provide enough background on the object approach. Let us move forward or, more specifically, upward and apply these principles to architectural frameworks.

Since the principles concerning objects are easily generalized, it is easy to see how they can be used at a higher level of abstraction. The use of these principles allows the concepts of frameworks to exist for objects and groups of objects that not only apply to the data but to the processes as well.

Object Frameworks

While the development and initial baseline effort to establish an object framework can be expensive in the sense of time involvement before the applications can be developed, it can also be purchased from many reliable vendors. The vendors have developed the generalized routines that are common to all object approach projects and captured them in object framework templates. The frameworks are easily implemented and easily extensible. This allows a company that is new to the object approach to enter into the object world in a facilitated manner and save in investment in setup and definitional efforts.

By having the generic superstructure of the object framework, it allows OO designers and programmers to leverage OO by having frameworks that span the spectrum of application activities and functions. Frameworks deliver built-in functionality at all levels and provide ready value when an application is being started. It is far more efficient than when this necessary functionality is being built piece by piece. It also ensures software reuse by encouraging framework usage, which in turn increases productivity and integration. Finally, it provides a development environment structured for object-oriented activity that ensures rapid application development and specification.

Object Framework Programming

The way object frameworks, in general, achieve these benefits over other development approaches is based on two fundamental principles. Frameworks are not simply collections of classes. Object frameworks provide infrastructure and interconnection in the design. It is these interconnections within a framework that can provide the architectural model and design for programmers and free them to apply their knowledge and skills to the business problem area. By providing process and data infrastructure, a framework significantly decreases the amount of code that the developer has to program, test, and debug. The developer writes only the code that extends or specifies a defined framework's behavior to suit the program's requirements.

But there are learning curve anomalies that need to be considered as well. The object framework method requires adjustment by even the most flexible developer because it automates or makes available to the programmer a significant amount of predefined functionality. It has this effect because the object framework drives the process, not the other way around. Using an object framework programming requires a shift in the programmer's activity mindset and logic.

In traditional procedural systems, the programmer's own program provides all of the infrastructure and execution sequence and as such makes calls to libraries as necessary. However, in object framework programming, the role of the framework is to provide the flow of control, while the programmer's code waits for the call from the framework. This is a significant benefit, since programmers do not have to be concerned with the infrastructure details but can focus their attention on their business problem area.

There is, however, a learning or unlearning curve of short duration associated with frameworks. This change in the responsibility of control can be a significant change for programmers who have experience only in procedural programming.

Pattern-Based Frameworks

Much focus in the industry today, from tools to products to the latest books, depicts and defines business modeling and reengineering with objects—for example, Andersen Consulting's Eagle Model, SES Software's Business Architect, Platinum's Paradigm Plus, and Rational ROSE, to name a few. Modeling methods based on objects have an advantage over traditional process modeling techniques because they facilitate the dialog between user and technical people; allow processes to be considered objects; and provide a mechanism to find "business objects." These techniques are being bundled and marketed as pattern-based frameworks.

Modeling and designing methods that focus on the business pattern analysis are very successful because these patterns are easy to implement as business architecture constructs. Pattern-based frameworks also provide a level of abstraction that is more appealing to business people—in other words, they don't have to understand object models to use patterns. An example from a TOGAF pattern framework website (http://www.opengroup.org/architecture/togaf8-doc/arch/chap28.html) follows.

Architecture Patterns in Use

Two examples of architecture patterns in use are outlined in the following subsections, one from the domain of an IT customer enterprise's own architecture framework and the other from a major system vendor who has done a lot of work in recent years in the field of architecture patterns.

- The *U.S. Treasury Architecture Development Guidance (TADG)* document provides a number of explicit architecture patterns, in addition to explaining a rationale, structure, and taxonomy for architectural patterns as they relate to the U.S. Treasury.
- The IBM Patterns for e-Business website gives a series of architecture patterns that go from the business problem to specific solutions, first at a generic level and then in terms of specific IBM product solutions. A supporting resource is IBM's set of *Red Books*.

- The following material is intended to give the reader pointers to some of the places where architecture patterns are already being used and made available in order to help readers make up their own minds as to the usefulness of this technique for their own environments.

U.S. Treasury Architecture Development Guidance

The *U.S. Treasury Architecture Development Guidance* document, formerly known as the *Treasury Information System Architecture Framework*, provides a number of explicit architecture patterns. Section 7 of the TADG document describes a rationale, structure, and taxonomy for architecture patterns, while the patterns themselves are formally documented in Appendix D. The architecture patterns presented embrace a larger set of systems than just object-oriented systems. Some architecture patterns are focused on legacy systems, some on concurrent and distributed systems, and some on real-time systems.

TADG Pattern Content

The content of an architecture pattern as defined in the TADG document contains the following elements:

Name
Each architecture pattern has a unique, short descriptive name. The collection of architecture pattern names can be used as a vocabulary for describing, verifying, and validating information systems architectures.

Problem
Each architecture pattern contains a description of the problem to be solved. The problem statement may describe a class of problems or a specific problem.

Rationale
The rationale describes and explains a typical specific problem that is representative of the broad class of problems to be solved by the architecture pattern. For a specific problem, it can provide additional details of the nature of the problem and the requirements for its resolution.

Assumptions
The assumptions are conditions that must be satisfied in order for the architecture pattern to be usable in solving the problem. They include constraints on the solution and optional requirements that may make the solution easier to use.

Structure
The architecture pattern is described in diagrams and words in as much detail as is required to convey to the reader the components of the pattern and their responsibilities.

Interactions
The important relationships and interactions among the components of the pattern are described and constraints on these relationships and interactions are identified.

Consequences
The advantages and disadvantages of using this pattern are described, particularly in terms of other patterns (either required or excluded), as well as resource limitations that may arise from using it.

Implementation
Additional implementation advice that can assist designers in customizing this architectural design pattern for the best results is provided.

TADG Architecture Patterns

The TADG document contains the following patterns.

Architectural Design

Pattern Name	Synopsis
Client-Proxy Server	Acts as a concentrator for many low-speed links to access a server.
Customer Support	Supports complex customer contact across multiple organizations.
Reactor	Decouples an event from its processing.
Replicated Servers	Replicates servers to reduce burden on central server.
Layered Architecture	A decomposition of services such that most interactions occur only between neighboring layers.
Pipe and Filter Architecture	Transforms information in a series of incremental steps or processes.
Subsystem Interface	Manages the dependencies between cohesive groups of functions (subsystems).

IBM Patterns for e-Business

The *IBM Patterns for e-Business* website (www.ibm.com/framework/patterns) provides a group of reusable assets aimed at speeding up the process of developing e-Business applications.

A supporting IBM website is *Patterns for e-Business Resources* (www.ibm.com/developerworks/patterns/library). The rationale for IBM's provision of these patterns is as follows:

- Provide a simple and consistent way to translate business priorities and requirements into technical solutions
- Assist and speed up the solution development and integration process by facilitating the assembly of a solution and minimizing custom one-of-a-kind implementations
- Capture the knowledge and best practices of experts, and make it available for use by less experienced personnel
- Facilitate the reuse of intellectual capital such as reference architectures, frameworks, and other architecture assets
- IBM's patterns are focused specifically on solutions for e-business—that is, those that allow an organization to leverage Web technologies in order to reengineer business processes, enhance communications, and lower organizational boundaries with the following :
  - Customers and shareholders (across the Internet)
  - Employees and stakeholders (across a corporate Intranet)
  - Vendors, suppliers, and partners (across an extranet)
- They are intended to address the following challenges encountered in this type of environment:
  - High degree of integration with legacy systems within the enterprise and with systems outside the enterprise.
  - The solutions need to reach users faster; this does not mean sacrificing quality, but it does mean coming up with better and faster ways to develop these solutions.
  - Service-level agreements (SLAs) are critical.
  - Need to adapt to rapidly changing technologies and dramatically reduced product cycles.
  - Address an acute shortage of the key skills needed to develop quality solutions.

  IBM defines five types of patterns:
- *Business patterns*, which identify the primary business actors and describe the interactions between them in terms of different archetypal business interactions such as:
  - Service (a.k.a. user-to-business)—users accessing transactions on a 24/7 basis
  - Collaboration (a.k.a. user-to-user)—users working with one another to share data and information
  - Information aggregation (a.k.a. user-to-data)—data from multiple sources aggregated and presented across multiple channels
  - Extended enterprise (a.k.a. business-to-business)—integrating data and processes across enterprise boundaries

- *Integration patterns*, which provide the "glue" to combine business patterns to form solutions. They characterize the business problem, business processes/rules, and existing environment to determine whether front-end or back-end integration is required.
  - Front-end integration (a.k.a. access integration)—focused on providing seamless and consistent access to business functions. Typical functions provided include single sign-on, personalization, transcoding, and so on.
  - Back-end integration (a.k.a. application integration)—focused on connecting, interfacing, or integrating databases and systems. Typical integration can be based on function, type of integration, mode of integration, and by topology.
- *Composite patterns*, which are previously identified combinations and selections of business and integration patterns, for previously identified situations such as electronic commerce solutions, (public) enterprise portals, enterprise intranet portal, collaboration ASP, and so on.
- *Application patterns*. Each business and integration pattern can be implemented using one or more application patterns. An application pattern characterizes the coarse-grained structure of the application: the main application components, the allocation of processing functions and the interactions between them, the degree of integration between them, and the placement of the data relative to the applications.
- *Run-time patterns*. Application patterns can be implemented by run-time patterns, which demonstrate nonfunctional, service-level characteristics, such as performance, capacity, scalability, and availability. They identify key resource constraints and best practices.

The IBM website also provides specific (IBM) product mappings for the run-time patterns, indicating specific technology choices for implementation.

It is the utilization of these business pattern frameworks, which are abstractions of the object frameworks just described, that allow the enterprise to be modeled in a manner that captures the current "enterprise entity" in its current state. It also allows that captured structure to be flexible and responsive to business change.

The integration of all of these into a single comprehensive enterprise object model will provide the basis for pattern-based enterprise architecture. While many individuals, such as Jacobson (1995), have published on the use of objects in business engineering and reengineering, only one has proposed the use of patterns in development of an enterprise model. Michael Beedle (1998) has proposed its use to create the enterprise model, verify this model using the Zachman framework, and subsequently use the model to reengineer the workplace using a new technique called business process reengineering.

Enterprise Data Model Implementation Methods

Although this will be covered in more detail in the specialty database section concerning data warehouses, we can briefly discuss these here. There are two primary methods for implementing the enterprise data model.

A *bottom-up approach* sets infrastructure standards and introduces governance processes to ensure adherence to those standards, while a *top-down approach* formalizes analysis of the current state with respect to business processes, application, data, and technology. Each approach entails senior management commitment and promises an improved relationship with the business as technology planning is brought in sync with business planning as concerns the data involved. Following are some of the benefits and drawbacks of each.

Benefits of Top-Down Approach
- Establishes a clear view of the existing data environment in the beginning.
- Emphasizes business issues with data at the outset.
- Establishes broad scope and vision for data at the beginning.

Drawbacks of the Top-Down Approach
- Top-down methods can become overly abstract.
- The data collection and analysis delay the introduction of governance.
- The formal methodologies require training to get started.

Benefits of the Bottom-Up Approach
- The method can have significant impact immediately.
- Early successes build credibility rapidly.
- Problems are tackled in priority sequence.
- Scope and complexity build gradually.
- It does not need a large central EA team at the outset.

Drawbacks of the Bottom-Up Approach

- The infrastructure origination of the effort hampers efforts to expand scope.
- A standards-based approach emplaces governance as a police action.
- The technology focus appears insensitive to business issues.
- Some areas in need of much improvement must wait for attention.

Preliminary Conclusion

In conclusion, we can look at the two methods and realize that, sometimes, neither works. In cases such as these, a hybrid or side-in approach may be taken. It selects the best characteristics of each implementation method and minimizes the negative aspects of each.

Hybrid Approach

A hybrid or side-in approach to enterprise data architecture implementation involves the purchasing of an industry standard model and implementing it and adjusting it to the company's needs. Based on the implementation, the data governance process and any enterprise efforts such as an enterprise data warehouse can be sourced from this. Subsequently, as projects are identified and implemented, they are brought into line with data governance policies and integrated into the emerging enterprise data architecture.

References

Alexander, C. (1979). *The timeless way of building*. New York: Oxford University Press.

Alexander, C. (October 24, 1964) *Notes on the synthesis of form*. Cambridge, MA: Harvard University Press.

A practical guide to Federal Enterprise Architecture by the CIO Council, Version 1.0. (2001, February).

Beedle, M. A. *Pattern-based reengineering*. <http://www.fti_consulting/users/beedlem>.

Bittler, S., Kreizman, G. (2005, October 21) Gartner enterprise architecture process: *Evolution* 2005.

FEA practice guidance. (2006a, December). Federal Enterprise Architecture Program Management Office, Office of Management of Budget.

FEA consolidated reference model document, Version 2.1. (2006b, December). Federal Enterprise Architecture Program Management Office, Office of Management of Budget.

FEA consolidated reference model document, Version 2.1. (2006c, December). Federal Enterprise Architecture Program Management Office, Office of Management of Budget.

FEA practice guidance. (2006d, December). Federal Enterprise Architecture Program Management Office, Office of Management of Budget.

Federal Enterprise Architecture Program EA Assessment Framework 2.0. (2005, December).

Gamma, E., et al. (1995). *Design patterns-elements of reusable object oriented software.* Reading, MA: Addison-Wesley.

Jacobson, I., et al. (1995). *The object advantage.* Reading, MA: Addison-Wesley.

James, G. A., Handler, R. A., Lapkin, A., & Gall, N. (2005). Gartner enterprise architecture framework: Evolution 2005. Gartner ID: G00130855.

James, G., Handler, R. A., Lapkin, A., Gall, N. (2005, October 25) Gartner enterprise architecture framework: *Evolution* 2005.

The data reference model, Version 2.0. (2005, November). Federal Enterprise Architecture Program Management Office, Office of Management of Budget.

Sowa, J. F., & Zachman, J. A. (1992). Extending and formalizing the framework for information systems architecture. *IBM Systems Journal, 31*(3), 590–616.

Zachman, J. A. (1987). A framework for information systems architecture. *IBM Systems Journal, 26*(3), 276–292.

Other Suggested Reading

Date, C. J., & Darwen, H. (1998) *The foundation of object relational databases.* Reading, MA: Addison-Wesley.

Larman, C. (2002). *Applying UML and patterns.* Upper Saddle River, NJ: Prentice-Hall.

3

ENTERPRISE-LEVEL DATA ARCHITECTURE PRACTICES

Enterprise-Level Architectures

Information is power in the modern world, and organizations with the most accurate and readily accessible data make the fastest decisions with the least negative impact. Making the best business decisions will positively affect the bottom line. This is something all businesses strive for. It translates into competitive advantage for the companies that are willing to invest in it. Of course, there is an investment, and often there is a slow initial start-up time, but it tends to accelerate once the initial setup activities have been accomplished.

In the next chapter you will learn more about the development of the organizational structures, objects, methods, and resources for implementing an enterprise-level information architecture, including the subarchitecture's enterprise-level system architectures, enterprise-level data architectures, and enterprise-level technology architectures.

Practice

- System architectures ensure that the current and future processing capabilities of the enterprise are not impaired during the development process.
- Technology architectures ensure that the enterprise is developing the right applications on the right platforms to maintain the competitive edge.
- Data architectures are the heart of business functionality. Given the proper data architecture, all possible functions can be completed within the enterprise easily and expeditiously.

System Architectures

An enterprise-level system architecture is an inventory mechanism that provides an automatic checklist of applications by function. This, taken in conjunction with an evaluation of each application within a scorecard range, allows strategic sequencing to take place in the mapping of new development applications (replacements) and remedied ones (reengineered). This ensures that development will take place when it is best suited to do so. Indirectly, it provides a matrix of application code to function, and in doing so provides some input into the reusability of the current code. The business systems architecture provides the mapping of current application systems to current data stores. All of these are of critical importance in maintaining control over one of the most expensive resources that the corporation invests in.

Enterprise Data Architectures

Enterprise-level data architectures ensure that the disintegration of integrated data stores is minimized. This ensures that current activity is sustainable while new development can take place. Also, using the same template also ensures that a foundation exists for the implementation of new techniques and technologies. They place tools and methods in relation to one another by virtue of an engineered structure. They also provide a way of quantifying risks and costing for or against implementing a new component of the architecture. In order to achieve the lofty objective of a corporate or an enterprise data architecture, it requires that organizational management address data as the critical resource and asset that it is.

Enterprise Technology Architectures

Enterprise-level technology architectures ensure that the enterprise is developing the right applications on the right platforms to maintain the competitive edge that they are striving for. Precious time in opportunity assessment is not wasted keeping a structure in place that provides a defaulting choice mechanism for each application. Also, the technology architecture provides a road map within each technology platform to ensure that the right tools and development options are utilized. This prevents additional time being spent extricating the application effort from previously experienced pitfalls.

But architectures aren't enough to ensure that the process and templates are used properly. Without the infrastructure mechanisms in place, the architectures, processes, standards, procedures, best practices, and guidelines fall by the wayside. We will cover in detail in the next chapter what groups are necessary and what roles they perform. With these data infrastructure mechanisms in place, the architectures have a chance of surviving the onslaught of the chaos brought about by changing priorities, strategic advantage, and just plain emergencies. We will cover the system and technology architectures with more detail in subsequent chapters, where they are more appropriately addressed.

Enterprise Architecture Terminology—Business Terms

We should take a moment to discuss some terminology and title structures to ensure that we understand those things that are involved in the infrastructure mechanisms. Detailed in the next few paragraphs are some of the terms and objects that we will be talking about.

First is a Business Entity Cluster (BEC). This is analogous to an Alexandrine "center" (as mentioned in the last chapter); a BEC is a consolidation or coalescence of data foci that deal with a "common" area of business subject matter within the corporation. Often business entity clusters appear to align themselves parallel to the abstracted division-level data needs of a corporation. While this is not a requirement, the situation often falls into place that way because it makes sound business sense. BECs are often expanded to the level necessary to cover all data foci in the enterprise's concerned applications that have been integrated or will be integrated.

Within these BECs are groupings or subclusters of entities that are denoted subject areas. It is of great importance to understand that this subject area orientation is concerned with the abstracted views of data independent of any lower process or business needs that are associated with it. They are specific as to data but independent of process. This is to ensure that while it will support the current business activity load, it is open and flexible for future down and outward specification. An example of a subject area would be finance or human resources.

As we descend one more layer we encounter business problem areas, which we can also refer to as data applications areas. These represent the collections of the specific data needed to support the business processes that advance the company's strategies and policies.

From the activity perspective, the Business Activity Segment (BAS) reflects a consolidation or coalescence of business activity foci within the corporation. Just as in the BECs at this level of abstraction, these are sympathetic in nature to the processes necessary for the organization process needs at the divisional level.

Within these BASs are groupings of subactivities known as functions. Another parallel can be drawn to the data side by realizing that functions are the process equivalent of subject areas in that they represent the abstracted process needs of the corporation at the departmental level. Functions are defined independent and without concern for the lower-level data needs. A function can be defined as an activity that has no start of completion other than with the life cycle of the corporation—for example, accounting or shipping. Again, these tend to resolve themselves to a departmental level of activity.

As we descend one more layer on the process side, as we did with the data, we come to functional process areas (FPAs), which can also be called process applications or simply applications. With this parallel structure in mind between process and data and the organizational levels associated with it, we can start dealing with composite objects and organizations specifically that address them.

The Enterprise Model

A compendium of the highest level of data and process models is an enterprise architecture model. This is a model that captures high-level business entities (BECs) and high-level business processes (BASs) that reflect the major reasons for the enterprise's (corporation's) existence. It is highly abstracted in nature and content, and it looks at things from the 50,000-foot level. There is not a great deal of detail, but the main subject areas are defined within their BECs and high-level functions are defined within their BASs. Further, external, subsidiary models deal with the specification of data at the application level.

In previous paragraphs we spoke of data architectures and system architectures as being part of the enterprise architecture. Other names we will use as synonyms for the manifest product of these architectures will be corporate data model and corporate activity model.

The Enterprise Data Architecture from a Development Perspective

The major premise here is that the enterprise data architecture (or an active copy of it) will be the source and repository of all development models. This ensures consistent development, minimization of disintegration, and enterprise data architecture concurrency. In the following paragraphs we will talk about the roles and responsibilities of various levels of management. We will do this in parallel with the different levels of data abstraction.

To do this, we will look at data and organization from a top-to-bottom approach. If we look at the major phases of a model-driven development process, we will see that each of these stages is definable, is discrete, and produces work products that are usable in the next phase of the development process. These stages are an analogous implementation of the Zachman framework stages. The first of these stages is planning.

Planning

Planning is the major function that provides a road map into the future that includes all strategic efforts and the ability to respond to competition-triggered or spontaneous events. By defining that road map into the future, resources can be planned for, expenses can be projected, purchases can be made, and deliveries can be completed on or near the time they are necessary to be completed. Models developed here will feed the analysis and design stage.

Analysis and Design

Analysis is a major function by which business requirements are investigated and documented in such a way as to be reusable for other purposes such as reference, validation, assessment, education, and traceability. By capturing the business requirements for each business area, the processing needs of that area are directly addressable and ensure that the knowledge of the business application is defined. This analysis is done independent of consideration of the organizational structure and the technology platforms available. This is to ensure maximum flexibility in choice for the target architecture. Models developed here will feed the transformation or translation stage.

Transformation

The transformation process translates the business requirements in a logical business model into a model that is "acclimatized" to the target environment it will be operating in. This translation includes DBMS specification as well as resource specification such as physical DASD storage for data and indexes.

Also included in this stage are those changes to the logical and physical model structure that will ensure good performance. The overall effort is to create the smallest physical "footprint" on DASD for the resulting database while still retaining all the original characteristics of the business requirements. Models developed here will feed the implementation stage.

Implementation

The implementation process moves the translated model into a physical environment. This includes the utilities that are run against the database, as well as mechanisms that are created to recover or secure images of the data for security and safety purposes. The implementation also allows active programs to execute their processes against the data store. This is known as the application function and is the only reason that the database exists. The application code or programs allow the business user to interact with his data in a formalized or ad hoc manner.

Practice

The following are the major factors in the success of the implementation of an enterprise architecture:

- Identification of subject area
- Identification of subject area drivers
- Naming and object standards
- A commitment to data sharing
- A data dictionary tool or lexicon
- Defined and controlled domain constraint data
- Proper organizational controls

Subject Area Drivers

Before we go much further, we must consider some facts about subject areas. Within each subject area lies a core or base entity that is the focus of the subject area—the nucleus of the Alexandrine "center." It is, as it were, the kernel of the subject area. It often is represented by an entity whose primary identifier can be readily correlated to the filing tab hierarchy that was used when the system was manually controlled. If the system wasn't a manual system, then it would be the file organization key, such as the key set in a VSAM database. These kernel entities and their identifiers are collectively known as subject area drivers. A few examples of kernel entities in a financial area are loan, account, and customer. In a manufacturing area, they would be product, market, sales, and inventory (both material and product).

This is because when changes are made to these entities, it most often ends up being propagated throughout the entire subject area. Knowing what subject area drivers are critical to an enterprise often allows subject areas to be skeletally defined and then fleshed out over time in the process of enterprise activity modeling. There are critical success factors for subject area implementation when this is done. Aside from the architectural dependencies we have just noted, there are others that are more indirect.

Naming and Object Standards

One of the most critical components of the architecture is a defined set of naming structures for all objects in the process. The identification process helps define which activities are associated with what data items, as well as specification as to what stage the object is in the design process. Object names should be the result of a consistent translation of the business reference to the object assigned in either a manual or automated mechanism that ensures uniqueness. The lexicon or data dictionary for the individual application must reuse the corporate lexicon in order to ensure data sharing opportunities. (A friend of mine in the industry once said, "The biggest problem with data dictionaries is that they are often written by IT people, not businesspeople. They tend to state the obvious (e.g., restate the name) rather than provide any real insight into meaning, domain of values, usage or source.")

Often there is an adjunct to a passive lexicon or data dictionary. This is an automated routine for the generation of database object names based on the known or defined standard. The names often consist of a root, one or more modifiers, and a class word. The root is the main descriptor of the name and tells the reader what the object is concerned with. The modifiers are qualifiers that amend or further define the root. The class word defines what type or class of object it is. An example would be:

Root = account
Modifiers = overdraft *and* limit
Class word = code
Therefore, the name would be "account overdraft limit code."

The routines themselves use algorithms to abbreviate the formal, long names that may be up to 30 to 60 characters long into something more acceptable to the programmer and DBMS limitations. The abbreviated names are then used in the creation of the database objects.

The initial start of these algorithms is usually a base pool of the appropriate industry abbreviations. If a known abbreviation is found, it is used in the name. If no abbreviation is found, the abbreviation algorithm is engaged to shorten the name. Because the algorithm always functions the same way, the names for similar or related objects have resemblance and consistency.

This algorithm can be used for data names in all stages of development but is most critical in the transformation/translation stage. Having standard names for the same objects ensures that there is consistency among all those involved in the design process when referring to specific objects. For example, developers can talk to database administrators and clients in the same language by using the same object names.

An additional character may be used in the physical names to indicate the object type when there are several that are derived from one. For example, a view of a table may have a "v" in the name at a particular node to indicate a view. An "I" may be used in the same situation to denote indexes.

Data Sharing

In order to accomplish maximum productivity in an enterprise architected environment, it is critical to define those things that are associated with the sharing of data. Among the most critical are the characteristics of the data itself and some of the problems that arise with multiple users of the same data. First, we will cover different data classes, and then we will discuss the sharing rules and limits.

Data Sharing Requirements

1. Data sharing should be defined as a policy and standard approach. In effect, all development must be sanctioned by management as being rooted in the subject areas and that a standard data-driven approach is defined and published by management.

2. Data ownership, data content security, and action sequencing must be resolved. Specifically, the ownership of data must be defined. Initially it must be defined at the entity level and subsequently at the attribute level. Ownership definition includes specification of all create, read, update, and delete (CRUD) categories. Also, data content security must be defined. This

includes the change rules concerning the data content as well as the release/distribution of the data. Finally, action sequencing must be accomplished to ensure that the shared data is accessed at the appropriate time in the attribute life cycle. This action sequencing defines in what sequence the data is updated, changed, or deleted.

3. A glossary of data sharing terms must be available for reference by the users of the data. This is most appropriately addressed by having a complete and comprehensive data dictionary.

4. Naming standards for entities and attributes must foster understanding of the data. The names of the attributes and entities must reflect the real business use of the data. No two attributes can have the same name. There must be one primary agreed-upon name for an attribute, and alias names should be discouraged in the long term.

5. Validation logic and translation rules must be defined for domains being shared. Valid values and ranges must be agreed upon and published for use in accesses of the domain data. Translation rules must be defined to minimize the proliferation of aliases.

6. The shared data model must be the simplest nonredundant image of the data that can be constructed (using canonical synthesis or CASE tools like Er Studio or ERwin).

7. Domain constraint data (valid value, valid ranges, translation, existence, and algorithmically derived data) must be separated from business data with no keyed relationships to the applications data.

8. Generalization hierarchies must be fully expressed (all super type–subtypes defined) in order to ensure that all data are available for sharing. This allows future or shared development to occur.

9. The logical data format must exist in a standard form (minimally, third normal form). This is generally documented in an ERD and associated attribute lists. This is true for structured as well as object approaches.

10. The stability of the business rules concerning the business data must be defined. If the business rules are not defined, the shared databases disintegrate into individual application databases reflecting singular business views.

11. The business need time frame for data sharing must be practical. It is inappropriate to have business users that have different data refresh requirements on the same database unless there is a lowest common denominator that they can share.

When the subject areas are defined, there are logical integration issues that must be addressed to ensure that current and ongoing activity can be coordinated. Resolution of these issues also ensures data sharing capability. As in all situations where data are gathered for common use, there are some considerations and "rules" that should be observed to maximize the use of the data:

- All subject entities must be added to an existing subject area. If a suitable subject area does not exist, it must be created.
- Project models must be reconciled to the subject area logical model in order to get into the release concept with implementation methods.
- The subject area logical model must remain as close to third normal form as possible. Collapsing and other forms of denormalization should not be done in the SALM but can and should be done in the appropriate application physical model.
- Relationships can exist between subject areas. It is, after all, merely a relationship between two entities within entity clusters. Optionality of relationships should be handled according to prevailing standards on the topic.

Data Dictionary–Metadata Repository

A data dictionary represents a compendium of all data definitions at the lowest level. That is, it consists of data attribute names and the definitions and characteristics associated with them. Normally it is established at the enterprise level but sometimes at the application level on an exception basis. While it is not necessary to compile this, it can be used as a guideline or source of new data names.

The enterprise level lets the pool of data attributes be reused throughout the enterprise, ensuring integrity of output while fostering understanding of the data. While it is critical to have a data dictionary of some kind, it doesn't matter how it is implemented. As long as it contains or references the procedures and policies that ensure that all development is assisted or implemented by way of a data dictionary, it will ensure success and data sharing.

Dictionary policies and procedures must be defined and publicized due to the need for the developer, the modeler, and the client to all agree on how to encode the requirement in the dictionary. It must be sponsored from IT management as well as client management, since it is often seen by the client as unnecessary overhead. But, as we have seen, once it is defined for the transaction system, it becomes available for the reporting and EIS systems that will follow later on. It will also provide a basis for data sourcing for the data warehouse that will eventually be designed.

Domain Constraints in Corporate and Non-Corporate Data

Domain constraint data fall into two levels of distinction. The first we can refer to as the corporate level; it represents that set of data that the corporation, as a whole, uses. That is to say, it is reference data for all departments in the corporation. This type includes company office tables, zip code tables, shipping tables, department cost codes, as well as other translations, and the like.

The second level of domain constraint data is those that apply to an individual application and represent domain limits for data unique to that application. Examples of these are permitted values for car color in the 1998 model year of General Motors trucks and postal codes for shipping locations for specific product types. Therefore, the second category is at a lower level or more specific level of detail. Whether the domain constraint is first or second level is immaterial when it comes to validation rules/policies and translation rules/policies. These two must be defined to ensure that the domain constraint is used properly and accurately reflects the true limits required by the business entity using it.

Organizational Control Components

The organizational components that engender full control of an architected approach to database design include data administration, database administration, and model repository management. In the context of having a comprehensive strategic data plan, having data architecture implies that the infrastructure of the organization is present and competent to handle the needs of the organization. Therefore, enterprise data architecture must include the mechanisms to support the models of the organization's data:

1. The capture and transformation of logical data models
2. The capture and retention of the physical data models and schemata
3. The process and means by which the physical models and schemas are implemented
4. The DBMS engines and DBMS extensions that will be used to support the architecture
5. The products used to manage the database, such as the tools and techniques that are used to ensure data integrity and quality on the platforms where they are housed

This is a tall order but critical to the success of the effective organization. Let us cover each of these areas in turn.

Data Administration

The data administration area consists of the personnel who are involved in the capturing of the business requirements from the business problem area. Also, they are responsible for integrating with and receiving model constructs and high-level definitions from the corporate architects and capturing these within reusable constructs such as case tools and data dictionary/repositories. They are also responsible for maintaining these model structures over time and ensuring that they reflect the business.

Data administration's focus is on managing data from a conceptual, DBMS-independent perspective. It coordinates the strategies for information and metadata management by controlling the requirements gathering and modeling functions. Data modeling supports individual application development with tools, methodology(ies), naming standards, and internal modeling consulting. It also provides the upward integration and bridging of disparate application and software package models into the overall data architecture. This overall data architecture is the enterprise data model and is critical in the organization's ability to assess business risk and the impact of business changes.

Database Administration

The database administration area is responsible for the structures that will be designed from the models that the data administration area produces. Also, as input they will take information about where the application will run and how it will be used in order to structure and organize it appropriately.

As the multitier architectures, data distribution and replication, data warehousing, stored procedures, triggers, and Internet data management bring new focuses to bear in the information processing community, the database administration area must respond to these pressures in a rapid and infrastructurally sound manner. Many organizations, through growth or unmanaged technology architecture, find themselves in the unenviable position of managing and controlling multiple DBMSs with anywhere from two to two hundred databases of each type. Keeping control of an armload of live eels is easier than managing this type of environment.

What can an organization do to counterbalance the entropy that results from these complex environments? What are the main problem areas? The following are some of them:

- *Multiple hardware platforms*, such as mainframe, server (database, network, and Web), and workstation

- *Different operating systems* that each have their own command set and interface
- *Different DBMS engines* that operate from different meta-model architectures and control management languages
- *Multiple physical locations* that distribute data across the street, town, state, or country
- *Middleware connectivity* that is used to connect all the different locations and hardware and operating systems
- *Data management tools* that can be used to move, massage, restructure, propagate, replicate, and maintain large structures housing the different types of data
- *Managing the application/DBA support interface*, which will provide the efficient development for the many applications that will serve the multitude of users

The depth of knowledge required by the DBA organization in these areas is substantial, depending on the organization's investment in each area. Because data is the focus in modern information processing, it is the core of the applications and in the applications of the DBMSs. Unfortunately, they are seen as bottlenecks in the process. This is simply because the complexity of the environment allows or promotes performance degradation and the breakdown of processes within it.

How does an organization manage to keep up? In the old days (a few years ago at the current speed of technological evolution), the DBA was a crotchety technologist who had unquestioned technical information and absolute authority over the data. This is not so anymore. Because of the speed of evolution, the technical absolutism has given reign to a conceptual knowledge of the internal structure of the DBMSs and databases. Technical knowledge alone is insufficient to ensure the success of the DBA function within an organization. Today, for example, business rules, relational optimization, access methods, integrity constraints, stored procedures, and user-defined functions exist within the database. The database isn't an owned thing anymore. It is shared by the DBA, the application, and the user.

The most that can be truly said today is that the DBA area owns the structure of the data and has a custodial responsibility for the data integrity and data quality. What tools does the DBA need in order to function properly? Simply put, they fall into three categories:

1. *Object management tools* that enable the DBA to perform everyday functions on the objects with his or her domain. Their functionality is limited to object migration, browsing, and modification.

2. *Utilities*, which are the tools that allow the DBA to maintain the databases. These maintenance functions include loading data, unloading data, reorganizing data, backing up data, recovering data, and validating data structure integrity.
3. *Performance monitoring tools*, which are tools that help identify and correct performance problems such as performance monitors, SQL analyzers, capacity planning and performance modeling tools, and systems adjustment tools.

These tools are necessary for the ongoing success of DBAs; make sure you have them on hand.

Setting Up a Database Administration Group

The most commonly asked question is, "How do I set up and develop a DBA organization?" Well, the rules are flexible and customizable, but the most common areas to consider are the following ones:

- **Build a centralized DBA area.** In other words, have an area that supports both production and development. This will keep maximum depth of support, foster cross training, increase communication, and provide continuity within the development life cycle (no transitions within the development cycle). It serves to ensure information sharing and creative solutions to major problems. Most crises are solved by the meetings held in the cubicle aisles and not in the conference rooms.
- **Place the DBA area in optimal position within the IT organization.** The DBAs are the custodians and stewards of the data asset for the organization and as such approach database design from a long-term and enterprise-wide data strategy perspective. Their client (application development and maintenance), however, approaches the data from a deadline-oriented, project-driven, and tactical perspective. This is a guaranteed collision that needs to be managed.
- **The DBA area must have significant autonomy in relationship to the client community.** If they do not have it, then their effectiveness is degraded and their expertise degraded to being merely rubber stamps to the application development area's whims. A truly strategic information resource management function should encompass both data administration and database administration and report at the CIO level. If this is not possible, then it should be a separate peer-level organization within the support groups.

- **Embed continuity of objectives in functional areas.** This continuity must exist among the DBA, the data administration, and model repository management areas. It is critical that these three areas have a seamless and rapid method for design development. If this is not done or is poorly engineered, it is a self-fulfilling prophecy: the design process becomes an impediment to the development process. It is an absolute requirement that these three areas work in tandem or lock-step, with the work products of the first feeding directly into the second and so forth. The policies and procedures should dovetail, and there should be no loose ends to prevent full closure of the design process. This will also provide a complete audit trail from the analysis stage through design and finally to implementation.
- **Publish standards for the development process and the implementation of databases.** These standards cover the naming of database objects, coding of SQL, use of triggers and stored procedures, commit frequency, and referential integrity, among others. This type of documentation should be in the developers' hands before they create the prototype or proof of concept databases. An education process may be necessary with the developers that allow questions and answers to take place that will allow ambiguity to be resolved. This should also have specific details as to how purchased software packages are handled upon selection.
- **Perform design reviews and preimplementation walk-throughs.** Design reviews should take place with the specific people needed for that level of validation. Architecture and scoping should be done with the user, analysis and design should be done with the application leader and team, and implementation should be done with operations and support organizations.
- **Implement service-level agreements.** The user customer should understand the operational climate of their application and database. Their service level should be defined and published with system documentation to afford future monitoring. The specific metrics that will be used to agree on successful performance should be defined and published. The following categories should also be addressed, such as responsiveness to error call, hours of support coverage, availability, maintenance windows, and recovery time.
- All of these and other specifics will help ensure the success of the database administration process within the IT organization.

Repository Management Areas and Model Management

The model repository management area is the group of personnel who are engaged in the maintenance and integration of all application models to the model inventory as well as to the corporate model. They are responsible for the maintenance of that data store that encompasses the data dictionary whether it is part of the modeling CASE tool or not.

An enterprise's information architecture must be capable of containing multiple levels of information (i.e., conceptual/planning models, logical models, and physical design models). The capture of information can be top-down, bottom-up, or middle-out, depending on the tools and methodologies being used.

Many current industry reports support the strategy of using multiple BPR tools. These reports state, "Using direct bridges between multiple modeling tools that have been purchased over time will in effect build a best-of-breed solution for large-scale enterprise modeling and may be the best decision given the amount of investment an enterprise has in a given set of technologies."

The model management policy must support a release-based system development methodology. A *release* is a group of business processes that can be delivered with a minimum of time and effort without compromising the options for the delivery of the rest of the business processes.

A model management strategy is of little use unless there are policies and procedures in place that back up the strategy. By this we mean that models that are generated at the application level are seeded from an enterprise model and are reconciled back to it. If there is no enterprise model to source from, it can be built by aggregation. This is a process by which the enterprise is built by integration of all of the modeled application views. Also to be considered is the history of the models, which represents the application requirements state as of a given date.

Also critical in this subcomponent of the infrastructure is the need for training of the user of the model management process. This includes those application personnel as well as repository personnel who are involved with the retrieval, update, and reconciliation of the models to the enterprise or corporate model.

Another area of significant concern is the area of human resources that are to be invested in the process from the user or client community. These subject matter experts (SMEs) are those individuals who have a complete and thorough understanding of the business processes and the business data. They are critical in the requirements-gathering phase to ensure that the true requirements have been met by the design and also to provide issue resolution when and if this occurs between the application developer, the data administrator, and the database administrator.

In summary, the enterprise-level architecture and model are dependent on the existence and coordination of infrastructure areas that maintain the currency and quality of the enterprise model, the subject area drivers, the data-sharing standards, the data object naming standards, the development and implementation methodology, and the rules that control the domain constraint data.

These infrastructure areas are the information architecture group, the data administration area, the database administration area, and the model repository and management area. Proper staffing and training are critical for success in initiating, implementing, and maintaining an enterprise architecture.

References

Although I have not cited any sources because this is excerpted from my own unpublished writings, the content of this chapter is rooted in the fundamentals expressed in the following books.

Fleming, C. C., & von Halle, B. (1989). *Handbook of relational database design.* Reading, MA: Addison-Wesley.

Tannenbaum, A. (1994). *Implementing a Corporate Repository.* The Models Meet Reality: John Wiley & Sons, Inc. New York, NY, USA.

4

UNDERSTANDING DEVELOPMENT METHODOLOGIES

Design Methods

Many software projects suffer from budget overruns, time synchronization problems, and the delivery of applications that do not satisfy the specified client requirements. Moreover, the developed application systems need to be responsive to change and yet be maintainable to reflect changing requirements. In order to address these issues in a structured manner, design methodologies were created. Many design methodologies have survived the revolutions that have taken place in the data processing industry, and they still provide methods of addressing these issues.

Principle

Methodologies provide guidelines for the application development process. They specify analysis and design techniques as well as the stages in which they occur. They also develop event sequencing. Lastly, they specify milestones and work products that must be created and the appropriate documentation that should be generated.

Computer-aided software engineering (CASE) tools are useful for supporting the software development process by providing heuristics encoded into their software that help with design decisions. They are also helpful with the preparation and maintenance of the design documentation, which often includes graphic as well as textual material.

Increasingly, CASE software tools are available with some capacity for code and database schema generation. Commentary on this subject will be covered in another chapter. In order to examine some of the characteristics of the existing methodologies, we must review when and where the methodologies arose and what problems were trying to be solved at the time. Practical discussion of the problems with some of these implemented methodologies will be discussed in a later chapter. The review covered here is to show the stepwise evolution to current significantly successful methodologies.

There are many different types of development methodologies that have been developed over the years since simple file systems were used in the 1960s and 1970s. They have all centered around how to address business activity and business data, and in what order. As you will see in the next chapter, the focus on data shifted from the separate business functions that use particular data to the data that are used by many processes. This shift dictated a data-driven approach in the requirements definition area in response to the business need. This has further been driven by the object oriented paradigm that focuses on all processes for a particular piece of data.

Why Do We Need Development Methodologies?

The heart of all development methodologies is the servicing of business needs. There was, and is, a business need to develop applications that utilize data responsively to the competitive needs of the marketplace. In the next chapter, we will cover some of the methodologies for application development, how they originated, and what benefit they supplied in the evolution of methods. We will start with the earliest of the designed methods and cover in brief the concepts of each. We will start from structured methods and go through structured programming, then go on to structured analysis, and finally we will cover structured design.

We will also cover a particularly successful structured design (information engineering) that originated decades ago but still is viable and in use today. It is an overall development control process that ensures success and integration (including application development templates and service-level contracts to ensure on-time development), as well as metrics to ensure accurate monitoring of the development process in its various stages. We will also briefly cover another competing method—the object design method—which has been used on smaller applications that requires significant interface with the user.

The Beginnings

There was a time when activities were always done by hand, and each work artifact was custom made. This applied to everything, including sculpting, painting, carving, building, tool making, and the like. For examples here, we will deal with an ordinary building activity: furniture building.

Furniture building has existed since man created places to reside in. Through the ages it became a profession as some craftsmen became quite good at it and specialization took place. The problem was that furniture produced by skilled craftsmen was very expensive. When the artisan died, there were only his apprentices who could repair or create another piece of the same style. The quality of the furniture varied significantly between craftsmen, and none of the pieces from the different craftsmen had interchangeable parts. Even the tools that were used to create and repair the furniture were custom made and varied from craftsman to craftsman.

All of this was challenged by the introduction of powered machines into the activities process. With the advent of the machine, custom craftsmen processes could be broken down into component activities and a machine used to create them. William Morris, the furniture maker, was one who recognized early that machines could, and would, eventually replace people in the manufacturing of furniture. He dabbled in using machines to produce furniture but was dissatisfied with the quality of the final product. He eventually chose to reject the concept at that time and return to hand designing and building his exquisite pieces that we cherish today. It was not until another furniture maker, Gropius, decided to use machines in furniture making that the machine was finally harnessed to compete in this way. The machines did come and they did replace the process, and in doing so, they lowered the prices of the delivered goods. It made sense from a price and repairability perspective. The conclusion we can reach is that market pressures will force the inevitable and that avoiding a design or process problem will only be a temporary measure. It has to be solved.

Structured Methods

If we advance the calendar forward to modern times and the age of computers, a similar problem can be seen. The same issues that had occurred in the furniture-making world (and other activities) held true in data processing. The structured methods approach evolved from the need to standardize things in order to maximize the process. To bring the craftsman-versus machine-made conflict into perspective, we can consider the efforts that went into the mass-production process that Eli Whitney first instantiated.

Eli Whitney, who resided in Westborough, Massachusetts, was adept at machinery making. Two of his inventions would have profound effects on the country: the cotton gin, which revolutionized the way southern cotton was cropped and processed, and his interchangeable parts, which would revolutionize northern industries and, in time, become a major factor in the North's victory in the Civil War.

Before Whitney's concepts were in place, every useful machine or mechanism was created by hand. That is, when a new one was needed, it had to be built from scratch. Each part was developed separately and then fitted together by the same single artisan. The same artisan had to do all the work, or it might not fit with the other components. The process was very slow, there was no separation of labor effort, and no power tools were available at the time.

When Eli Whitney was contracted in 1798 to develop rifles for the new army of the colonies, he analyzed the conventional procedure and saw where it was failing. Using this knowledge, he created a procedure we have come to know today as the American system of manufacturing, which is comprised of the use of power machinery, the use of interchangeable parts, and the division of labor. This would set the stage for the nation's subsequent Industrial Revolution.

Whitney created a process where all the components could be manufactured separately according to a planned standard of size and shape. When the time came to demonstrate that he could create the rifles, he and a small group of skilled workmen assembled a rifle in minutes rather than the many weeks that had been required for each rifle before.

Principle

Standards must be defined because assembly implies that all pieces of a particular type are uniform. All of any particular part must be interchangeable between constructs. A defined procedure or method has been defined for assemblage. Each assembled product is evaluated or measured against a representative standard.

Other structured processes followed suit, such as assemblage from preconstructed modules. These concepts have been in use since that time. They were structured procedures to ensure an assembly process could take place rather than the handcrafting or being built to order process.

As seen from these time periods, these are not new concepts. But when the data processing industry began its evolution and change, the concepts found new ways to be applied. Let's examine the sequence of the evolution in data processing.

Structured Programming

Structured programming was the first implementation of structured techniques used in data processing. The advent of structured programming began in the early 1970s and was due primarily to the efforts of Dijkstra (Dahl et al., 1972). They put forth the ideas of defining levels of abstraction and the definition of stepwise refinement.

Briefly this can be described with the concepts stated in the following paragraphs. Traditional application analysis started with application processes that were in existence at the time; improvements to these processes were derived by meeting with the client and arriving at new output products from the application. The analyst would then begin to work backward to define the data and the data structures to hold the data. This would continue until the business need was met.

The newly proposed program construction techniques involved the assessment of the program code itself. There was a formalization of the standard structure of the programs, and evaluations were introduced to complete the concept of how to best sequence the functionality within programs. This rigor would reduce redundancy within the programs and allow some commonality when dealing with multiple programs. The uniformity introduced would lend itself to easier maintenance. In addition, these concepts were applied to the connectivity of programs and their linkages into larger programs.

Structured Design

The second evolutionary step that occurred in structured techniques was structured design. The structured design movement began in the mid-1970s. Due to the efforts of Yourdon and Constantine (1975), with their definition of structured design, and Jackson (1975) and Orr, with their respective design methodologies, by 1975 the structure philosophy had made some gains and inroads.

These, plus the improvements seen as a result of structured programming, fostered a renewed interest in applying more structured concepts in other areas. The renewed interest in structured concepts was applied to the problem-solving process of the programs and their interfaces. Where the structured programming concept addressed an instruction-level view of the program, the structured design focused on the concept of the program module as a building block. It advocated a top-down approach of program development in module form, with the top modules being developed first. It also advocated the packaging of logic into modules, ensuring that problem isolation for program failures or "bugs" was enhanced.

By ensuring that the modules were tested as they descended down in the processing hierarchy, the application could be tested as it was developed rather than waiting for the entire application program to be coded prior to testing. It was also tested as a whole once completed, but the process allowed a more gradual ramp-up time with better division of labor in the development process. More could be done with fewer people over time.

Structured Analysis

The structured concepts reached their peak in the structured analysis approach, which is currently in existence in many different forms. In the structured analysis approach, the current application system was captured in the "data flow diagram." The technique itself advocated the separation of the logical design and physical implementation. To achieve this, the existing data store was viewed as the old physical model, and a new logical model was derived from it. If there were no previous system in place, then the manual process would be analyzed as if it were one and documented as so. This new logical design was then focused on *what* was done rather than *how* it was done.

Changes could then be applied to the logical model that encompassed the client's desired changes. The changed model would become an even "newer" new model and be translated into a new physical model for implementation. As a result of the impact this approach had on the evolution of the relationship between the business problem and the program solution, the concept of modularization was refined. This refinement gave uniformity to program module structure, interface and communication restrictions between modules, and quality measurements. Later, some of the significant findings during this time were useful in forming the conceptual roots of object oriented design, which we will cover in more detail elsewhere.

Still Having Problems

In the late 1970s, there were still problems in developing quickly created, efficient programs and data stores that provided the necessary response time for the application client. The problem wasn't in the programs, and it wasn't really in the design. Where could the problem be? Simply put, it was occurring when there wasn't enough time spent in evaluating before a creation effort began. The seeds of the failure were in the starting parts.

Something was wrong with the basic premises that the efforts were beginning with. Not enough analysis was taking place before building. There was no way to know when analysis was complete. By the late 1970s, multiple views of structured analysis were being fielded. Along with this, there were efforts on the data structure side by Edgar Codd (1970) with the normalization and relational theory. The time was ripe for analyzing the true cause of the poor application quality.

Requirements Definitions

By this time, the true source of problem solutions had been traced back to the poor definition of the requirements. Because these were used as the primary form of metrics for the problem solution to be measured by, it would seem necessary to apply some standardization to this area as well. By use of the data flow diagram, where data to be reused later were defined in "data stores" and the use of a "data dictionary," the requirements were more understandably captured. It is captured in a manner that is understandable and acceptable to the client as well as the analyst.

Problems with Structured Approaches

Despite all of the advantages of using structured techniques, there were problems inherent in the complete path of structured techniques: structured programming, structured design, and structured analysis. They primarily were based on the evaluation of the current application system, be it automated or not. They were based on the procedures that would aid in automating the current application but not for enhancing the application. They would also fall short in that situation where integration was desired. Data in any corporation is to some degree redundant, but using structured techniques propagated the creation of additional redundant data stores.

The result was that each analyst was utilizing her own models and dictionaries without coordinating with other analysts. The result of this was that data that should have a common name ended up having different names and characteristics, even though it was the same data. By the same token, common logical data structures, by now called entities, ended up being composed of different data. As time went on, it became an increasingly complex effort to manage, but it was attempted with some manner of success through the later part of the 1970s. This too, however, would soon end up failing but not for the poor definition of the requirements. It would be brought about by a revolution within the evolution: the computer information revolution of the 1980s.

Personal Computers and the Age of Tools

By the early 1980s, a small, quietly evolving "life form" exploded into an evolutionary niche reminiscent of the rise of mammals in earth's prehistory. That life form was the personal computer or microcomputer. The prodigious expansion of computers during this time frame led users to be more data literate and aware of its usefulness. Added to this awareness was the increased development of databases. And also thrown into the mix was an explosion of competition in the business world. What was happening was that new processes needed to be in place sooner, ensuring competitiveness in the marketplace.

Applications couldn't be developed fast enough, even with all of the structured approaches in place and in use; the pace could not be met. The search to produce things faster created a flurry of new languages, new report generators, database tools, query tools, and code generators.

The awareness finally occurred when the decision was made to use computers to help design computer processes. By encoding the structured methods of the earlier years into tools that could be used for design, speed of development could be gained. They could be used to alter structured diagrams, maintain data dictionaries, and automate the data modeling that had been developed—all of which brought speed to the design process.

All of these tools are in use today but in a more robust form because they too evolved in order to produce even faster developed applications. These robust tools are regarded as a new breed of tools that fall into the category of CAD (computer-aided design) products. Although this is an old term that came about in the early days of structured techniques, it was applied thoughout the 1970s and 1980s as a generic class of automated tools that produced applications faster. This era saw the interconnection of design tools to the implementation tools for databases and the code generators for application code creation.

In theory, one could capture user requirements and generate an application directly, without contact with a programmer. In fact, there are still problems associated with requirements capture, and unless the structured concept is taught to the client, the requirements may still end up being fraught with gaps and failures.

Engineering Concepts Applied

The structured concept has basic characteristics that need to be understood in order to understand the intrinsic functioning of the CAD tools today. The first characteristic is that of *abstraction*. To do this is to view something by itself without reference to common connections. When it is applied to a person, place, or thing, it allows the intrinsic traits of the abstracted entity to be viewed without reference to its placement or use. Just as you can understand the true meaning of a word by examining it out of a sentence, doing the same for an entity allows more detailed examination.

The second characteristic is *structured approach*. This is exactly what it seems to be. It is a step-by-step process that has been defined that ensures that a procedure or method is followed and that the work products of one step are used as input to the following step. This also referred to as stepwise refinement. By following the step-by-step approach, all projects are in definable stages at any given point of time. When the input products of each step and the output products are defined, then reusability and sharing are by-products. These steps and processes are repeatable. When they are not deviated from, they educate the developers into a faster methodology with each new application designed.

The third characteristic has to do with *component isolation*. This is separation or distinct isolation of the overall problem into a series of problem components so each can be addressed in turn without dealing with the complexity of the whole. Business problems had become so complex that it was almost impossible to entertain the entire business problem, never mind the abstractions of it. By solution of all of the isolated problem components, the resultant solutions can be integrated and the complete solution set produced.

Which brings us to a related fourth characteristic: *hierarchical ordering*. Hierarchical ordering is the next step to be done after component isolation. The hierarchical ordering of the solution components is done in such a way as to allocate each problem component to a layer in order to get integration. As the name implies, there is a hierarchy that allows the solution components to be viewed as layers. From the top, as each layer is removed, the subordinate layers with more detail can be viewed. When the solutions are integrated at the lowest level, each higher level can be viewed in an integrated manner. So whether following top-down or bottom-up approaches, the integrated result can be achieved.

Other Principles Utilized

Other principles of using computers and computer logic to design systems were in the process of manifesting themselves at this time as well. These also helped with the further definition of how best to develop applications. The first principle was that of *obscuring,* which was used as a modification of the breakdown process or decomposition activity necessary in structured design and structured analysis. This allowed *only* that data necessary for use by a detail process to be defined with that process. This fostered unit-level process specification and therefore facilitated modular programming.

The second principle concerned the *separation and regrouping* of logical things together physically. This allowed programs to deal with data at a particular location within the program without navigating all over the place. It aggregated processes together so the data only needed to be touched by the program code once.

Finally, there was the principle of *logical independence.* This was a premise asserting that data should be defined in its logical state as if it were not operated on by any process. This allowed the data to be defined without the constraint of having some process to use it.

The Birth of Information Engineering

All of these principles plus those of the structured techniques went into the formalized process that became known as information engineering. Two people central to this methodology were James Martin (1981) and Clive Finklestein (1981). This methodology took a fundamentally different approach from all the methods and techniques that had preceded it. By bundling all the known advantages into a methodology package and changing the central driving themes, it was possible to bring new forces to bear on the problems in data processing.

A common premise that was true in all corporations was that they had the data they needed to run their business (otherwise they would be out of business). Another thing was basically true: data within a corporation, once defined, tended to stay stable in its definition. New uses were found for existing data, and, rarely, new data was added, but most of the time it was stable. Lastly was the basic fact that business processes evolved very quickly. New ways to use data for competitive purposes churned the application need.

Information Engineering recognized that data has inherent properties of its own, independent of how it is used. It also recognized that some data are related to other data independent of use. The information engineering methodology embodied all the aforementioned principles, facts, and concerns into four basic tenets in its operation (1989).

- The first tenet is a principle of rigorous analysis. This basically states that data have an inherent structure. Analysis of this structure must be completed before process logic is defined. As a follow on, it should be captured for future use and reference.
- The second tenet, data independence, states that the inherent logical structure of the data should be captured in model form independent of how the data are used by any process and independent of how they will physically be implemented.
- The third tenet, strategic data planning, was a product of all the burgeoning systems being developed without a game plan. It states that there must be planning, definition, and structuring of data throughout an enterprise in order to facilitate data reuse and data exchange among many processes.
- The fourth and last tenet of information engineering, the principle of end-user access, states that end users should be facilitated in their quest for access to their data. This is a result of the clamoring of all professionals in the industry to have access to data that might increase their competitive advantage.

Information Engineering as a Design Methodology

We have examined some of the behavioral tenets of information engineering. Let us look at some of the characteristics it has when in use:

- It applies the structured techniques on an enterprise-wide basis rather than on a project basis. Instead of having many projects making up their own model according to their own standards, a common approach is being used.

- It progresses in a top-down fashion from the highest level of data abstraction to the lowest. For example, it deals in descending order with:
  - *Corporate systems planning*—A formal procedure and plan for definition of that set of existing and planned applications that provide the corporation to ensure competitive edge in the marketplace.
  - *Corporate information planning*—Another formal procedure and plan that identifies that set of information at a high level, which will be required for the corporate systems planning and will be used to "seed" all subordinate business area analysis:
    - Business area analysis (BAA)—Procedure and plan to deal with analysis of the major subject areas within the corporation.
    - Systems design—Application design procedures for the design of all applications within a BAA.
    - Construction—A set of procedures that creates the application physical structures that will be used to house the data, as well as that set of procedures that have captured how it will be used.
    - Implementation—A set of procedures for implementing the application, which may or may not utilize a code generator to do so.
- As it progresses, it builds an increasing store of knowledge about the enterprise, its models, and application designs. Although it may take time, the process will capture all the necessary data and processes that allow the corporation to run its day-to-day operations.
- It provides a framework for application development. By using models and defined procedures, it facilitates an organized step-by-step process for application development. It utilizes a repository for the accumulated knowledge that will be reusable for subsequent efforts.
- The corporate-wide approach allows maximum coordination and integration between separately developed applications. This maximizes reusability of both code and design. With the formalized application development process and the dictionary/encyclopedia that is required by information engineering acting as a repository for requirements and model caching, this maximizes the opportunities of data sharing while assuring the minimum set of data definitions.
- It involves clients at all of the preceding stages to a high degree. By encouraging and advocating client involvement in the requirements process at all levels of interface from top to

bottom, the methodology ensures that the true requirements have been met. This ensures that both IT and non-IT know the processes and deliverables for all tasks. It also ensures that any application created using these methods will meet the usage requirements of the client.

- It facilitates the evolution of different applications and, in turn, the evolution of the corporation. By developing applications faster and more responsive to client needs and ensuring the maintenance of these applications is minimized, it allows the corporation to respond more quickly to business pressures in the open market. The corporation can venture into fields that it couldn't before and trust its data in doing so.

- It identifies how automation can best achieve the strategic goals of the corporation. By assessing what needs to be automated and in what sequence, it provides a strategic pick list that allows the corporation to make the wisest decisions concerning the allocation of its human and financial resources.

The Synergy of Tools and Information Engineering

Parallel with and integral to the development of information engineering, the use of computers to aid in the design process allowed larger, more complex problems to be addressed. Simply put, it was because the problems had become too large for the human brain to retain all the necessary information. Definitions, layouts, character representations, report requirements, and identifiers were among the hundreds of pieces of information to be retained. Additionally, the requirement to retain graphics as well as textual data added an additional level of complexity to the solution. To do the designs properly, computer automation and the use of design tools were required.

As another factor in this crazy equation of the 1980s was the fact that with the use of computers increasing phenomenally in business, everything was needed more quickly. Decisions had to be made more quickly, data needed to be found more quickly, reports created more quickly, transaction response needed to be quicker. Speed was of the essence, but not at the sacrifice of accuracy and integrity. Be there first, with the best data, using the least resources to win in the marketplace.

Automation was the only way to cope—automation of both the application and application development process itself. In order to do this, some marriage of method and machine was necessary to ensure that business problems could be solved as fast as possible. The result would be a structured, formal manner that would allow reuse and produce repeatable results.

The information engineering methodology utilized the integrated efforts of everything that existed at its inception to formalize, within tools and without, a method for proceeding forward. As a result, almost all current CASE tools that are used in the design process acknowledge or inherently have manners of designing according to IE standards.

The IE approach has proven successful in recent years, holding sway over other development methodologies. Because it dealt with the corporation as a whole, it provided a common answer to many problems being faced by corporate management.

Problems with Information Engineering

But in the world of quick results and instant response, the effort sometimes took too long to establish. In order to truly implement the full IE foundation, the investment is significant, sometimes up to a full year to define the strategic data plan alone. Another six months or another year in creating the information strategy plan would follow this year. It is a long time frame to be laboring without some form of payback.

It is true that there is formality that provides limits and methods to the corporate environment where there may have been no methods or, worse yet, conflicting methods. There is also true architectural definition that puts companies in a much more responsive position as to change in the market or business climate.

Many companies regarded this as too steep an investment before any return would be seen at the application development level and chose not to use it. They felt the pain in the business process area, and that is where they wanted the relief. They understood that there are things they have done to get them in the mess, but what they wanted was a way out, not a list of the steps to be implemented in order not to have this happen again.

What they wanted was a solution at the application development level. Further, they wanted the application-level solution to be usable as a future construct toward that total environmental solution proposed by IE. In the configuration that was being used at the time for information engineering, it was all or nothing.

In those companies that did adopt it and fostered its growth and used it, an undercurrent of resistance began to form. It began to be regarded as a bottleneck to development. This is true to a degree in that until the practitioners were skilled, it took longer to achieve the goal. But in many companies it got a bad rap just because it set boundaries and limits on what was being done. It became just another obstacle in the path of disciples of the application development method of the month club.

Also of concern is the overall fact that when beginning with the corporate level and descending downward, one must have the staff and commitment to ensure that the process is followed and that the requirements are met. Many companies didn't have or want a corporate architecture group, a data administration group, a repository/encyclopedia group, and a database administration group. So much infrastructure and expense required supporting it. Along with this, policies, standards, and procedures had to be defined and propagated. There were education classes to be conducted, and tools and workstations to be purchased and installed.

At the application level, there is the view that traditional IE is best suited for designing transaction-processing systems. They feel that management information systems and data warehouses are not favorably treated if done in an information engineering manner. This is truly a misconception because without the high-level definition involved by IE, the true scope of an MIS reporting database or data warehouse could not be defined. Without the architecture in place, the decision support was only available at the application level, not at the enterprise level.

So information engineering was a right idea but possibly in the wrong flavor. Many companies in the business world needed a different flavor of the original. It is a flavor of the methodology where the burden of building the entire infrastructure to support the effort wasn't required to be shouldered by the initial project setting down the path.

Implementing the Best of IE while Minimizing Expense

It is to that end that a new flavor of IE is suggested that takes the best of both worlds and accomplishes the most with it. Simply put, it is the implementation of IE from two vectors at once: top-down and lateral. But this must be done in a sequence that minimizes cost.

The first step or stage should be the top-down definition of the information strategy plan (ISP). This is an attempt to determine the objectives of the enterprise and what data are needed to support it. The steps that we detail following this step may be done without doing ISP but it would be like building a house on top of gelatin. It would be unstable and shaky. The ISP can be accomplished with some degree of completion within several months if the SWAT team approach is taken. The information strategic plan must break down the enterprise into its major subject areas, and within these the business entity types must be defined. At the same time the business processes must be captured at the same level. In this same phase an additional step must be taken to identify major subject area drivers and inter-subject area relationships.

The data modeling phase would be next in the modified approach. It would be a lateral phase as opposed to a top-down phase. By *lateral*, we mean using data and process modeling to develop the enterprise repository by accretion or addition to the whole. This would be accomplished by adding and integrating the modeled data and process results to the repository with each application designed and implemented. Where the top-down approach was too limiting, it is far easier and less costly to build the repository content one application at a time and integrate the results to the whole. The process or activity analysis can then be further used in the interaction or mapping phase.

This phase is the mapping of processes against data, which then validates both the data model and the process model. It will ensure that all the business problem requirements have been captured in the solution data and process models. These will then enter the last stage of the modified version of IE: repository integration.

This last stage allows the integration of the captured business requirements into a repository for future use. By setting up the mechanism to integrate applications by subject area, there is a scorecard or inventory of what has been done in each subject area and what needs to be done. Additionally, this allows a buildup or ramp-up time for the other infrastructure functions to be created before they are needed. By the time that many applications needed to be integrated, the standards, policies, and procedures associated with this new brand of IE would be in place and be in use. Also, the repository and data and database administration staffs would be in place and be trained as well. In the following chapters we will cover the model-driven approaches that will accomplish a streamlined methodology in an optimal manner, including object design.

References

Codd, E. F. (1970). A relational model of data for large shared data banks. *Communications of the ACM, 13*(6), 377–387.

Codd, Edgar 'Ted', (1970). A relational model of data for large shared data banks, communications of the ACM, *13*(6), (June 1970).

Constantine, L., & Yourdon, E. (1975). *Structured design.* New York, New York: Yourdon Press.

Dahl, O.-J., Dijkstra, E. W., *C. A. R. Hoare,* (1972). *Structured Programming.* New York, New York: Academic Press.

Martin, J., & Finkelstein, C.: *Information Engineering, Savant Institute, Carnforth*: Lancs UK (1981).

Finklestein, C. (1992) *Information Engineering—Strategic Systems Development.* Addison-Wesley, Sydney: Australia.

Jackson, M. A. (1975). *Principles of Program Design.* New York, New York: Academic Press.

Martin J. *Information Engineering—books 1–3* (1989). Englewood Cliffs, NJ: Prentice Hall.

Orr, K. T. (1980). Structured programming in the 1980s. In: *Proceedings of the ACM 1980 annual conference ACM '80* (pp. 323–326). New York: ACM Press.

DeMarco, T., (1979). *Structured Analysis and System Specification.* Englewood Cliffs, NJ: Prentice Hall, ISBN 0138543801.

2

THE PROBLEM

5

BUSINESS EVOLUTION

The Problem of Business Evolution

This chapter describes the importance of the underlying business structure in relational database design, including business units, business politics, culture, and standards and policies. It explains optimum organizational policies and procedures structure for successful database design. As in all processes there are some general functions that are maintained in the business process that make it work more effectively. These are the functions, developed over time, that have applied to all businesses from the smallest store to the largest megacorporation. In the beginning, all businesses were started and run by one individual. The time it took for them to become megacorporations may have been brief, or they may still be in flight. Examining some of the base concepts involved by using a small business as a model may be helpful.

In a small business, the owner has all information about his or her business at hand. He knows who his best customers are. He knows their accounts and his customers' creditworthiness. He knows his own inventory levels and who and where his suppliers are. He even is aware of his suppliers' lead times. He knows the level of activity and the turnover and can establish his market base to ensure his own profitability.

By providing a reasonable product or service at a reasonable price, the owner knows that she will survive as long as she has no market overlap with others in the same business and there is a need for her product or service. She has established the direction of her company by choosing to service or produce a product that her market needs. She has provided a channel for sales either by inviting the customer in or by delivering the service or product out to them. Finally, she has provided objectives in the form of the quality of service or integrity of the product to the customer.

When the business owner is successful, his business grows. The volume of his sales increases. The profits roll in. He works at ways to ensure the best response to his customers' needs. He finds better suppliers and more quality material to make his products with. This increases his sales, as he soon becomes known as a purveyor of quality goods for a minimal price.

Expansion and Function Separation

Soon he cannot handle all of the positions and functions himself and has to hire a staff to fill the roles that he cannot. He separates his activities into each of the functions that he used to perform and trains someone to fill each role. Each appointee handles the data associated with his/her specific area or function. As he/she operates in the subsection they are responsible for, they become familiar with the data associated with the function and manage their own data. Further growth is the result of this efficiency that the business owner has put in place. He has more product, more sales, more profit, more sales, and so on. And this goes on until individuals cannot handle the functions anymore. It has become too much work for a single person again. Each appointee then has to select new people and train them. These people increase the efficiency and result in more sales and more business and so on. Growth is rampant, and the separated functions evolve into departments and the staff has increased manifold.

At this point in time the functions are still the same, but the scope and context of them have changed significantly. No longer is it possible for the one person to know all of the business data. Each functional area keeps its own information and makes sure it handles its own piece of the business. The owner has no real control. It is delegated out to the people who control the functions for him. In order to make sure everything is working right, the owner makes sure that sales data are sent to inventory control and accounting to ensure that billing is taking place. He wants to make sure that everything is going to run smoothly.

Separate Function Communication

In actuality there is the beginning of a crisis. In one function or department, such as inventory control, there is an immediate need for the data concerning what has been sold to the sales and marketing department and to what customer. This ensures that inventory is kept at "just in time delivery" levels, which will keep expenses down. It also provides a basis for customer service if there are problems with the product. When this occurs, reporting procedures are introduced to record sales, extraction from inventory, and profits. These data are then sent to other departments as reports to ensure that the other departments are kept informed. But physical reports are limiting, time consuming, and because most of the work is manual, prone to error.

Manual Data Redundancy

But now the company is keeping two or three or more redundant sets of customer data: one for the sales department, one for the invoicing department, one for the inventory department, and one for the accounting department. Since the communications of the changes to the common data have not been instantaneous, the information in the different departments is now not equivalent and now not accurate. The business can continue to flow the reports and even develop electronic feeds between computer systems to ensure sharing of data at the earliest possible point to keep integrity. Unfortunately, that is not a solution because data for the different areas are designed differently and accuracy is lost. Data and information slip through the cracks, and some of it is not retrievable. Data gathered by customer service on a returned defective product may not get to the sales and marketing, new product, or quality control areas in a timely enough fashion to solve the problem before more products go out the door. Maintenance and change control on the manual version of this structure/process is rigid and incredibly complex. Automating it to an electronic solution produces computer feeds that are subject to the same problems, delays, and missing data. Let us examine the company's data requirements at this stage of its evolution.

Each department, though keeping its own unique data due to its separated function, must keep some common data for use as well. A good example of the common data shown thus far is customer data. As each department has its own procedures for acting on their own version of data, they also each have activities that act on the data that are common—that is, customer data.

Additions, deletions, and updates to customer data that are common to other departments may need to be made by individual departments. How can they communicate the changes? Obviously, distributed reports are a poor method, and electronic feeds are better but still not instantaneous. The solution is to share it.

Practice

Suppose you had a requirement to allow ten people to touch a basketball in ten minutes. Each individual must touch it and do what they need with it. In most cases they would need to touch it, but one or two would need to sign it or mark it for posterity. Each individual in the group was designated as a Ball Toucher or a Ball Signer. The simple solution would be to pass the ball from one person to the next until all have touched or signed the ball. That is a fine and a good solution. But what happens when there are many more balls to be touched? Based on the speed of the passing and the time for touching or marking, the process would be slowed. A single limit would soon be approached that could not be surpassed. It is the limit of the process and is reflected in the maximum number of basketballs that are in transit at one time.

What would happen if the Basketball Processing Co. management got together and said, "You are taking too long. We need to get more throughput?" They might be right, so you have to find a way.

The way to solve management's problem is to put each ball in one place on a moving line and move it past a point in the process where all Touchers or Signers can touch or mark it at the same time. Of course, some etiquette might have to be worked out as to who needs to do what first—Signer or Toucher—but it is easily worked out, and the process is sped up hundreds if not thousands of times.

Departmental communication problems, data redundancy, and delayed incorporation of data changes can result in the inaccuracies in the data used throughout the company. Brought about by the separation of the functions that occurred with the growth of the business, we see that common data, customer data, has now been disseminated. This is true not only within departments but throughout the company. This data redundancy and inaccuracy have introduced a serious problem to management.

While the operational management that oversees the day-to-day operations only needs the data within their departments, top management needs a cross-departmental look at specific data. This specific data are the data that have been analyzed for a defined purpose.

Management Organization and Data

The head of the organization must now look at selected data or metrics data to evaluate how profitable her company is. She must look at information about her company. The improved data systems and the sharing of data make it now possible for the head and the management to draw on vast reservoirs of data that have been accumulated but been heretofore inaccessible. The technology has helped the business owner in her rise from a simple company to a large one with many departments. It helped her to gather, manage, consolidate, and summarize the data for management use. But in order to do this, there needs to be a more consistent approach to development of the information systems and processes and how and where the data are stored.

Data Planning and Process Planning

Data analysts and process analysts are people who are facile at defining the specific data and processes within a given business area. For example, if they were to visit the inventory control department, they would talk to the users and management and define the best ways to improve the process and data use for that department. However, if they were to go on to a second department, such as sales and marketing, after the implementation of the changes to the inventory control department, the analysis and redesign for the second business area might come in direct conflict with the changes already made.

What they really wanted was a single set of data that would serve the data needs of both departments, but what they got was the data of one and then the conflicting data of the other. This conflict appeared because the data needs of both were not looked at prior to any implementation or development, and moreover they were looked at from the perspective of the processes they had to serve. The process perspective on a finite set of data will only select that set of data that will serve that process, thereby excluding data that might serve other or follow-on processes. Management tends to want to develop single application systems to minimize costs and then single-thread the development of these to control the cost.

What they did is called "stovepipe" development, and its long-term impact is devastating. Organizations do change; they must change in order to survive. Applications developed in a monolithic or stovepipe manner are custom-built to the specifications that they were given. Each one is developed sequentially. The systems they introduced with such fanfare become crippling ball-and-chains that hindered the effective action of the company and its responsiveness to the market pressure in the industry. Often the applications are so mutually isolated that they cannot be made to reconcile without manual processes. This action is seen by the information technology department as unresponsive and overfunded. Databases that were touted as being the savior of the user and business are now viewed as inadequate. When this happens, information technology and databases are found to be limiting factors in the ability of the organization and business opportunities and customer service suffers.

Corporate Architecture

What is needed is a form of corporate architecture. Most enterprises have not reached the potential that they could have. They have often used old methods and used process-oriented solutions. Instead, they should have used a more datacentric approach that took into consideration the strategic future of the organization.

What has happened in the small company that evolved is not unique. In fact, it is rampant in the world of business today. In 1979, Richard Nolan (1979) of the Harvard Business School wrote an article for the *Harvard Business Review* entitled "Managing the Crisis in Data Processing." In it, he described stages of data and processing awareness in companies from his analysis of many major companies. While this assessment is 30+ years old, the problems still exist. The lesson has not been learned or understood as to how to maximize efficiency.

In Nolan's article he defines six stages of growth, which we will examine in detail:

Stage 1: Initiation
Stage 2: Contagion
Stage 3: Control
Stage 4: Integration
Stage 5: Data administration
Stage 6: Maturity

These are covered in a little more detail following as to how they affect or reflect the growth aspect of the organization.

Stage 1: Initiation. The first few applications to handle the company's data are developed. These are mostly cost-reducing applications such as payroll, accounting, order control, billing, and invoicing. As each application is implemented, users and operational management start identifying additional business need. The information technology department is small and is a job shop. Overall, information technology exerts no control during this stage.

Stage 2: Contagion. This is when the burgeoning requests for new applications that seem to spread by contact begin to move into swing. This stage is characterized by growth—big and fast. As the user demands for new applications increase, information technology finds itself unable to keep up with the growth. It soon degrades into a period of uncontrolled growth, with each application being built without reference to or consideration of the other applications. The result of this is the proliferation of redundant and replicated data and processes. There seems to be no control, and there is no common focus or planning. Integration is lost, and bridge systems and manual reconciliation units have to be created.

Stage 3: Control. Information technology at this point has recognized that it needs to introduce something to curb the runaway development. The lax controls of Stage 2 have had their impact. Users are frustrated and angry at their inability to get information. Management cannot get the information they need for decision support. There are application backlogs, and application maintenance costs are sky-high. Information technology attempts to again control by restructuring the existing applications, instituting a database management group, and formalizing planning and control by introducing development methodologies. Application development slows while the information technology is restructuring and rebuilding.

Stage 4: Integration. Existing applications are retrofitted. The use of models becomes the center of application development methodology. The users get more information out of access to the data and thereby increase their demands for more from information technology. Information technology expands to meet the demand, and costs spiral upward.

Redundant data and lack of company-wide data analysis frustrate the attempts for the information technology area to develop control and planning applications. Information technology becomes aware of how important the database is in the restructuring and retrofitting process. This represents a fundamental change in the way the applications are built. The change is from simply automating procedures to the examination and consolidation of data for processing. The integration of the data moves the company and information technology into Stage 5.

Stage 5: Data administration. This is the organizational artifact of the integration of the data and the applications. In this stage, organization-wide strategic planning is implemented, information resource management is emphasized. A top-down development methodology is defined that is datacentric and based on stable data models. The reporting data are spun off into reporting and decision support databases. After effort, final application retrofitting is completed on existing applications. Finally, as the company starts to approach Stage 6, applications start to emulate the organizational processes.

Stage 6: Maturity. In this stage, organization-wide data analysis and data modeling have been completed and implemented. Applications mirror the enterprise's function, and the corporate structure has changed to allow for an architect approach to be fostered and followed.

Using Nolan's Stages of Growth

Nolan's stages of company growth enable us to determine the stage that a company's data processing has reached. Different divisions and departments may be in different stages, so a multitiered strategy may be needed to approach the problem at an enterprise level. Datacentric analysis and design techniques can be used to identify the critical data to all levels of management and process throughout the company. It can then be organized into a single corporate model or kept as separate subject area data models that reflect the business function areas.

But this begs the question: What if a company is in the throes of, say, Stage 2 and wants to jump to Stage 4 without going through Stage 3? Is it possible? The answer is, of course, it is!

Nolan's six stages of growth are a valuable representation of the data processing history in most corporations. By review of what the problems were for each stage and by avoiding them and targeting the goals of the appropriate stage, a company can avoid the problem areas that others have become bogged down in. Modern software and methodologies can also help avoid certain stages of the growth pattern.

If we were starting a company's information technology from scratch, the steps necessary would be a compilation of what we have seen in the various stages. The higher the level entered on, the better. The reason for this is that in the highest level (Stage 6), form follows function—that is, the organization is constructed in the best possible way to process the data. The form of the organization follows the function the enterprise is fulfilling.

In the case of a start-up company with the luxury of ramp-up and planning time, the necessary time to do strategic requirements planning and appropriately design enterprise-wide data architecture could be taken. As noted before, it is really impractical to have corporate architecture at the detail level. Therefore, the need is to define the corporate information groupings within that corporate architecture that would represent the data and functional areas. Subsequently, it is necessary to perform specification within these subject areas in order to develop the applications and databases necessary to support the detail business process of each of these subject areas. When this is completed and the development of these architected subject area databases is pursued, the company would be able to enter the Nolan Sequence at Stage 5.

When viewing the Nolan Sequence, it is important that it be viewed from bottom to top. This shows the increases in the level of efficiency of processing of data, the minimization of cost of processing and storage, and the increased responsiveness to market pressures. It is easy to see why new companies strive for the architected approach: it's cheaper in the long run. But what if a company can't come in at the top of the Nolan Sequence?

Problems with Older Organizations

An older corporation has many more problems getting to Stage 5, primarily because there is much more analysis of data and processes that must be done. These will take much longer to analyze, resolve conflict, and integrate. Second, the cost of converting all the code that currently runs against the old data structures is prohibitive unless done over a transitional path via migration. In order for any action to take place in an older company, bridges need to be built between the past and the targeted future so when reprogramming takes place, the future structure will already have the correct method and structure and the data conversion is ensured. For the older company, living with a patchwork of old structures and new structures is inevitable. Sometimes the load can be lightened by taking reporting data and separating it from the transactional systems data and allowing the transactional structures to be changed with minimum impact to the user reporting use.

A serious problem, however, in most old corporations is the dedication to the old methods. Most of the developers in older companies' skills are geared toward sequential processing and structured analysis. Some managers easily admit that they do not trust databases and prefer flat file processing. Other company infrastructure elements, such as standards and policies, adhere to the old methods. Many of the information technology staff in this type of environment believe that the user community will not buy into the new approach. On top of all of this is the situation where you have an old-line client manager who is barely speaking to information technology because of its failure to solve his problems. This is why some companies never get beyond Stage 3 or 4. Sometimes the human and educational problems are just too much to overcome.

In those companies that do have a commitment to their own future, there is a strong desire to do the informational analysis that will provide them the working framework from which to respond to the future.

Business Today

Business today is a world of burgeoning markets, increased competition, and shrinking profit margins. We live in a world where Internet companies are sending phone calls and phone companies own Internet backbones.

Banks are making headway ventures with heretofore unopened financial products, and insurance companies are merging with banks. Health insurers are merging with provider organizations to keep their costs down. Technology companies are opening doors to other technology companies to assume greater market share in related areas. Alliances and joint ventures abound. Why own just part when you can own some of your own suppliers as well as the distributors?

These create tremendous pressures within organizations to develop a business structure that is nonredundant and responsive to the business pressures. Pressures on the business are from within as well as from without. Stockholder pressure makes many business decisions (whether the board of directors admits it or not). The strategic response needs to be reactive. It has to react differently to encroachment than it would to a market blending. (External strategies will not be covered here, since we want to focus on the problems within the business.)

Businesses have had to become cost-controlling, focused, and attentive to the market need. With increased competition comes the need to be innovative and evolve. What can be done, and when will it end?

Analogy

An analogy here is appropriate. In the country of Nicaragua, there is a lake that was once part of the ocean. Lake Nicaragua, covering 3,150 square miles, is a lake almost as big as a small sea. It is the twenty-first largest lake in the world. As noted before, it was believed to be an inlet from the ocean that, by virtue of a volcanic eruption and earthquake, was isolated from the ocean and became landlocked.

Unlike other landlocked marine environments, it did not increase in salinity—quite the contrary. Over the years it became desalinized by rivers and is now a freshwater lake. It is a very big lake. What happened to the marine creatures that were in the inlet? Some died, and others lived and adapted. The sharks that were in the inlet at the time of the eruption and earthquake survived and adapted and are now true freshwater sharks (others live in tidal and brackish estuary and river waters).

When in the ocean, these sharks were the same as their brethren in all respects, including size, speed, and appetite. What do you suppose they evolved into in the lake environment—where there were fewer food resources, being pressured to evolve from salt water to freshwater and in a closed environment? They evolved into a somewhat smaller, faster shark in response to the pressures of the environment.

They learned how to hunt the freshwater fish that were coming down into the lake from the rivers. They would have to adapt in order to survive, and so they have. It is a wonderful lake today, with the sharks fully adapted to the freshwater. Through it all, the target food species would be evolving in its own response to the increased aggression. It would become faster, more elusive, and harder to catch and would develop camouflage. It would continue in a dynamic state, assuring that all pressures on all species were met and equilibrium established. Nature would find a balance, just as we must do in this critical time of increased competition.

While the case of the sharks may seem to be a poor analogy, please take the time to understand it. We live in a dynamic business world where competition is becoming sophisticated and intense. The customer has more choices, and therefore big businesses have no choice but to evolve. They have to become leaner and more efficient. They need to become quicker to respond and more attractive to the customer. The old and slow businesses that depended on brute force and massive size will not survive very long without financial hemorrhaging. The death will not be the brutality of consumption by the competitors but it either will be a death of starvation as its food supply (the customer base) is consumed from underneath it by smaller, quicker competitors, or it will be the bleed-out of financial resources as the company tries to keep its bloated business line afloat.

In order to get the customer, companies need to slim down and become more responsive to what will help achieve their objectives. As to the questions "What can be done?" and "When will it end?," they need to be examined individually.

When Will It End?

Let's take the easy one first: When will *it* end? *It* refers to the dramatically changing business environment. The answer is that it won't end. It will continue to dynamically adjust to the pressures that are affecting it both externally and internally. It will adjust even if the pressure is intense and unexpected. An intense response will come, and the equilibrium will be reestablished. Another new force will come and upset the equilibrium, and another response will be the result.

It will evolve because it must. It will go through cycles of merger and divestiture, and product changes and diversification. Companies will become giants. We are seeing this now with the merger-mania that has overtaken the marketplace. At some point in the future, these merged giants will break up into smaller pieces, not because of government regulations but because of competition forces and the inflexibility of their own weight. Government meddling will only cause another force that needs to be met with in order for equilibrium to be established. The speed at which the mergers take place has become so rapid in the marketplace that many of the newly merged organizations wait for years or longer to merge data processing facilities for fear of the extensive expense. Worse yet is the possibility of divestiture of divisions of the merged organization; this would break apart the newly merged information technology department.

Government regulation and antitrust actions will do nothing but temporarily cripple the giants, leaving more room for the smaller companies to grow. This is all in response to what is happening in the marketplace. There are no hard and fast rules that anyone can apply that will ensure that a company will survive. The only thing that is sure is that the environment will change, and the only variable in the change equation is really the rate of change.

What Can We Do about It?

As for the other question—What can be done about it?—there are many things that can be done about it. The knee-jerk reaction to this from the 50,000-foot level will be, "We know our own companies better because we have made them lean and mean, we know what business we are in because we have analyzed and designed it for precisely for the purpose it is serving, and we know where our businesses are going."

Businesses have to deal with where their organizations are going by better strategic planning. Many books have been written about strategic planning, but unfortunately, many of these books are dry and not applicable because they don't deal with the real-world basis of the commercial world. If a strategy is to be viable, it has to start by using reality as the foundation for it. Most of the literature in the market is based on the development of corporate objectives. The existence of the organization, with its current products, markets, and channels, is assumed, and as such is taken as fundamental. These are then used to project forward for corporate goals and objectives. Because there is no detailed analysis of the current environment to validate the future assumptions, there is a basic flaw in the objectives, goals, and strategies developed. They have no basis in reality. It is the right idea with the wrong implementation.

For example, it is well known that many inefficient processes and functions are made tolerable and even efficient by the use of undocumented procedural workaround efforts made by employees. Employees maximize the effectiveness of poor-quality processes because they don't want to waste their time.

When the current state of the corporations is used as a basis, and projection is done forward from that state, then all of these undocumented efficiencies will not be included in the formulations of the strategic plans and efforts. The resulting plan will have overlooked efficiencies that will result in implementation of a software product that will not handle the current business needs or the future ones as well.

Generic Subject Areas for Corporate Architectures

The Practice box shows the generic subject areas necessary to define a corporate architecture. These corporate subject areas are appropriate for any organization that has a fundamentally open but core ideology that embraces its mission and purpose. By keeping the generic structure in the corporate data architecture, the business flexibility is present to pursue expansion in any direction desired. The structure will be there to hold any new market or products that are ventured into as the company evolves.

Practice

The following are the architectural clusters of information entities that almost all corporations need to keep. Their contents are defined in more detail following.

External organizations would contain entity clusters and entities such as:

- Vendors
- External agencies
- Third-party service and administrators
- Product resellers

Customer would contain entity clusters and entities such as:

- Customer
- Customer activity
- Customer contract
- Customer listings
- Customer address
- Customer requirements

Finance would contain entity clusters and entities such as:

- Accounting
- Billing
- Collecting
- General ledger
- Accounts payable
- Accounts receivable
- Taxes

Regulation would contain such entity clusters and entities as:

- Regulatory bodies
- Federal, state, or local governing agencies

Sales and marketing would contain entity clusters and entities such as:

- Sales
- Products
- Services
- Service bundle options
- Bids and bidding
- Promotions

Business strategy and planning would contain such entity clusters and entities as:

- Plan
- Strategy
- Business operation
- Business architecture

Locations would contain such entity clusters and entities as:

- Address of company operations
- Address of company properties
- Address of company

Service delivery would contain such entity clusters and entities as:

- Service providers
- Service channels
- Service components
- Service processes

Equipment would contain such entity clusters and entities as:

- Hardware
- Software
- Third-party software packages

Plant would contain such entity clusters and entities as:

- Production facilities
- Warehouse storage
- Manufacturing sites
- Distribution mechanism

Supply would contain such entity clusters and entities as:

- Supply vendors
- Supply disbursement
- Logistics
- Inventory

Human resources would contain such entity clusters and entities as:

- Employees
- Job descriptions
- Managers
- Management hierarchy

Product would contain such entity clusters and entities as:

- Product offers
- Product disclosures
- Product liabilities
- Product specifications

Corporate Information Groupings or Functional Areas

In the following paragraphs, these groupings are analyzed to see how each of these affects the business and their importance to the organization's bottom line. While all of these do not occur in all companies, the ones that do not are generic enough to apply to the functional areas that are not specified by one of the following categories.

They are referred to as strategic business subject areas because they represent the infrastructure area functions that maintain the integrity of the business. By extension of this mindset and premise, the detail process and data are the result of the analysis of these infrastructure strategic business subject area functions. These subject areas can be the organizational template for a new company or the target structure for a corporation trying to move toward a higher stage of development.

As noted in Nolan's stages and the descriptions along with them, there are methods and steps that can be used to migrate from one stage to the other. This migration can take place as long as the critical analysis and integration take place at the appropriate time by the appropriate level of the organization within these subject areas.

External Organization

This strategic business subject area refers to any party, public or private, that the company deals with in the course of doing business, regardless of the role it plays (customer, partner, vendor, government department or agency, trade association, or charitable organization). This is core information about that organization, not its relationship to the company or its performance in regard to that relationship. For example, it would not contain business inter-action rules for the companies, but it would contain deliverable and definition info, and contact information examples.

Customer

This strategic business subject area refers to any organiza-tion or private party who buys services from the company. If you are a telco, it is a telecommunications customer, either public or private. If you are a financial institution, it is banking, stocks and bonds, or fund management. If you are a manufacturer, it is the user or purchaser of the product, either retail or wholesale. This subject area includes all entities having to do with prospects for such purchases, current purchasers, and former purchasers as well as customer contracts, complaints, claims, and accounts.

Finance

This strategic business subject area refers to a collection of services to manage the company's financial assets including general ledger, accounts receivable, fixed asset evaluation, cash management, and costing. This subject area includes all enti-ties having to do with accounting, with the exception of invoic-ing and its associated entities. This is because they are part of the business process. The finance systems are the support systems of the money control processes such as accounting, general led-ger, and payroll. These exist to insure that there is control over the finances that flow into and out of the company. They are maintained under a classification called corporate or finance systems and are usually controlled with very strong security and the integrity issues surrounding them are paramount. This is not for frivolous reasons; it is important that this level of attentive-ness be maintained due to federal and state business laws, the commercial code, and other codes of business operations. These reasons ensure that the company's resources are protected from legal and illegal access or destruction.

Regulation

This strategic business subject area concerns the statutory law or government agency rule that licenses, governs or restricts the company's operations. It may involve compliance reporting, such as for the Internal Revenue Service, state treasurers, or others, such as for the FAA. There are voluntary regulatory agencies as well such as the AMA. This subject area includes entities having to do with employment, environment, operations, finance, or safety.

Sales and Marketing

This strategic business subject area refers to collection of the company sales prospectus, competitors, customers, other parties, marketing geography, and other factors, which are treated as a unit from the company's perspective. It also includes all those entities and processes associated with the sales activity at the company. These functions exist to ensure that there is a constant income to ensure growth. Within marketing there is a subarea that consists of functions that deal with new products and also another subarea that deals with the maintenance and change control of existing products.

Business Strategy and Plan

This strategic business subject area concerns the statement of direction and an associated implementation plan for a period of one to five years. This subject area includes all entities having to do with goals, policies, objectives, directives, guidelines, standards and procedures, organization structure, budget performance and metrics, and business requirements from the highest level to detailed procedures. It is the most underpopulated subject area in most businesses today, mainly because of the misunderstanding of its purpose. It has to do with what tools you have in place to deal with the impact of change.

These infrastructure mechanisms allow the organization to anticipate and interpolate signals in the marketplace and adjust their process in advance of the change or at least to have a plan to deal with it.

Location

This strategic business subject area concerns the geographic location mechanisms and procedures used by the company in providing services to its customers. This subject area includes all entities referencing equipment such as customer addresses of all kinds, service location addresses, reference locations, and so on.

Service Delivery

This strategic business subject area concerns the efforts to accomplish and the results of all services performed in the servicing of a customer at the company. This subject area includes all related topics such as work orders, product orders, service requests, repair requests, maintenance, negotiation processes, billing/invoicing, and account maintenance. It is the primary processing area for what the enterprise does as a profit mechanism. It is the enterprise's reason for being.

Equipment

This strategic business subject area concerns powered or non-powered vehicles or service machinery used by the company to provide services and maintain its networked infrastructure. This subject area includes all entities referencing equipment. Examples of these are telephones, lines, circuits, PBXs, and maintenance equipment.

Plant

This strategic business subject area concerns any location used by the company to conduct business. This subject area includes all entities referencing office buildings, yards, and terminals where equipment units are assembled or dissambled. They represent the physical structures associated with the enterprise.

Supply

This strategic business subject area concerns the company material inventory, its suppliers, and all related events. This subject area includes topics such as vendor contracts, support capability, vendor performance records, purchase orders, supplier invoices, material inventory, and office support systems.

Human Resources

This strategic business subject area concerns any person who is, was, or potentially may be responsible for the execution of tasks at the company. This subject area includes all entities relating to employees, potential employees, pensioners, and related compensation, as well as career planning, succession planning, and benefits and support programs.

Product

This strategic business subject area concerns the actual or planned products and service products that the company offers to internal and external customers. This subject area includes all related topics including price, schedule, product requirements, complaints, and promotion and advertising requirements.

Business Strategies

This strategic business subject area contains information pertaining to analysis of the external business environment and defined business and marketing strategies. Growth strategy is a subarea within this area that deals with expansion growth and mergers and acquisitions. This exists to ensure that the software inventory in the company environment is maintained and controlled in order to assess the impact of the merger or acquisition on the functionality of the current company. It also provides a prioritization or selection criteria as to whose functionality will serve the merged company better.

Corporate Knowledge

One of the largest problems today, other than the inability to architect solutions, is the fact that the body of corporate knowledge is dwindling. It is a fact that as the baby boom generation grays and heads toward retirement, the generic knowledge of how things work is rapidly vaporizing. No longer available are the generalists who understood the business flow and the need for integration. No longer is the corporate architect available. Everything today is focused on the specialist who provides the coverage for the latest evolving niche.

Information technology as a rigid framework for development has exploded, and there are a myriad of products and methods to fill the void. Who is to say what is right for the company? Who will make the choice as to what platforms will be used and what hardware? What are missing are the generalists who were the interpreters, the architects, and the designers that made sense out of the chaos.

Whether it was because business schools didn't think that information technology architects or architecture knowledge would be needed in their headlong rush to make management a science independent of its application, or whether the information explosion itself left everything in chaos remains to be seen.

The fact remains: there are not enough people at the management level who understand the overall workings of businesses. Poor strategic decisions concerning data, hardware, and software are being made without a real understanding of the facts.

Management has become a neutered mechanism that allows and foments the assurance that a manager with no technical competence can tell a technical person he is wrong when all facts and reality point to the technical person being right. Companies need to address this issue within their own domains as it leads to inability of their applications to survive the disintegration of the integrity of their data resources.

Eventually it leads to the complete failure of the company to compete with others that are trying to move up Nolan's stages. It also leads to the technical brain drain to consulting organizations and the loss of corporate knowledge that will be sorely needed in the far more competitive future. It is a vicious irony that when these knowledge resources are needed most, the finances of the companies will be sequestered. It is then that a company with more insight and more responsive capability will get them.

Organizations need to identify their need for this resource, recruit carefully, and nurture these individuals carefully. These people will be management's answer to the need for understanding when their current management has no skill or capacity to adapt to a fulminating technology world.

References

Humphrey, W. S. (1989). *Managing the software process*. Reading, MA: Addison-Wesley.

Nolan, R. L. (1979). *Managing the crisis in data processing*. Cambridge, MA: Harvard University Press.

Other Suggested Reading

Date, C. J. (2000). *A retrospective review and analysis*. Reading, MA: Addison-Wesley.

Date, C. J. (2000). *An introduction to database systems*. Reading, MA: Addison-Wesley.

Nolan, R. L., & Croson, D. C. (1989). *Creative destruction: A six-stage process for transforming the organization*. Cambridge, MA: Harvard Business School Press.

Roetzheim, W. H. (1988). *Structured computer project management*. Englewood Cliffs, NJ: Prentice Hall.

6

BUSINESS ORGANIZATIONS

Purpose and Mission of the Organization

Once the stable data foundation that is being used by the organization today has been defined by adequate analysis, then a projection can be made of the data foundation that will be needed in the future. In order to perform this current organizational analysis, a review must be done of the prime purpose of the organization's existence: its purpose and mission.

The purpose and mission of an organization may appear to be obvious. In fact, it may be too obvious. So obvious, in fact, that it is never documented and is assumed to be present. For example, the purpose of a school is to educate. The purpose of a store is to sell retail goods. The purpose of a bank is to make money by accepting and storing other people's money at one rate of interest and lend that same money out at a higher rate of interest.

Looking at the mission and purpose of an organization, the reason for their being is easily seen in more detail. There was a time when management was not so short-sighted and ruled by the price of the organization's stock in the marketplace. There was a time when management understood the process and was an integral component of the process. This was a time when management was not regarded as a science unto itself but as a mechanism to control the business to ensure profitability.

From this era, Peter Drucker (1993) states that by defining the purpose and mission of an organization, management establishes the three most important reasons for the organization's existence, and even more importantly, where the organization will go in the future. Drucker identifies these questions as:

1. What is our business?
2. What will our business be?
3. What should our business be?

The answer to each of these questions is not obvious and rarely easy to get to. But it is critical for management to address them continuously if they are to stay competitive in the marketplace, manage more effectively, and maintain profitability.

Drucker states, "There is only one reason for a business organization: to create a customer." This was true in the 1970s, 1980s, and 1990s, and it is true today. The organization's customers are a major part of its reason for being. Without identifying the customers and their needs, we would be unable to completely define the mission and purpose of the organization. Even if the customer base changes all the time as businesses reinvent themselves, the mission and purpose should be such that it can and does adapt to the changes.

Ideology, Mission, and Purpose

As Jim Collins and Jerry Porras (2004) note in their book *Built to Last,* companies that survived while their competitors failed were not motivated primarily by profit but by a core set of ideals. They state, "In short, we did not find any specific ideological content essential to being a visionary company. Our research indicates that the authenticity of the ideology and the extent to which a company attains consistent alignment with the ideology counts more than the content of the ideology."

An organization that exists without an ideology that defines its mission and purpose drifts like a ship without a rudder; it cannot control its own destiny. It is subject to the currents of the marketplace without any resistance and direction. Eventually the uncontrolled movement will bring it into trouble by forcing it to respond to events and tasks that were never part of its original intention. When it is in these troubled times, even an excellent management team cannot save the organization from foundering.

The core ideals, purpose, and mission must be defined and documented, not in agonizing detail but in a manner in which it can be readily referred to in the future. Here is a list of the core ideology values from *Built to Last*:

GE
- Improving the quality of life through technology and innovation
- Interdependent balance between responsibility to customers, employees, society, and shareholders
- Individual responsibility and opportunity
- Honesty and integrity

Procter and Gamble
- Product excellence
- Continuous self-improvement
- Honesty and fairness
- Respect and care for the individual

Sony
- To experience the sheer joy that comes from the advancement, application, and innovation of technology that benefits the general public
- To elevate the Japanese culture and national status
- Being a pioneer; not following others but doing the impossible
- Respecting and encouraging each individual's ability and creativity

Disney
- No cynicism allowed
- Fanatical attention to consistency and detail
- Continuous progress via creativity, dreams, and imagination
- Fanatical control and preservation of Disney's "magic" image
- "To bring happiness" to millions and to celebrate, nurture, and promulgate "wholesome American values"

Wal-Mart
- "We exist to provide value to our customers"—to make their lives better via lower prices and greater selection; all else is secondary
- Swim upstream; buck conventional wisdom
- Be in partnership with employees
- Work with passion, commitment, and enthusiasm
- Run lean
- Pursue ever-higher goals

Motorola
- The company exists "to honorably serve the community by providing products and services of superior quality at a fair price"
- Continuous self-renewal
- Tapping the "latent creative power within us"
- Continual improvement in all the company does—in ideas, in quality, in customer satisfaction
- Treat each employee with dignity, as an individual
- Honesty, integrity, and ethics in all aspects of the business

Hewlett-Packard
- Technical contributions to fields in which we participate ("We exist as a corporation to make a contribution")
- Respect and opportunity for HP people, including the opportunity to share in the success of the enterprise
- Contribution and responsibility to the communities in which we operate
- Affordable quality for HP customers
- Profit and growth as a means to make all of the other values and objectives possible

It is understandable from the essence of these core ideological values that they provide a basis for a mission and objectives to continue in spite of changing times and business climates.

By keeping a tenacious grasp on the ideology that best suits the business organization and by answering Drucker's three questions, it is possible to ensure that the organization can define what the business is now, what it will be, and what it is capable of becoming. Organizations do not stand still. They grow and respond dynamically to pressures in the marketplace. If they do not adjust and grow, then they are dying or soon will be. But it is not just growing and adapting that is critical; it is sustaining that core set of ideals that foster the mission and purpose.

Design with the Future of the Organization in Mind

Taking this core ideology-sponsored mission and purpose down into the structure of the organization, particularly the information technology department, can have very positive ramifications. Organizations need application systems to handle the processing of the data to accomplish the mission and purpose. The development of an application system (and the data store that is an integral part of it) is not an idle undertaking. It may take months or even up to a year to develop it fully. If management loses focus on the mission and purpose of the organization and instead focuses on the development of only what the business needs *now*, when the project is completed in a year, what has been produced is a system that can handle last year's business.

Too often this is how it is done. In the interest of solving the immediate problem, management usually ends up just developing the short-term solution. After many years of this, the results are cobbled applications that are mostly exception code and data stores that are fragmented and disintegrated. An organization that has become lost and inflexible will never be highly profitable in a competitive marketplace.

While all organizations don't evolve rapidly, and thus do not suffer the indignity of systematic degeneration, the world is rife with rapid change, and most organizations must deal with the change as it comes. If the management concentrates on defining what the organization and data requirements are *now* and ignore where they will be tomorrow (or five years from tomorrow), they will find themselves in the trouble they wish so much to avoid. They may end up being able to change the applications enough to squeak by. But the data will have been structured in a way that the evolving organizational needs are served less and less by it until that structure is barely usable.

Without taking the time to do strategic planning and proper data architecture, the application will have a defined shelf life that is measurable by the ability of the data architecture to serve the business. These go hand in hand with the core ideology of the mission and purpose. Architectures correlate directly to the mission and charter. They are the artifact of direct translation of the mission and purpose statements applied to the business problem at the time.

It is only by examining the major functions and information necessary to support the mission and purpose that the best way to structure the organization can be seen. By examining products, services, markets, and channels, it can be determined, with some degree of integrity, how the organization can best go about the prime objective of "creating a customer." Based on this, the structure of the organization can be "adjusted" to best achieve it. This does not necessarily state that "form follows function," but it does allay itself to the principle that if an organization is focused on its ability to identify the customers' needs and develop products that suit those needs, it will continue to survive in the marketplace.

As part of the examination process of the necessary major functions and information, it is critical to consider the business plans and business strategies. This is when the second and third of Drucker's questions can be responded to. It is necessary to make sure that the future is considered when designing or adjusting the structure of the organization and developing control mechanisms. By ensuring that the company is lean and effective, it is also necessary to examine what products, markets, and channels will be used in the future.

Generalize for Future Potential Directions

Strategic requirements planning targets future products as well as today's products. All alternatives for the **product, services, markets, and channels** must be examined in order to develop a mechanism that is generic enough to handle all of the different types. By developing the structure to handle the lowest common denominator, the business structure has the flexibility to respond to what the market needs when it needs it. This minimizes or pushes to the lowest level the requirement to "specialize."

When business management "specializes," they overly focus on the process. When this is done, the organization will train people for, hire people for, or manage specific areas without reference to other areas within the organization in order to maximize control and measurability. By embracing specialization, the organization micromanages specific areas. What this does is minimize the growth of the staff as well as the organization. Personnel in the organization do not want to be pigeonholed to a specific task and then told exactly how to do it. This would remove any possibility of them bringing something new to the work and also limits their view of the big picture. This is happening today because of organizational mistakes associated with specialization.

This specialization also results in overstaffing as more personnel are hired for specific areas that might be similar or related as natural extensions of these specific areas. It introduces functional redundancy as well as personnel redundancy, which cuts into profitability. Specialization is a form of structural rigidity and compartmentalization that prevents adaptability to future needs and so must be resisted at all costs. It is no wonder that many organizations are looking for downsizing options when they made the mistake in the first place. Worse yet, they are looking at outsourcing as a saving option. We will cover outsourcing and downsizing as options in the next chapter.

By "generalizing," management allows the organization to be more flexible in adapting to pressures that face it. Keeping the core ideology supported mission and purpose in mind, management needs to design the organization in such a way as to ensure its ability to evolve. By designing for the generic approach, the newer areas of evolution provide the growth areas for current personnel and on a natural learning foundation from their previous skills. By structuring the organization for flexibility, it will allow it to determine what the marketability of new products might be. It will also help in the estimation of the cost of their development. The people within an organization that provide this capacity are the strategic planning group. This area was covered in previous chapters from a different perspective.

Unfortunately, strategic planning is usually the purview of the "innovation and research" departments of organizations. In the brutality of the cost-cutting efforts in recent years in business organizations, these research and planning groups have been the first victims. The second victims have been the information architecture. Often, the reasons they give for their sacrifice is, "It takes too long for the efforts of the aforementioned departments to affect the bottom line of the organization." It is unfortunate that business organizations feel this way because these are the two organizational areas that will help keep the organization profitable for years to come.

In order to be successful, an organization really needs to have the products under development before the bulk of the need arises in the marketplace. In order to do this, they need to have defined the need and quantification for their product, retooled their current manufacturing mechanism to set up development of the product, and then delivered the first release of the product. There is no time to respond quickly if there is no strategic basis to react from.

To quote Drucker, "From the definition of its mission and purpose, a business must arrive at objectives in a number of key areas: It must balance these objectives against each other and against the competing demands of today and tomorrow. It needs to convert objectives into concrete strategies and concentrate resources on them. Finally, it must think through its strategic planning—that is, the decisions of today are the business of tomorrow."

Organizational Structure

From the **mission and purpose** it is easy to see that **objectives** are the primary embodiment of the lower-level specification of the **mission and purpose**. Objectives are fundamental to an organization. While this may seem like an old concept, it is still true. It has been buried in the flurry of responses that try to come up with quicker ways to react to pressures in the marketplace. Business **objectives** determine which way we should structure the business. They determine what the activities will be and what we will do in order to achieve the purpose.

In some ways, business objectives are like a road map: They provide guidance as the organization moves into the future, allowing an alternate path if necessary to keep moving. Unlike a road map, however, there is no specific destination for an organization in mind. Contrary to this, what is needed is just the guidance mechanism that keeps the movement in the right direction. It also keeps the organization profitable in spite of the direction it might be following at the time. Using a road map, the optimal path will always be chosen and all other alternatives discarded. This kind of discarding is not something that can be done by an organization. The prudent thing is to be mindful and to capture and retain information about alternatives, since they will prove invaluable in the future.

What Are the Basic Functions in an Organization?

So how **should** management structure organizations best handle the functions that make up their business process? There are three classes of functions that generally take place in organizations:

- *The operating function.* This is the work done that manages what is currently present in the organization and exploits the potential of the processes and data and resolves problems with the day-to-day operation of the organization.
- *The upper management function.* This is the work done that manages where the company is going, plots where it should go, and measures the progress on the chosen path by use of defined metrics.
- *The innovation or research function.* This analyzes and develops alternatives for the future for the upper management function of the organization.

The operation function management of the organization is easy to identify. Management of this type is the head of the line functions of the organization. Examples of these are the head of accounting, the manager of production, and the head of MIS.

Upper management of the organization are also easily identifiable: the president and board, or executive team, or some other leadership team that ensures that the administration of the organization is taking place appropriately within the organization.

The innovative or research management is not so easy to identify. In a lot of companies it has been folded into the upper management function, while in others it is a small group that advises from a distance. In some companies it is given token recognition but has little or no influence.

Objectives from all of these classes of management help codify the strategies as well as provide the blueprint for mapping of the necessary information. An information plan concerning the data architecture can be developed from these requirements and can be passed down to the subordinate business management structure.

The Information Needs of Management

As noted before, the information needs of management fall into the three functional levels of management. Operating management reflect the organization as it runs today. The existing procedures and data have been defined and established by middle management and operating management and reflect the operating needs of the organization. It allows operating management to carry out the day-to-day operations and responsibilities. Reporting procedures provide the necessary information to make decisions at this level.

While operating management is concentrating on today, innovative management is concentrating on tomorrow. Innovative management is concerned with what products, services, and activities the organization will be working with in the future. It is concerned with the information about trends that are happening now and comparisons with the experiences of the past. By analyzing these, they can project the trends into the future. The need is to assess the viability of products and services, and in order to do this, they need market analysis and sales analysis data to base these on.

Top management, historically, has not received their data when and in the format that they need it. When they asked for information, they received reams of report pages that did nothing for them. This was the data in the undigested form. What they needed was a more analyzed form of the data. Instead of needing to know what the status of today's deliveries is, they need to know if there is a downward trend in a particular product line. This is a need that was never really answered and has been solved time after time in the business world by more and more sophisticated mechanisms. Over time, this problem has been addressed by the development of decision support systems, management information systems, and executive information systems. Now data marts and data warehouses are addressing it.

The information technology area is a business group (often kept with the other service organizations within the innovative management group) whose sole responsibility is to service the need to the operating management group, the innovative management group, and the top management group in all of their business needs. It also exists as an adjunct support group for the tools and warehouse data that are maintained for all groups in the organization. (Chapter 22 covers data warehousing.) The data organization or information technology organization will be covered in the next chapter of this book in greater detail to examine its current inadequacies and what can be done to make it more effective.

Organizations Don't Know What They Don't Know

Continuing with the breakdown of the organization using a "data-driven" approach will help generate information plans for each area. By doing this, the information requirements of the organization are being defined independently of their primary use and thereby allow them to be "generalized" for the multiple users within the organization. It is important to define these as independent of the processes they are currently associated with. It may sound illogical, but organizations only know what they know, and conversely, they don't know what they don't know.

Management may understand how the business works today, but if they design and adjust their organization to maximize its potential on this basis, they will only be left behind in the marketplace. It is unfortunate, but the latter will kill the business very quickly. By taking a data-centered or data-driven approach, the organization defines the data and how they will use it. The definition allows them to integrate the future use (soon to be defined by strategic planning) along with current use without damaging the data structure or the organizational structure. This approach maximizes the responsability of the data architecture and the enterprise.

An information plan for the operating function would include an analysis of all the data requirements used for the day-to-day activity of the company. These would be captured in high-level data and process models that were easily relatable or organized in the subject areas mentioned in Chapter 5. These would include the corporate grouping or subject areas of customer, supply, product, service delivery, sales and marketing, and location.

An information plan for the innovative function would include an analysis of the entire data requirement of the research and development function of the organization. These would be captured in high-level data and process models that were easily relatable or organized in the subject areas mentioned in Chapter 5. These would include the corporate grouping or subject areas of business strategies and to some degree sales and marketing. The innovative function shares this subject area with the operational business function.

An information plan for the top management function would include all of the data requirements used for this function in the organization. These would be captured in high-level data and process models that were easily relatable or organized in the subject areas mentioned in Chapter 5. These would include the corporate grouping or subject areas of external organizations, regulation, finance, staffing, and human resources.

After the data requirements are in this data architecture, the "business views" can be defined for each subfunction within each function area. The business views are nothing more than the composite of those data pieces that are needed for each business process for that area.

In summary, what can be seen is that throughout the history of data processing, the business processes have driven the method of application development. It is because of the strict focus on the implementation of these processes and the lack of consideration for future use of the data that most applications today are accepted as being produced with built-in obsolescence. With this inattention to strategic planning and resulting information planning within subject areas, the enterprise has little assurance that their mission and purpose are truly being adhered to.

It is not a hopeless case, however. Organizations can make the evolutionary changes that will provide the capacity to jump stages in the Nolan Sequence simply by even partially adopting the data-driven approach and beginning to refine their application development methodology. Of course, the strategic planning and information analysis must be done for the affected business area within the organization to some degree. What usually happens is that it ends up creating a small residence of data entities in many of the corporate grouping or subject areas of the data architecture that have been mentioned. A business organization can begin an enterprise architecture with the implementation of a single application. It may seem small at first, but as each successive application is sourced from and is integrated back into the data architecture, the corporate groupings' population expands. From experience it takes no more than four applications to completely define some residence in all of the subject areas.

It can start small but be built up over time as long as the focus is on a shared data architecture. It is as simple as sourcing the new application project's information from the data architecture. Then, as each new application project is developed, the data are integrated with the data architecture. By this method the corporate groupings are built by accretion and not by static analysis.

Information Strategy for Modern Business

Just as Nolan had suggested, a new look at the way information is used is critical to the way the organization can capitalize on its information asset. In their book *Information Revolution*, Davis, Miller, and Russell (2006) report on new ways to use information to grow your business. I have excerpted and restructured some of their findings in the following paragraphs. Other explorations of this subject area are encouraged in the referenced material.

In order to move forward, in many cases an assessment of where you are is critical. When reassessing your information management strategy, seven business realities must be considered.

Business Reality #1: Business Cycle Times Are Shrinking

The productivity tools that facilitate your organization to design, develop, and deliver faster than ever are also doing the same thing for your competition. Computer-assisted design, e-marketing, and other technology-based advantages such as these also have a darker side. They shorten business cycles into a fraction of their previous time-to-market. At one point in time, this was measured in years; now it is measured in weeks. In the intensity of the competitive Internet-fueled marketplace, today's window will close on tomorrow's opportunity. This rapidly changing environment demands agility and on-the-spot decisions. Survival and profitability require up-to-the-minute understanding of the big picture and constant innovation.

Business Reality #2: You Can Only Get So Much Juice Out of a Turnip

In the recent past, organizations invested significant time and money optimizing operational processes and implementing enterprise resource planning systems to produce much-needed cost savings and competitive advantage. In actuality, so did the competition. Operational optimization for efficiency's sake is like squeezing a turnip. The first time you squeeze it, you get a significant return on investment. The next time you get a little less. And the next time even less. The absolute best you can accomplish with an ERP solution is retaining parity with your competitors.

Business Reality #3: The Rules Are Different

The rules are different; there is no more "business as usual." There was a time when the business world could operate like a fairly played game of Monopoly. March around the board acquiring more through corporate mergers, and accumulating wealth. But the rules are different now. The winner of today's game would not be the one who accumulated the most real estate and utilities. It would be the one who invents transatlantic travel, time-shares, adjustable rate mortgages, frequent flyer miles, tourism, and online ticketing

But there are still old rules present that existed when business *was* as usual. The old rules that still apply are money counts, and profitability matters. Customers are number one. Competitors are hungry. But some of the methods that were used under business as usual have created problems. Some of these new problems are the mergers and acquisitions increased corporate influence and revenues but also increased the difficulty of keeping agility and enterprise-level perspective. Productivity of human advancements that increased yields into tighter and tighter turnaround cycles also ratcheted up baseline expectation from company management and customers.

Information technological advancements that generated gigabytes of data also are now drowning the systems that were supposed to capture and retain that data. And the technologies that were supposed to be cure-alls failed to resolve the root business issues because of the interdependency of people, knowledge, process, and culture.

Business Reality #4: The Only Thing That Is Constant Is the Unending Volatility of Change

Change is endemic; it comes around more often and more rapidly than ever. Volatile markets destroy companies for having poor business models and punish their management harshly for indecision. Conversely, volatile markets reward a company's agility and a willingness to take calculated risks. But how does a company embrace meaningful change and realign the corporate strategy to match this? How does one choreograph corporate change while minimizing risk and maximizing returns? In reality, organizations need to harness and drive change rather than react to it. They need to focus on creating value for the organization in the future rather than depending on historic results to carry them through.

Business Reality #5: Globalization Both Helps and Hurts

The Internet and corporate virtual networks have transformed the smallest organizations into global entities. On the plus side this means that the marketplace is as widespread as the reach of the communication networks. The organization's suppliers and other partners can be strategically chosen from the locations with the lowest costs. You can attract the best and brightest talent for collaborative teams without requiring them to relocate.

On the minus side, globalization means that your customers are increasingly crossing borders and expect a response to their needs in the country in which they operate. Process and quality control are now complicated by continents being spanned, different languages being spoken, different international standards being imposed, and cultural differences having to be understood. New international outsourcing and marketing operations also raise the complexity of doing business.

Business Reality #6: Penalties for Ignorance Are Harsher Than Ever Before

The penalties of not knowing the facts about organizational financial data are harsher than ever. As a result of the recent high-profile corporate accounting debacles, the SEC now holds chief executives of public corporations personally accountable for the veracity of their financial reporting.

The Sarbanes-Oxley Act requires that top executives personally swear by their financial statements. Executives who certify statements they know to be false can face criminal charges, fines, and jail terms of up to 20 years. If there is any doubt, just ask ex-WorldCom chief executive Bernie Ebbers. In July 2005, Ebbers was sentenced to five years in prison for his role in an $11 billion accounting scandal. At its core, the law does not require anything more than ethical business conduct. However, as corporations become more complex and operate at higher speeds across virtual geographies and markets, it is harder to offer up a snapshot of the financial accounting that is not accurate, and it may have nothing to do with malfeasance.

Business Reality #7: Information Is Not the By-product of Business but the Lifeblood of Business

Information is not a by-product of business but is the lifeblood of business. The natural outcome of business realities 1–6 is that more organizations have to be faster and more responsive than ever. They have to be more innovative and adaptable. They

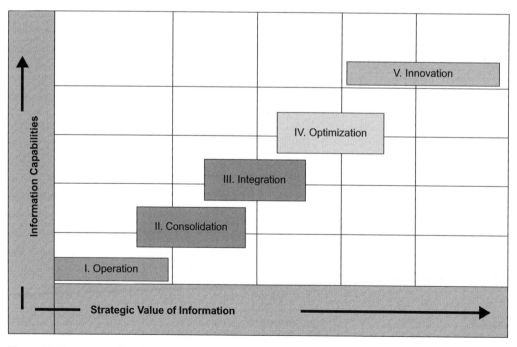

Figure 6.1 The stages of business evolution.

have to achieve more with less and have more profit in their short tenure as the market leader. The common foundation required for all of this is based in information.

Decision makers must have up-to-the-minute access to intelligence above all of the influences and the issues that can affect their decisions. The climate of the new economy requires autonomy based on the broadest possible perspective inside and outside the company.

Companies must extract maximum value from the information they have about suppliers, customers, competitors, and global markets. This information is essential in order to know what the market wants, how to supply it as efficiently as possible, and how to promote it in ways that will maximize market share.

Business treatment of information passes through five stages as the organizations mature (Figure 6.1). In most cases they never get past the midpoint before internal stress and external pressures cause them to lose focus. We will review the evolutionary stages and their characteristics. Figure 6.1 shows the five stages, and Table 6.1 defines each stage, much like Richard Nolan did in his work decades ago.

Maximizing the Value of Information

Success in managing information as a strategic asset is dependent on the integrated function of infrastructure, process, people, and culture. Ideally they would all be working in harmony. A company's maturity depends on these dimensions, but it can also be represented in a business evolutionary model that includes five stages:

- *An operational level.* The operational enterprise organization focuses on individual day-to-day activity. It might be a startup or mature organization struggling with the here and now operational problems or an entrepreneurial organization with a strong leader. While these types of organizations seem different, they share similar characteristics.
- *A consolidation level.* The consolidated enterprise organization has a department-level perspective. At the consolidation level of business evolution, organizations have consolidator information and management across functional areas. They have unified departments and implemented solutions that satisfy the department-level needs. Also at the second level of evolution individual departments within the organization have consolidated their own information into silos that serve department-level needs. Within this organization there is little regard for an enterprise plan as our priority.

Table 6.1 Locations of Internal Forces in an Organization

	Infrastructure	Knowledge Process	Human Capital	Culture
	Definition: The hardware, software, and networking tools and technologies that create, manage, store, disseminate, and utilize information.	Definition: The policies, practices, standards, and governance that define how information is generated, validated, and used; how it is tied to performance metrics and reward systems; and how the organization supports its commitments to strategic use of information.	Definition: The organization's human assets and the quantifiable aspect of their capabilities including their recruitment, training and ongoing assessment.	Definition: The organization and human influences on information flow. The moral, social, and behavioral norms of the organizational culture as embodied in attitudes, beliefs, and perceptions about information being an enduring strategic asset.
OPERATIONAL LEVEL				
Characterized by individual data ownership and control when used to control daily processes.	The operational infrastructure relies on manual system or unnetworked distributed PCs. Intranet capabilities, collaboration tools, and governance processes are missing or limited. Analytical tools are present but they tend to be client-based rather than server-based. Information costs are high due to redundant processes, duplication of interfaces and extracts, and inconsistent data processes. Separate transactional systems support fragments of the total operation.	The operational knowledge processes are uniquely individual. Peers in the same department work in different ways. Information mavericks emerge. Information management focuses on day-to-day operations and not long-term plans. Information processes are variable and undocumented.	At the operational level, people work autonomously in unstructured environments information mavericks are common. Tend to be outgoing and risk tolerant. Differentiate them through subtle internal competition and motivate them using individual recognition. They see change as an evil threat to the status quo.	At the operational level, cultures reward charismatic leaders and PC renegades and create a gratifying working environment for them. The environment is internally competitive and lacks consistent evaluation and performance criteria. It is an everyone out for themselves information culture.

(Continued)

Table 6.1 (Continued)

	Infrastructure	Knowledge Process	Human Capital	Culture
CONSOLIDATION LEVEL				
Individual perspective is replaced by departmental or functional level standards, metrics and perspective.	The infrastructure applies department-level hardware, networking, and software. Data stores and decisional applications are designed and developed. Even though some of these tools such as modeling and mining may exist, they are not used consistently and are still a problem across the organization.	At the consolidation level knowledge process consolidates data and decision making at the department level. Peers in a group do the same work in the same way they use systems and processes that are consistent within their department. Two departments often come up with different results.	At the consolidation level mavericks and data wizards still reign supreme, but they are more likely to be middle-management, competing with peers for recognition from the boss. They selectively align themselves with loyal team players rather than individuals.	At the consolidation level in an organization, culture embodies an us versus them mentality where each department pursues its own interests and people are rewarded for contributing to departmental goals. Incentives are based on departmental goals even at the enterprise expense. Tribal knowledge and internal politics distract the company from staying focused on the marketplace.
INTEGRATION LEVEL				
Characterized by the consolidation effort being expanded and propagated to the enterprise-wide process, including standards, metrics, and perspectives.	At the integration level information management processes are formalized under a central point of control. A streamlined, enterprise-wide infrastructure, including software, hardware, databases, and networking, eliminates redundancy and enables a single version of the terms. IT processes are	At the integration level knowledge process shifts from an operational focus to an analytic focus that reports not only what was but what is and what can be. The organization will mobilize resources around markets and customer relationships	At the integration level people collaborate well within their peer groups on an ad hoc basis but they also think outside the functional unit about the greater good of the enterprise with a	Integration-level culture places a high value on the quality of information for enterprise-wide performance results. Information is viewed as a corporate asset. Information is widely accepted as an essential tool to operate the

(Continued)

Table 6.1 (Continued)

Infrastructure	Knowledge Process	Human Capital	Culture
defined and provide audit trails and integrity and accountability.	rather than functions and product groups. Information processes are predictable and repeatable performance management is automated.	holistic view that enables them to understand and appreciate how their efforts contribute to enterprise goals.	business and create value throughout the enterprise.

OPTIMIZATION LEVEL

Characterized by an organization that is aligned with the markets it participates in and gains market leadership by using predictive insights about customers, suppliers, and business partners.	At the optimization level the information structure represents an enhancement to the level III infrastructure rather than a new framework. It provides complete context for all decision-making and makes it available as the natural course of business rather than as a constant process. Business systems are linked across the supply chain from back-office functions through customer touch points enabling communications data sharing and continuity across functional areas and extended business relationships.	At the optimization level the knowledge process focuses on maximizing performance and efficiency and incrementally improving the quality timeliness and availability of information. New quantitative metrics, real-time analytics and closed-loop feedback processes fuel continuous movement of those business models. Integrated customer information is analyzed to detect patterns, predict behavior and understand customer needs for consistent and immediate customer response.	At the optimization level people are driven, diverse, adaptable, and thrive on new challenges. They prefer creative challenges to predictable tasks and are not afraid to take risks. They bring diverse intellectual skills to the table, and use historical and predictive analysis to increase the effectiveness of their organization in an ever-changing marketplace.	The organization at the optimization level empowers individuals to continually make incremental improvements and gives them feedback information in order to do it well. Managing change becomes a competency. Internal competition has been replaced by collaboration and interdependency. Access to internal and external information provides broad understanding, allows communities of interest to share experience and fine-tune the business process.

(Continued)

Table 6.1 (Continued)

	Infrastructure	Knowledge Process	Human Capital	Culture
INNOVATION LEVEL				
Characterized by an organization that has reached the optimization level and sustains the market leadership and revenue growth by continuing creativity and renewal.	An organization at the innovative level has an infrastructure that is sophisticated and flexible as well as being extensible to meet any integration or expansion challenges that the organization might encounter. It has a rich suite of analytical tools by which new ideas can be tested and refined in virtual environments. It provides network for creativity including methods to organize and foster ideas and manage emerging work products.	At the innovation level knowledge process uses extensive analytics to model the future and minimize risk while fostering constant innovation. New business models are regularly created, simulated and tested. Collaboration crosses familiar boundaries and is enterprise-wide, and employees continuously offer new ideas, and in fact, they are encouraged to do so.	At the innovation level people are proactive, creative thinkers with entrepreneurial mentality. They hold various roles within the organization yet can be pulled together for quick interdisciplinary teams. They focus on moving the enterprise forward. They constantly contribute new ideas and foster viable ideas from concept to revenue as quickly as possible.	The culture in an organization at the unabated level embraces thinking outside the box where the only bad idea is an unspoken one. While not all ideas make it to fruition, the organization generates a significant amount of its growth and development of new ideas.

- *An integration level.* Organizations at the integrated enterprise level share an enterprise-wide perspective. Organizations at this level have acknowledged the strategic and competitive value of information and have defined an information management framework to satisfy organizational-level objectives. Rather than focusing on individuals or departments, IT solutions enhance the organization's capacity to create value for customers and stakeholders
- *An optimization level.* Organizations at the optimize enterprise level are agile, adaptable, and efficient. Organizations at

this level have been optimized for efficiency while constantly realigning and adjusting to changing markets. Access to current information is immediate. When the market grows or jobs increase, organizations at this level quickly adjust and re-optimize to the adjusted bussiness model.

- *An innovation level.* Organizations at the innovative level create continuous and sustainable growth through innovation. Organizations at this level institutionalize innovation and transform the enterprise from an operational and reactive one and IT into a consistent proactively self-renewing company. This type of organization creates sustainable growth by continuously generating new products and services.

Forces in the Organization

- *Infrastructure:* IT architecture.—the hardware, software, and connectivity that supports information flow
- *Intelligence tools:* The applications used to transform raw data into useful knowledge
- *User access:* The flow of meaningful intelligence to the users who need it
- *Knowledge process:*
- *Degree:* The extent to which processes are defined and enforced
- *Consistency:* The extent to which processes are uniform across the enterprise
- *Metrics:* The types of measures that the company tracks to gauge its success
- *Human capital:*
- *Skills:* The capabilities that are sought or nurtured in the company's knowledge workers
- *Motivators:* The intrinsic and extrinsic forces that drive people to do what they do
- *Dynamics:* The nature of interactions among individuals.
- *Culture:*
- *Rewards:* The compensation structure, both formal and informal, and how it shapes behavior
- *Adaptability:* The company's acceptance of or resistance to change
- *Dynamics:* The nature of interactions among teams and with the upper management
- *Attitudes:* The collective personality and engendered by the corporate culture

Table 6.1 shows the locations of the internal forces in the organization mapped against the levels of evolution the organization will go through in its utilization of information for growth purposes.

The goal of any organization is to reach the innovation level with all of its internal power foci. It is almost an impossible task to sustain long term. The reason for this is that dynamic factors are always at work. Factors such as financial cycles, internal factors such as human attrition and reorganizations, and infrastructure changes such as new software and hardware platforms all lead to dropping from the innovation level back to the optimization stage, or even further back. However, if an enterprise organization embraces the evolution, the higher performance level can be regained.

References

Collins, J., & Porras, J. (2004). *Built to last*. New York: HarperCollins Publishers Inc.

Davis, J., Miller, Gloria J., & Russel, A.: (2006), *Information Revolution*. Hoboken, NJ: John Wiley and Sons.

Drucker, P. F. (1993). *Managing for the future: The 1990s and beyond*. Plume/ Penguin Books, New York, NY.

7

PRODUCTIVITY INSIDE THE DATA ORGANIZATION

Information Technology

It is appropriate now to cover a different problem area. This will be a high-level review of the relationship among organizational structures, information technologies, and productivity. Initially it will cover trends in information technology, trends in organizational change, and a brief overview of what has been called the productivity anomaly. Then it will cover the impact that information technology change may have on the organization, obstructions that prevent effective use of information technology, and ways to eliminate these obstructions to best use information technology.

What Is Information Technology?

Information technology can be broadly defined as the use of computers, software (operating system/tools and application), communications, and networks to ensure that the information needs of an organization are being satisfied. This can be regarded as a baseline concept, although there are many different definitions of what information technology might be.

The implementation of an IT organizational structure has occurred in two stages. The first stage (phase 1) started in the 1960s and involved the use of computers as a solution to mathematical and logical problems. The second stage (phase 2) of the revolutionary change started in the 1970s and involved the improvement of the man–machine interface and the use of the computer for other than the initial reasons it was introduced (that is, high-speed numerical processing).

There is an important difference that has been defined by Thomas Landauer (1995) between the two phases in the information technology revolution. In his work he points out that computers in the 1960s handled stage 1 tasks very well. Many examples can be referenced that have resulted in significant savings and efficiencies in this area. Manufacturing and banking institutions provide the best examples of this type of usage.

Phase 2 activities began in the 1970s and included such current activities as spreadsheet processing, word processing, management information systems reporting, OLAP processing, and data warehousing. It is in the second stage that the computer was being used for purposes it wasn't originally envisioned for and that do not see the savings and efficiency advantages that were evident in the first stage.

Trends in Information Technology

Many projections that were posited in the early 1980s indicated that the future would be built on the usage of computers. The projection of one in four people in industrialized countries interfacing with a computer each day seemed alarmist and overreactive at the time. Yet today, in the new millennium, industrialized societies are interfacing with computers at a rate that has exceeded that.

Increasing business dependence on automated processing has forced organizations to invest higher and higher budgets into information technology for seemingly less payback or return. This dependence and the resulting required investment are occurring at a very bad time. The business marketplace has become extremely competitive today. The company that delivers the new product in a new field will make first blood and garner the lion's share of that market. In response to the increased need for performance, hardware vendors are selling more computer power for cheaper dollars. They are also selling disk storage at decreasing prices and increasing the amount of data online by enormous amounts.

If this is all true, then why is the cost of information technology going up in the face of all the lowering costs and hardware technology breakthroughs? Many believe it is the software that is causing the problem. Off-the-shelf software has become more expensive to purchase. Vendors are trying to recoup their investment in a shorter period of return by levying high licensing fees. Software development companies have to develop products that meet the need or develop the market and generate the product. All of this is expensive. This is passed on to the buyer in order to cover costs. To aggravate the situation, the alternative effort of developing code has also become more expensive to write because of higher personnel costs (this will be covered soon as being one of the major costs of information technology today).

Vendor Software Development

Let's look at software development costs for a moment. In the speed of the technological evolution in hardware, new changes have to be made to the software to take advantage of the new hardware options. The cycle time of a hardware change has been faster and allows computers to speed up. Since the invention of the integrated circuit in 1958, the number of transistors that can be placed inexpensively on an integrated circuit has increased exponentially, doubling approximately every two years (Moore, 1965).

Likewise it has become an annual event or even twice a year that software releases come out. This is to take more and more advantage of the hardware leaps that have taken place. The structuring of software purchase and licensing fees has gone up as well, increasing the overall cost. All of these things have increased dollar payout for businesses. This payout is offsetting the savings that were gained when hardware prices were lowered with the technological advances. The end result is that costs in information technology are still rising.

New market strategies have been developed where the price of keeping abreast of the latest release of the software became critical. It is often said that the latest options in the releases solve all the problems. It only becomes clear commitment to the next release that does indeed solve all the older problems … and also brings on a raft of new ones. Users are becoming angry, and budget-meisters are concerned about where it will end.

The Other Option

The other scenario, developing code, has become more expensive due to the lack of knowledge of the latest software technologies. Knowledge of the latest skills usually involves hiring gurus or high-priced consultants for knowledge transfer to the employees that will perform the coding work. Unfortunately, the knowledge transfer is not always the best, and often the consultant walks out the door with little or no skills embedded in the retained personnel. This is a subject covered in greater detail in this chapter.

Additional costs associated with the computer and software are formal and informal training, setup, maintenance, and upgrading the costs for workstations. Although no estimates are available for this type of cost, it is the feeling of many that these peripheral costs exceed the cost of the main computers and networks.

Trends in Organizational Change

The term *organizational change* is relatively broad and can apply to strategies, to company structures and even to the business practices of an organization. Some researchers have defined organizational change as including the following:

1. Competitive strategy, which is the set of business efforts that ensure viability in the marketplace.
2. Structural characteristics of the organization, including hierarchy, functional lines, and organizational boundaries.
3. Work processes, including flow of work, job design, and work allocation. This involves the work within the information technology department only.
4. Human resource practices, which includes human resource practices within information technology and the use of suppliers and contractors.
5. Industrial relations practices that involve the strategies that interface with external organizations for government, regulatory, or labor management practices.

Trends have affected all of the preceding areas and in doing so have affected the organization in the form of organizational trends.

Some of these organizational trends include the following (listed in the order of frequency that they appear to be used by organizations):

- Reengineering or changing the processes within the organization
- Reliance on increased functional flexibility or, to put it another way, cross-training of current personnel for multiple tasking and sharing
- Downsizing, resizing, or rightsizing, which are sobriquets for removal of personnel (covered more in the next chapter)
- Increased integration or the collapse and integration of redundant structure and process within the organization that either increases or decreases centralization
- Adoption of flexible working hours as a motivational incentive for employees
- Delayering or the elimination of layers of management within the organization hierarchy
- Increase in overtime utilized by the organization
- Increase in use of temporary or consulting help

All of these organizational trends are being implemented because no one is happy with the return on investment of their information technology dollars.

There seems to be a law of diminishing returns operating when it comes to information technology within the organization. Many have called it a productivity problem, whereas others consider it a productivity anomaly. It is simply that the expected efficiencies and savings are not evident in the IT environments.

Productivity

But what is the problem with productivity? Why, when more dollars are being spent on information technology than ever before, does it seem that companies are getting less in return? What exactly is this productivity issue? Is it perception or reality?

Let us start with the premise that productivity is the creation of the product in the most efficient manner that will ensure a profit margin for the company. It is measurable as the variance between cost to produce and sell and the total of sales. But information technology does not produce a salable product. It produces a product that supports the production and selling of the real product. Still, even when IT costs are bundled into the production costs, it can be measured. Unfortunately, the IT costs have not been dwindling as part of the production costs but have been growing.

The overall production efficiency gains that were felt in the sixties did not propagate through the decades through today. In fact, the efficiencies seem to be declining according to some studies despite the proliferation of information technology and computers throughout the economy and business world.

Looking into history, it is easy to see that emerging technologies transformed the economies, improved productivity growth, and raised living standards. Examples of these are the diesel and gasoline engines, turbine generators, and other contributors to the industrial revolution. This emerging technology transformation continued and propagated through the first part of the twentieth century as exemplified by the use of railways and electrical power. But this latest emerging technology, the information technology that encompasses both computer and software, does not appear to be following in the same footsteps. Despite massive investments in information technology, it appears that productivity efficiencies and savings have slowed since the 1970s.

Explanations for the Anomaly in Productivity

The possible reasons for this anomaly can be clustered into several categories:

- *Business has evolved and has become more complex, but it is truly using the benefits.* The expected gains in productive efficiency are present, but they are not showing because business hasn't figured out how to assess them properly.

- *Businesses are still evolving.* The expected gains in productive efficiency have not been realized because business doesn't really know what it is yet. When business gets past the learning curve of the computer, it will be able to truly measure productivity.

- *It is just evolutionary change.* This indicates that the expected productive efficiency gains are not here and shouldn't be expected because computers and IT are merely tools and not all that important to the original idea of productivity.

We will cover each theory in detail and see how they address the problem and how they are related to organizational structures.

Business Has Evolved and Is Using the Benefits

According to this theory, the benefits of information technology have been actualized, but measurements have failed to capture them. This viewpoint has several aspects to it. One aspect of this view is that in the nonbusiness area where there is no measured output of a product, productivity is zero. For example, productivity gains from information technology use in government, education, and health areas (as opposed to manufacturing) will not show any productive efficiency gains by the standard measurement techniques.

Similar problems exist in the financial and services sectors. These two areas have made significant information technology investments but have shown little productivity gain according to the standard definition. Perhaps it is because finding the right metrics is harder to accomplish or the true cost of information technology can't be delineated with enough specificity.

So either measurement problems are more difficult to solve or the number of the areas affected has grown. One argument that supports this is that in areas where the output is measured very well and the investment in information technology has been significant, such as the telecommunications industry, the productivity gains have proven to be substantial.

The implication then is that in areas where large investments were being made in information technology and there were no metrics defined, the output was poorly assessed or not measured at all. Therefore, there are productivity savings and efficiencies present; they just haven't been made visible. Complicating this is the nonmeasurability of some of the components of information technology investment that have made life better in the generic sense. Examples of these components are conveniences to the public (ATM access for banks), access to more information (World Wide Web), and new services (e-mail and instant messaging communications).

Businesses Are Still Evolving

According to this theory, information technology has the potential to enormously increase productivity, but there are barriers that have prevented this from happening. Over time, when the barriers are removed, the productivity will be realized and the train will finally arrive. Some things posited in supporting this scenario are poor organizational structures, poor data architecture design, and marginal usefulness of computer systems.

There is some merit to this theory because there have been lagging periods after a new technology implementation that allowed the customers to adjust to the change. For example, it took several decades for television to be propagated before the explosion of its use began to occur. Part of the increase in speed of the propagation of television was the drop in price to the consumer, which helped foster distribution and transmission.

Another factor noted as being a roadblock is a familiar one: poor organizational structures. As noted in previous chapters, poor organizational structures only make matters worse. To paraphrase one observer in the field:

> *At best, a computer system merely reinforces the processes and hierarchies that are already present in an organization; at worst, they amplify them. Bad systems, when automated, simply let you make more mistakes—faster. As successful organizations have found, real productivity gains are only ever realized when certain critical enablers are present. These are a sense of shared vision and mission, clear communications, stable and understood processes, and a fervent zeal for continued improvement.*

An additional factor implied supporting this theory is that there is insufficient training to fully exploit information technology gains. As seen with the evolution of the hardware and software in the industry, the rate of change is accelerating and it is very difficult to keep a workforce fully apprised of all the nuances without spending inordinate amounts of time on training.

A final supporting concept for this theory is that the computer is failing the test for commercial usability and usefulness. Thomas

Landauer (1995) indicates that "the usability of the computer is poor because of lack of standardization and is fraught with excessive complexity (i.e., the user has too many features and options to learn)." He also indicates that its "usefulness is limited, as rarely more than a small number of the features on computer are used fully." His belief is that computers will be realized for their capacity to be powerful tools for the service economy through task analysis, iterative design processes, and trial use.

It Is Just Evolutionary Change

The final theory for explaining the productivity anomaly is that the computer and information technology are just not that important. It purports that computers and computer systems just aren't as productivity enhancing as originally believed. In short, there were high expectations based on the first wave of productivity, but it turns out they are just tools.

Concepts that support this are the lack of widespread organizational change with the implementation of advances in information technology, the underestimation of information technology operations costs, and the confusing scenario of the accelerating technology change. For certain areas there can be no doubt that information technology has had a fundamental impact. Some of these are the airline and telecommunications industries. But for other nonspecific industries and business, it did not fundamentally change the business process. It only facilitated the automation of something. For example, the users of spreadsheets, word processing, e-mail, and the Internet have not been significantly or positively impacted by these improvements. In fact, in some ways they have negatively affected the productivity.

Examples of this antiproductivity are spam and junk e-mail (jokes, memes, chain letters) and the Internet (non-work searches), which degrade the productivity in all information technology departments to some degree or another. From another perspective, the cost of the information technology operations and the computers may have been underestimated. This cost covers the upgrading of networks, purchasing of monitoring tools, technical support, and the training of employees to create or use new computer applications. It also involves the degradation of expensive human resources rather than inexpensive ones. (Executives and senior staff now are forced to spend more time understanding and using information technology in order to use the new control tools.)

The confusing scenario of accelerating technology change is based on the fact that the pace of technology evolution is accelerating. Computers, both hardware and software, are symbols of this. According to that concept, there should be a corresponding improvement in productivity. But what if information technology has really not been accelerating but is instead just moving forward at a constant velocity? It sounds paradoxical, but the "perception" of its acceleration might be based on the proliferation of so many products and options in the marketplace. The net result would be that the fragmentation within that technology would be dispersed and distributed over a wider range, thus giving the appearance of less productivity.

Information Technology and Its Impact on Organizations

There have been four basic impacts predicted by the pundits in the industry for the impact of Information Technologies on the organization:

- Information technology changes many facets of the organizational internal structure, so it affects the roles, power, and hierarchies in the organization. By virtue of this, it should end up eliminating the middle management in an organizational structure. In fact, two distinct results have occurred associated with this: There has been an increase in organizational management centralization in some industry cases and the opposite decentralization in other industries. It does indicate that information technology is searching for an optimal identity that will allow it to evolve where necessary.
- Information technology will stimulate the formation of solution-focused teams that along with communication tools will become the primary organizational form. This would flatten the top-to-bottom hierarchy significantly. Peter Drucker (1998) speculated that the symphony orchestra might be the model of the organization of the future. Within this model, each player would be responsible for his or her own specific piece of the entire work, with minimal guidance from the conductor. While this might be desirable, it has not happened, and probably never will, due to top and senior managements' inability to deal with strategic rather than operational issues. Live for the now and manage to the stock price is de rigueur.
- Information technology will force the disintegration of organizations due to steadily decreasing costs of interconnections

between businesses. Therefore, companies will have to change their organizations to a market-based form that will use external service-based organizations to perform the work requested by the hierarchical organization. This purports that the organizational structures are being degraded through the crumbling of boundaries between businesses. This crumbling is facilitated by the combined effects of increased electronic information flow, use of common databases, and tight electronically bound interorganizational processes. This has evolved partially as market pressures have increased within different parts of the industry. Unfortunately, the metric being used is how the market share is being affected by the stock price instead of just competing for market share.

- Information technology has proven that improved communication ability and improved data accessibility lead to increased system integration across product line function and geographic lines. Therefore, the change to the organization is predictable and expected. According to this, with integration of data and process comes the natural progression of integration of organization across functional, geographic, and product boundaries. This remains to be seen as businesses and organizations coevolve.

Why Invest in Information Technology?

With any and all of the preceding theories being true to some degree, why and to what degree will organizations invest in information technology? As pointed out before, organizations invest in information technology to provide a flexible, adaptable environment for future business, improve the integrity and stability of the data and the processes the organization depends on, and improve the quality of products and customer relations.

The positive effects of information technology have been felt by the shrinking of time and distance to nil. Geographically distributed processes can now be completed across countries and time zones with impunity. It is understandable that organizational history is imbedded in the use of common databases by many users and can be maintained over long periods of time.

Telecommunication has opened wide the communications options of organizations. Prior to the recent years, mail and telephone were the only methods of communication. Now we have fax, e-mail, cellular phones, cellular modems, voice mail, paging, handheld computers, texting, and videoconferencing, all of which have added many channels to the communications options.

Information access has increased through the use of integrated database systems and new access mechanisms and search engine tools via the Internet. Information technology has proven it is possible to reduce the number and levels of management and therefore has flattened some organizational hierarchies. Some theoreticians insist that hierarchies (and the power-broking they entail) are inherent in human nature and will continue despite any efforts to the contrary. This is perhaps too cynical.

Also, as a result of information technology investment, there has been a decentralization of decision making. Organizations originally concentrated their decision making in the upper levels of the organization. As seen in previous chapters, it is critical that the decision-making power needs to be delegated downward for the best efficiency of the business process. In conclusion, the effect of information technology and the investment in it have been very positive—that is, as long as a chosen focus is decided on, the path to the future is architected, and it is embraced from top to bottom in the organization.

Ineffective Use of Information Technology

One area of easily observed concern is the negative attitude taken by individuals in relation to changes made by and for information technology. Many executives and midlevel managers are ambivalent to information technology. Older senior executives often feel particularly uncomfortable and threatened by information technology. In doing so, they end up not using it correctly and thus fulfill their own prophecy. Employees other than management may also feel threatened, particularly if there is the possibility of job loss or the fear that the technology will be too difficult for them to understand.

Another impediment is the absence of synergy among the organization, the individual, and group efficiencies. Changes in individual efficiency do not necessarily indicate group or organizational productivity. Some of the specifications of these barriers are as follows:

- Choosing slower forms of communication. An example may be using e-mail to communicate rather than speaking or instant messaging (which can be up to five times faster).

- Formalized communication. An example is that communication is maximized when both parties are at the same level of knowledge and understanding. It is lower and slower when one party has to teach and communicate to the other at the same time.
- Quality versus quantity. So much energy is expended on reediting text, fine-tuning print fonts, formatting, and embellishing presentation material that it consumes any information technology savings on the task.
- Increased requirements for skill and complexity. The frequent introduction of new hardware and software to information technology leads to rapid skills obsolescence or imposes major learning burdens on workers.
- Generation of more work by computers. Despite what it may seem, computers may actually increase paperwork by producing information faster to the worker than it can be reasonably used.
- Administrative overhead. The technical support required to keep information technology operating may lead to hiring high-salary employees, which eats up any cost savings.
- Management control. Information technology is often charged with providing organizational management with performance data. This data usually fosters managerial control but does nothing significant to the decision-making capability or productivity.

Other Impediments to Organizational Efficiency

These are also a series of factors that nonspecifically affect the productivity of information technology in the organization. These are possible areas of concern when productivity is ailing for reasons other than what has been pointed out so far.

- Poor-quality training provided to users
- Lack of ongoing user support availability
- Limited extent of user involvement of the user in new application development
- No reward mechanism for using the new applications
- No job security for the workers
- Poor coordination between groups using the applications
- Political conflict within the organization (turf battles)
- Absence of a willingness to accept the new applications

Organizational Impediments to Information Technology

In order to overcome some of the impediments in organization, changes in management behavior must be made. It does appear that management has been misunderstanding the measurement of information technology. Most management appears to measure information technology by one or two criteria instead of several. Moreover, they often do not share the results in detail with the information technology group, so there is no feedback or results to allow the information technology department to make changes. A gap between hostile camps soon develops.

Tom Peters advocates approaches that would radically slash payrolls and eliminate certain structures and organizational levels altogether. Peters sees little role for management except to stay out of the way of the new organization that must act for the most part autonomously. His view could be considered similar to the reengineering efforts of the 1990s. These efforts claimed that the fault was not with the technologies but rather in the business processes, which still reflected organizational thinking from a previous time. Peters feels that the right business structure must first be created and then automated.

One form of the radical reorganization that has been taking place is downsizing. Although it is covered in greater detail in the next chapter, it should be covered here from the perspective of impact to the organization. Management often orchestrated the downsizing, believing that the productivity that would increase would help them to reduce some of the costs they had been incurring. However, in many cases the downsizing did not have the desired effect, mainly because the managers making the downsizing decisions did not have an adequate understanding of the big picture for the organization or were focused on whether or not they themselves were 'safe'. They ended up reducing the workforce but not the work—making already workload-taxed workers more overtaxed. Thus, as a result, many of the wrong people, levels, or functions in the organization were cut. In most cases, long-term costs increased because of downsizing.

Technological Solutions for Information Technology

It has been noted that information technology has not made the hoped-for improvements for the productivity of managers.

However, managers that do not have as many repetitive tasks as their subordinates can be made more productive with the use of management, project, and communication software.

Bruce Love (1993) identified the nature of the problem as being twofold: the problems with the information itself and the nature of the information technology organization. He identifies three obstacles to exploiting information as a resource:

- The prevailing limits and vision of information
- The limits of supporting technology
- The nature of information, its sheer size, volatility, and the difficulty associated with managing it

Although these points are not covered here in detail, further reading of his work is suggested to have a better understanding of his perspective.

Many arguments can be made with respect to what will best serve to increase productivity after the introduction of information technology. One suggestion is that the managers must make changes to increase their own productivity, and it in turn will increase their subordinates. Among the actions the managers may take is the introduction of new organizational structures to facilitate the productivity effort. However, there are also solutions that suggest that the problems with information, software, and technology must be addressed first. In both cases they represent opportunities to help solve the problem.

Human Resource Issues in Information Technology

There have been studies that show that aligning human resource efforts and information technology implementations solves many of the problems that result in productivity loss. It appears that a synergy was created when new human resource practices were implemented along with information technology changes. This synergy was best seen in an environment where the workers had a voice in their own futures. It also appears that human resources is involved in resolving internal conflict issues that deal with the politics of the organization. It is said that organizations that are the most profitable tend to be the healthiest and least internally conflicted. They are comfortable with their goals. The organizations that espouse this decide how they want to run themselves, decide how they will handle their people, and finally decide how they will handle information technology. In these healthy companies, information technology decisions come after the more fundamental issues are handled.

Paul Strassman (1995) states that firms can improve their information productivity by maximizing their knowledge capital, which is making the best use and reuse of their knowledge workers and their own acquired corporate knowledge.

Quality of the Workforce

Another human resources issue is the changing of the quality of the workforce. The new worker is less motivated to learn and acquire knowledge than the older worker. This is not because they are less qualified but because the educational process has focused on specialization of tasks rather than understanding the concepts of the whole process.

New workers are less inclined to focus on improvement and broad-scale problems without incentives and motivation because they have a different work ethic that is more results-based and material than that of older workers. There is also a sense of entitlement in the newer generations of workers that has been instilled as the "me" generation has passed on its heritage of self-focus to their offspring. All of these factors introduce a different flavor into the blend of the workforce and can create gaps and conflicts between younger and older workers.

Summary

As in the case of most complex puzzles, there are several solutions. It can be said that the different theories specified earlier in this chapter really are facets of the problem that contribute to an overall explanation. It is, however, easier to understand the different theories. This is because they deal with the measurement of expected results, which are real components.

In many situations, computers are workhorses for activity. They reduce human effort. Based on definable indicators of output produced, the introduction of computers and computer systems has facilitated both growth and productivity. In areas such as telecommunications, these gains are measureable. In banking, finance, and parts of government administration, they may not be. If the same rule-set that the others are measured by is applied, these other areas would look stagnant when they aren't. Output measurement appears to be a major part of the productivity problem.

Maximizing the Use of Information Technology

A major conclusion that can be gained from the material in this chapter is that information technology is not a panacea. That perspective must be understood. In terms of importance, it ranks below the fundamental issues such as human resource strategies and must be integrated after the fact into these strategies.

Michael Scott-Morton (1991) concluded, "None of the potentially beneficial enabling aspects of information technology can take place without clarity of business purpose and a vision of what the organization should become. A clear mission visible to, and understood by, the organization is a well-known prerequisite for any organization change. However, when the issue at hand is organizational transformation, enabled by technology, it appears particularly important to invest a large amount of time and effort in getting the organization to understand where it is going and why."

It appears that two major conditions have to exist for a successful organizational transformation to take place. The first is that the organization has to align its corporate strategy and information technology. The second is that the organization must have a robust information technology infrastructure in place, including electronic networks, and understood standards and procedures.

A final conclusion from Scott-Morton (1991) is, "One root cause for the lack of impact of information technology on the improved economic performance of organizations is the organization's unwillingness to invest heavily and early enough in human resources. Changing the way people work can be extremely threatening and therefore takes a great deal of investment. There must be investment in new skills, in psychological ownership of the change process, and in the safety net under the employee so there is no fear of taking prudent risks. These investments are required to be taken throughout the organization, as management itself is part of the change. The ultimate goal is to give all employees a sense of empowerment."

Without looking at the entire organization as an enterprise, which is an organism unto itself, the problems cannot be corrected. Specifically the problems have left information technology underutilized and left wide gaps between departments within the organization. This only foments the political strife and turf battles that are so destructive.

References

Drucker, P. F. (1988, January–February). The coming of the new organization. *Harvard Business Review*, volume 66, 45–53.

Moore, G. E. (1965). Cramming more components onto integrated circuits. *Electronics Magazine*, volume 38, number 8, April 19, 1965.

Landauer, T. K. (1995). *The trouble with computers: Usefulness, usability, and productivity*. Cambridge, MA: MIT Press.

Love, B. (1993). *Enterprise information technologies: Designing the competitive company*. New York: Van Nordstrand-Reinhold.

Morton, M. S. (1990). *The corporation of the 1990's: Information technology and organizational transformation*. New York: Oxford University Press.

Peters, T. (1992). *Liberation management: Necessary disorganization for the nanosecond nineties*. New York: Alfred A. Knopf.

Strassman, P. (1995). *The politics of information management*. Information Economics Press, New Canaan, Ct.

8

SOLUTIONS THAT CAUSE PROBLEMS

Downsizing and Organizational Culture

While the average worker has become numb by the near daily accounts of new layoffs, a *New York Times* (1996) national survey finding is perhaps more telling: Since 1980, a family member in one-third of all U.S. households has been laid off. By some measures, downsizing or "rightsizing" has failed abjectly as a tool to achieve its principal goal: reduce costs. Downsizing for the sake of cost reduction alone is now being looked on as shortsighted. Considering downsizing from the perspective of increased global competition, changing technologies, and the changing nature of work provides an interesting insight. It is clear that downsizing can be seen both as a response to and as a catalyst of organizational change.

From the business perspective the most significant effects of downsizing are cultural within the organization. This is an indistinct connection between downsizing and organizational culture because there are different variations and approaches to downsizing. Proactive downsizing is planned in advance and is usually integrated with a larger set of objectives. This is often done in the case of well-thought-out merger processes. Reactive downsizing is typified by cost-cutting in order to meet budget goals. It is usually done after periods of inattention to organizational or productivity problems by management. It is also the most demoralizing forms of downsizing.

Downsizing can range from involuntary reductions to resignation incentives and job sharing. There are also different options of deciding who remains and who leaves. There are different modes of downsize planning—from secretive sessions by management to solicitation and discussion of ideas from employees. There are different standards of notice of terminations, from same-day terminations to generous 90-day or longer notices. There are even differences in intent. Reductions can be planned to create as little a break as possible from what they have known in the past, or they can create deliberate disruption to the status quo.

Downsizing Defined

The term *downsizing* is problematic in its usefulness. Often, because it is associated with "giving people the axe," it is not a term that many want to use. Some researchers are concerned that downsizing has become closely associated with the concept of organizational decline and its negative effects. Cameron (1994), for example, defines downsizing as a positive and purposive strategy: "a set of organizational activities undertaken on the part of management of an organization and designed to improve organizational efficiency, productivity, and/or competitiveness."

Downsizing, when it is defined this way, falls into the category of management tools for achieving desired change, much like *restructuring* and *reengineering*. Clearly, this viewpoint is extremely broad. Downsizing very likely will impact or impinge on in-place change efforts such as the introduction of "total quality management," "reengineering," or "reinventing" initiatives. They are not the same as Cameron's definition.

Very few organizations implement downsizing in a way that improves their effectiveness. Most organizations deteriorate in terms of levels of quality, productivity, effectiveness, conflict, low morale, loss of trust, and rigidity. In order to look at this subject objectively, downsizing can be simply defined as a reduction in the size of the workforce.

Culture Change

Changing an organization's culture is a messy business. Studies have indicated that this change becomes tougher as organizations become more established and successful. The very basis for a company's earlier success can hinder necessary changes under different market conditions. Also, research supports the idea that organizational culture change is a multiyear effort, thus making the implementation more complicated.

If the definition of culture change is broadened to include both intended consequences and unintended consequences, then it is a statement of fact that downsizing is a catalyst for culture change. Organizational theorists like Lewin (Ash, 1992) and Argyris (1992) have insisted on the need for a destabilizing element in any change process. The existing status quo is conceptualized as a stasis state in which forces resisting change and forces pushing for change have found equilibrium. They feel that in order to shift the balance, the situation needs to be destabilized. Euphemistically speaking, people have to be shaken to get their attention so they will be aware of a need for change.

Downsizing qualifies as a destabilizer of the status quo even under the mildest circumstances, such as where departures are voluntary attrition. Management literature abounds with examples of burnout, depression, anger, and betrayal as common responses by survivors of layoffs. However, not all responses are negative. Some people appear to get "charged up," finding new excitement in their work, being challenged by the prospect of "doing more with less," or saving the organization. But these people are usually in positions of power or those who were happy they had "dodged a bullet."

In any event, it must be acknowledged that downsizing has changed the unwritten contract of employment. No longer can the employer offer job security. The "new" contract is conditional employment. Sometimes training and development opportunities provide some amelioration to this situation.

From a broad cultural perspective, downsizing can be seen as the embodiment of the "creative destruction" inherent in capitalism. Although many management personnel feel that downsizing is not easy to watch and people will get hurt, they feel that this is the way the market takes care of itself. Bridges (1994) and others warn the rank and file that only the foolish will let their fates be decided by those they work for. The wise ones will think and act like private consultants even if they fall under the label "employees."

The symbolic aspects of culture change associated with downsizing should not be overlooked. The very act of downsizing creates an appearance of leadership that is taking charge. An older example of this is the Clinton-Gore program in the U.S. government. They made the claim that by eliminating 272,900 federal jobs, they had reduced the cost of government. They were applauded for achieving the goal. The symbolism associated with the change weighed more heavily on people's minds than the costs, which included contracting out at a much higher price for services previously provided in-house. In fact, they expensively outsourced the work to the private sector, and there were no savings, only increased taxes. It was the appearance of change that was exciting to the media.

Speaking of politics, the political aspects of culture change within an organization that are associated with downsizing are also very dramatic. Downsizing represents a shift in power toward top management and shareholders. The unspoken message is that management isn't afraid to decide who "has a future" with the organization and who doesn't. The message is clear: "If you want to continue to work here, you will have to work harder and more responsibly, be a team player, and so on and so on."

Organizational-Level Analysis

If there is a right way to downsize, it is through careful examination of the organization it will be applied to. Organizational-level analysis emphasizes the need to plan, analyze, and implement downsizing carefully, since it must have the desired effect of improving and streamlining work processes. Key assumptions in this analysis include an engineered notion of organizations, in which the parts are examined to improve the fit with the whole. Organizational survival must be seen as a prime directive. Along these lines, some research has revealed some interesting things.

In one of the key early works on downsizing, Tomasko (1990) identifies corporate cultures based on mistrust as a leading cause of excessive staffing. American corporate culture, he contends, rewards winners, not losers; places control at the top of the agenda; and causes people to believe that it is better to hide mistakes than admit them. In consequence, staff groups are formed to serve as watchdogs. Managers respond by attempting to gain control of even more bloated corporate bureaucracies. Tomasko's solution is to use downsizing to create a flatter, leaner organization in which a team environment prevails and people trust one another to contribute to common goals.

In the 1990s Cameron and others conducted extensive studies of downsizing in terms of the number of organizations involved, breadth of investigation, and time span. Their conclusion was that downsizing was a necessary and positive approach to becoming more competitive. Also, it was an appropriate response to the disproportionate growth in the white-collar workforce over recent decades.

The successful companies in their study not only reduced the work force but also engaged in organizational redesign and systematic efforts at quality improvement. Successful companies engaged in downsizing as a purposeful and proactive strategy.

Several books in the industry addressing culture change in management explicitly state what many will not state: that part of the *intentional* aspect of downsizing in the midst of culture change is the infliction of pain on at least some to get the attention of all. This is the therapeutic "slap in the face" that has been referred to.

Tichy and Sherman (1994) talk of avoiding the "boiled frog phenomenon," in which frogs boil to death while the water slowly changes from cold to boiling. Kearns and Nadler (1992) conclude, "You also have to create dissatisfaction with the status quo. Otherwise, why are people going to work hard to disrupt it? And you cannot wait around until everyone feels induced pain from the marketplace, because then it's too late. So you need to have induced pain. You need to throw a few punches here and there."

Other analysts defer praise for downsizing. These analysts argue that an organization does not exist only for profits; that is, profits should be viewed as a means to other ends, rather than as the only end. They believe that shareholders have taken over too much of the power. Their opinions are that institutional shareholders have gotten greedy and have imposed a gouging price on the multitudes of employees who have lost their jobs. These opinions surmise that any realized performance increases may be at the expense of hollowed-out companies.

Downs (1995) expresses an even harder view. He decries the public acceptance of a "culture of narcissism," in which corporations have only one objective: profit. Part of this culture of narcissism is reflected in the increase of senior executive salaries by 1,000 percent between 1980 and 1995, the same period of time in which record layoffs were amassed. And this increase hasn't slowed. To quote CNN from August 30, 2005:

> If sky-high executive pay at publicly traded companies gives you vertigo, you might want to read this sitting down. In 2004, the ratio of average CEO pay to the average pay of a production (i.e., nonmanagement) worker was 431-to-1, up from 301-to-1 in 2003, according to "Executive Excess," an annual report released Tuesday by the liberal research groups United for a Fair Economy and the Institute for Policy Studies. That's not the highest ever. In 2001, the ratio of CEO-to-worker pay hit a peak of 525-to-1. Still, it's quite a leap year over year, and it ranks on the high end historically. In 1990, for instance, CEOs made about 107 times more than the average worker, while in 1982, the average CEO made only 42 times more.

Organizational/Individual-Level Analysis

The analysis at the organizational/individual interface should be focused on healing the effects of downsizing on those who remain in the organization. Research in this area has provided documentation of the harmful effects downsizing can have on the "survivors"; these effects have been described in terms of lower morale, high stress, and a employee mindset marked by anger, envy, and guilt.

Brockner and colleagues (1994) studied the "fairness" of layoffs from a procedural justice perspective. Their results showed a link between perceived fairness of the layoffs and the survivor's commitment to the organization. Among the fairness factors Brockner examines is the connection with existing corporate culture.

Organizations such as IBM, which have traditionally had a policy of averting layoffs, are likely to be perceived by employees as violating a personal contract and therefore seen as more unfair when they finally do resort to layoffs. When the conversion by IBM to the downsizing corporate mentality occurred, it was viewed as a betrayal by many who had worked there for decades.

Downsizing's Impact on Culture

For organizations, particularly the IBMs of the world that long resisted layoffs, it is hard to imagine that the organizations or their cultures have remained anything close to intact. Answers must be defined for the following questions:

1. *For whose benefit does the organization exist?* It is clear that organizations do not exist today for the well-being of rank-and-file employees as they once did. With the stock market driving business choices the way it does, it seems clear that the shareholders have the upper hand. They are partnered with CEOs who received an average pay raise in 1995 of 23 percent (*Washington Post*). Look at who is making money and who is not.

2. *What are the basic assumptions among people about working relationships in the organization?* The basic assumptions about working relationships have changed. Many of the assumptions have changed in ways that cannot be well assessed. It appears, minimally, that relationships are less "familial" and much more competitive than in the past. What is the value of commitment and loyalty? What is the impact of discarding the concept that the organization is a community—even a family? How will that play out in terms of cooperation given to others as opposed to "backstabbing" in the intense competition for scarce resources? There are no answers to these questions. The only conclusion to be reached is that things have changed, not how they have changed or to what degree.

3. *What are the basic assumptions the organization and the employee make in relation to each other?* In order to really understand downsizing, it is necessary to look beyond the

stated rationale for reductions. How many organizations admit, for example, that one of the key objectives of a layoff is to dump the "dead wood"? There is much more than meets the eye. It is intuitively plain that IBM today is in the same business as they were in the past. It will take time and study to know if these new organizations are as habitable for modern workers as they were in the past.

A Different Approach to Culture Change and Downsizing

How can senior management steer an appropriate course? This is not an easy task. In the private sector, the stock market seems to well reward a tough approach to downsizing. For example, AT&T's Robert Allen was criticized about, but still received, his pay package of $16 million during 1995, the same year he began to downsize 50,000 people out of their jobs This has occurred at other organizations time and again. Overall, the media have given friendly coverage to downsizing.

While being moralistic about changes in organizational culture is best resisted, there are still many leaders who wish to accept responsibility for the "moral" or "spiritual" fabric of the life of their organizations. For those persons, the leader needs to examine just how well the type of downsizing proposed fits with the values and beliefs he or she would like to see carried forward. It may require the leader to put aside the technical rationale for reductions provided by external consultants. It may also require reconsidering the implementation strategy devised by a legal team in conjunction with an outplacement service.

Summary

It is evident, even definitional, that senior management's mind-set will have a great deal to do with how downsizing is implemented in an organization. It also seems, beyond question, that downsizing acts as an organizational destabilizer and thus as a catalyst for cultural change. Whether the resultant cultural change is beneficial to the organization as a whole is open to speculation. Because downsizing is a relatively recent phenomenon at the white-collar level, time will have to differentiate between short-term effects and reactions and the longer-term consequences. Perhaps less bloated bureaucracies will free people to get more work done and to interact more positively. Perhaps a whole generation of management thinkers understated the value of loyalty and commitment that accrued over long and stable employment tenure. Time will tell the story.

Outsourcing

What is outsourcing, and why does outsourcing jobs make sense? Outsourcing information technology functions can include a number of different components of the information technology department, including the following:

- Disaster recovery
- Network management
- Maintenance of operating system
- Maintenance of application software
- Maintenance of hardware
- Web creation, maintenance, hosting
- E-commerce development

Some of the information technology functionality can more easily be outsourced than others. One of the easy functions to outsource is maintenance. This can be done to vendors for which there are reasonable connections. For example, maintenance of hardware can rest with the manufacturer or vendor from whom the equipment was originally acquired.

Alternatively, there are many firms that can function in this area. Hardware maintenance provided by a third party is often set up as being bundled with the lease for that equipment. Disaster recovery is a functional area where outsourcing is more critical than with any other. It can be successful if implemented correctly.

A good disaster recovery plan is imperative to lowering the risk of a system failure due to any number of causes: natural disasters, power outages, fires, and floods. The problem is, while initially easy to develop and set up, disaster recovery plans are seldom maintained or tested well by internal functions. Disaster recovery plan maintenance and testing tend to become low-priority tasks, as there are always more pressing current issues to deal with and resolve.

If the disaster recovery strategy is not maintained as a living evolving strategy, then failure is imminent. By the time information technology typically gets around to testing and maintaining the disaster recovery plan, situations typically have changed so dramatically that the plan is obsolete and, therefore, useless.

Network management and upgrades, web development and hosting, and e-commerce development are growth areas where very few companies can justify the expenditure for additional personnel. These areas of information technology are changing so rapidly that it takes cutting-edge expertise to manage and develop. Education must be constant in order to keep up on the latest developments with the technology.

When outsourcing to the expert consultant or service group/ vendor, you take some risk. The expert is going to demand top compensation and can, in times of a seller's market, hold an organization hostage for higher pay. This approach is typically fatal to their employment with that company, but they can easily move to another. They are opportunistic feeders. They walk out the door with no knowledge transfer taking place. Then the hiring company is stuck reorienting another expert to the methods and background.

In some cases, the cost of having all information technology functions in-house may be justifiable. As an example, the hardware maintenance of some equipment may be able to be performed by an internal employee whose job function might include being the contact person for the company and the outsource vendor(s). That person might perform maintenance on hardware, perform daily backups, maintain system job queues, and ensure that maintenance and upgrades to application software are performed by the outsource vendor(s). A person with this skill set is easier to find in the market, less likely to leave, and less risky to the internal in-house function.

Another area where in-house personnel could be justifiable includes software application upgrades. This is true in packaged applications with no modification to the source code. If there are modifications, a cost justification needs to be made to employ an internal programmer to maintain upgrade applications or outsource the function to a firm with programming expertise. They simply apply the patches or upgrade supplied.

In-house programmers of this type are seldom cost justifiable in small firms, but they may be cost effective in large organizations with a large amount of modified code. Even in these instances, turnover and the risks associated with it should be considered—especially for "business-critical" applications. It all comes down to cost/benefit analysis of each function and determining the level of risk you are willing to accept.

With some of these caveats in place, some of the positive aspects of outsourcing can be discussed. There are a number of benefits to outsourcing the information technology function. Only continual education and exposure to the latest products and developments in the market provide expertise to outsourced information technology professionals. Firms providing outsourcing services must provide their employees with the necessary expertise in many areas or they will face dissatisfied customers.

Contracts don't last long if the servicing agent doesn't have the skills. Internal information technology department employees must be afforded this same degree of education in order to be retained. Many companies consider the combined costs of salary and benefits, employee turnover, recruitment fees, and education investment a virtual wash when compared with outsourced information technology services fees. So there is no real saving there.

Generally, the outsourced information technology services are considered a lower risk. Under no circumstances should development be outsourced to outside vendors. We will cover this later, but as stated, outsourced information technology services should be those considered to be low risk.

Availability of resource is a second benefit to outsourcing. The vendor will also more likely have a pool of employees from which to draw (redundancy in an internal information technology staff is impossible to maintain except in the largest of companies). An indirect benefit of nonemployee staffing is the related human resource cost benefit. By outsourcing, you are hiring a company, not an employee. Administrative headaches and costs of maintaining an employee for low-risk tasks are thereby eliminated.

Another benefit of not having an employee is the savings of costs of training and ramp-up. While it is true that these costs are to some extent included in the fees the outsourcing firm charges for their services, the risk and probability of higher than average turnover within a company should be recognized and addressed.

Maintaining outsourced services can also increase the reliability of a company's system. The chances of a good outsource vendor going out of business is less than that of an employee in the information technology staff leaving the company.

A further benefit of outsourcing information technology is that control of the systems rests with management. The vendor providing services works for the company and, in most cases, doesn't get involved with internal company politics and hidden agendas. Control is maintained outside the information technology function. The risk of the system being left abandoned or neglected is reduced.

While there is less risk with a large internal information technology department, few firms can afford the cost of a department large enough to employ people with the required degree of expertise in all areas of information technology. Additionally, many companies have asked themselves if they really want to be in the information technology business. Many would rather concentrate on their core business, improving their processes and capitalizing on current market trends and technologies.

Out-of-pocket costs may be somewhat higher than that you would pay an employee. You may have to pay travel costs and per diems to get an outsourced resource on site, but these costs can be negotiated. Picking the right outsource resource should cost no more than hiring an employee. Unfortunately, many companies do not spend enough investigating an outsource vendor.

All information technology outsource firms are created equal. They are as different as the employee candidates you interview. To minimize the risk of hiring a "bad" vendor, be sure to choose a firm with expertise in most, if not all, of the software you use. Inexperience in one area should not preclude choosing the vendor if other important qualifying factors are present. It is also important to ask for a copy of the vendor's errors and omissions insurance.

Most important, choose a firm with good references and a history of long-term relationships. There are many firms that come and go from the marketplace. Above all, recognize three things when negotiating contracts with the outsourcing companies:

- Outsourcing companies do not grow the way the hiring company does. They may be able to handle the business now, but what allowances will they make for you when growth exceeds expected rate? You may have to bear the burden of their expansion costs.
- If you do not specify everything that can possibly happen in the contract period, there is usually a three-year window in which you have the ability to maximize the outsource. The first year is the honeymoon in which everything goes well between you and the vendor. The second year, the vendor has discovered all the problems that you didn't tell him about and what made you consider outsourcing in the first place. You have discovered that the small clause in the contract allows the vendor to charge for everything not nailed down. The honeymoon is over. At the end of the third year, by mutual consent, you consider a new arrangement with a different partner.
- An audit after the three-year period would indicate in most cases that you have saved very little and you still have the same original problem you had when you outsourced. Actually you are a little more in the financial red, since they have been doing the maintenance and the people or the new vendor hasn't a clue as to what has been done to the code. A new learning curve has to be traveled. And it will be at the company's expense.

In summary, outsourcing is good if you can do it as a complete package and if you are a small firm that can readily use it. Large firms will find it more profitable to keep projects and information technology in-house and only outsource the less frequently used functions such as disaster recovery, human resources, and administrative systems.

Rapid Application Development

Consider briefly the progress of the past 30 years. During the 1970s, the age of "programming productivity," the creation of new languages, tools, and development methodologies enabled programmers to improve their productivity by orders of magnitude. During the 1980s, the age of "software quality," the focus was on software processes and continuous process improvement. Quality results have been published in the literature for the past couple of years and indicate improvements in an order of magnitude range along several vectors (decreased defects, increased productivity, decreased cycle time, decreased number of personnel required to achieve results, and decreased percent rework after release).

The decade of the 1990s was the age of "Internet time." The advent of the Internet and associated new software technologies (for example, Java and framework development) enable software developers to field products in cycle times of six months or less. The combination of best practices that have evolved over the past 30 years in productivity; including approaches, quality improvement, and technology are impressive and match progress in other fields of engineering. Taken collectively, they form an assortment of tools with which to attack software development. While the progress is real and arguably impressive, the reasons for failures in software development are largely the same today as they were 30 years ago.

A 1988 U.S. Air Force science study concluded that there were three common risks that were cited for failure (where failure ranges from excessive cost and/or schedule delays to never fielding a system):

1. *Staffing risk.* If a team of developers, end users, and systems maintainers had not worked together before and did not learn to communicate effectively, they were not likely to develop a successful system without schedule delays or cost overruns.
2. *Technology risk.* Teams that pursued a new technical approach (for example, the first foray into client-server computing) found that the lack of experience with a new technology, architecture, or development approach contributed to failure.
3. *Requirement risk.* By far, the most often-cited reason for failure was poor management of requirements. This risk was characterized by frequently changing requirements, requirements that were not well understood, and requirement proliferation.

The bottom line is that experience counts. An experienced team that is developing a similar system to one that it has previously developed with a customer and end user with whom it can communicate well is much more likely to produce high-quality systems on time and at cost.

Rapidly Developed Prototypes

To commercial companies, rapidly developed prototypes were often "throwaways." These prototypes were often too fragile to scale into a tested, deliverable system. But they served a critical purpose: they enabled businesses to quickly capture requirements and depict them in a meaningful way to end users. The tools of the day allowed them to work interactively with end users to evolve a more complete understanding of those requirements. In effect, they provided a means of communication through which a development team could discuss and reach common understanding of the requirements.

Many have criticized rapid application development (RAD) as lacking rigor, leading to fragile systems that do not scale, and serving to raise end user and management expectations to unrealistic levels. These criticisms are valid unless a more disciplined approach to RAD is followed that couples RAD with the lessons learned in productivity and quality. A newly proposed approach to disciplined RAD would entail these steps:

1. Prototype-based requirements capture
2. Architecture design and analysis
3. Component specification with maximum reuse
4. Rapid development of integral modules
5. Frequent testing with end users and systems personnel
6. Distributed with support tools to allow for evolution

The progress in software technology now makes this approach much more likely.

Step 1 addresses the major source of risk described: requirements. Prototype-building tools allow rapid development of cases to illustrate system operation. These in turn are useful for defining requirements. Because end users and management often see ways to improve their work processes as a result, this approach has also proven useful in business reengineering. Thus, prototype-based approaches provide a useful way to do requirements analysis.

Steps 2 and 3 address technology risks. As in other engineering fields, it is useful to define the architecture early during system development and to conduct analyses to assess attributes such as data throughput, usability, and security issues. Too many poor-quality applications are being attributed to misunder-standing technical constraints until realization of the software system in executable code. Recent advances in software architecture development and analysis (for example, see Brockner et al., 1994) provide an engineering basis for early architecture specification. In addition, a lesson learned from reusable software development is the criticality of software architecture in which to embed reusable software components. Components that do not exist or that cannot be easily retrofitted into the architecture can be developed using a rapid prototyping approach (step 4). Requirements and architecture provide design constraints to bound and guide the development of these modules.

Steps 5 and 6 are also very important. It is critical that end users and system maintainers participate regularly in testing. Although listed as a separate step (a final test before delivery needs to be done), it is also useful to use prototype-based test data to assess the output of each step.

Lastly, since requirements often change over the life cycle of the system, it is important to consider how systems will be used and will likely evolve. Then plan for that evolution. The structure in the preceding approach comes from having well-defined and well-understood processes. In addition, training for new employees and continuing education for all employees is an important aspect to ensure that the development team can cope with technical change.

So how can the first decade of the new millennium be characterized? Trends suggest that there will be more powerful computing coupled with a low-cost, high-bandwidth communication infrastructure. There will be continued downsizing of organizations and more outsourcing. There will be marketplaces for reusable objects and software components, such as architecture models and warehouse structures.

References

Argyris, C. (1992). *Knowledge for action: A guide to overcoming barriers to organizational change*. San Francisco: Jossey-Bass.

Ash, M. G. (1992). Cultural contexts and scientific change in psychology: Kurt Lewin in Iowa. *American Psychologist, 47*(2), 198–207.

Bridges, W. (1994). *Job shift: How to prosper in a world without jobs*. Reading, MA: Addison-Wesley.

Brockner, J., Konovsky, M., Cooper-Schneider, R., Folger, R., Martin, C., & Bies, R. (1994). Interactive effects of procedural justice and outcome negativity on victims and survivors of job loss. *Academy of Management Journal, 37*.

Cameron, K. S. (1994, Summer). Investigating organizational downsizing—fundamental issues. *Human Resources Management*.

"CEOs at major corporations got 23 percent raise in '95," p. c1 (March 5, 1996). *Washington Post.*

Downs, A. (1995). *Corporate executions.* New York: AMACOM.

Kearns, D., & Nadler, D. (1992). *Prophets in the dark: How Xerox reinvented itself and beat back the Japanese.* New York: HarperCollins.

Tichy, N., & Sherman, S. (1994). *Control the destiny or someone else will.* New York: HarperCollins.

Tomasko, R. M. (1990). *Downsizing: Reshaping the corporation for the future.* New York: AMACOM.

3

THE PROCESS

9

DATA ORGANIZATION PRACTICES

Fundamentals of All Data Organization Practices

Over the next several pages are discussions of some of the fundamental practices that have to take place in any software engineering development process. As there are many different methods that are focused on many levels, there will be no specific focus until there has been a more detailed discussion of each of the methods. Suffice it to say that these following points need to be in all methods to some degree or another whether they are embodied in a technique or are a significant separate step. Each will be covered in some level of detail so as to provide an understanding of what the subject is and how it benefits the development process.

Subsequent to the discussion of the fundamental practices, the rest of this chapter will be dedicated to a discussion of the different techniques that are currently used and their advantages and disadvantages.

Corporate Data Architecture

With all this terminology in mind, let us try to understand the human components of the infrastructure required to make architectures work. This is best initiated by covering the roles and responsibilities of those involved in the infrastructure and then relating it to the objects previously discussed.

The first of these is a corporate data architecture group. It is specifically charged with the responsibility of creating and maintaining a corporate data model and a corporate activity model. That is, they have the responsibility to define all the BEC's and BAS's within the enterprise down to the subject area level. The reporting structure for this group should be independent of any function and they should be considered as a corporate resource as opposed to a strictly defined information technology resource. This corporate data architecture should be independent from, but facilitative of, whatever methods are in use in the corporate venue.

Corporate Data Policy

The following are some basic corporate data principles or policies that must be in place and adhered to in order for the effort to work. These have been discussed before and have been defined in different contexts in other chapters of the book, but it is appropriate to recap them here to ensure the understanding that all data must be viewed by the corporation in a manner that will promote its care and maintenance. This takes commitment from both the maintainers and management. The following tenets indicate the primacy of the concern:

- Data must be assembled and maintained in an integrated manner in order to support the evolving business needs and to insure customer service of the highest quality.
- Data, and the structures and constructs used to develop and house it, are renewable and reusable assets for the corporation and as such need to be secured in the most prudent manner possible.
- Data must be of the highest quality and integrity possible to ensure that business decisions made using it are responsive to the needs in a dynamic and competitive business environment.
- Data must be stored or placed in the structures and locations most appropriate to its optimal utilization and safekeeping by using the best options available in the technology forum.
- Data ownership policies and custodial responsibilities must be defined in order to ensure the accountability of the needed quality and integrity within the organization.
- Data must be captured, validated, scrubbed, and utilized according to industry-wide standards and methods using accepted tools and techniques that ensure consistency.

Architecture Team

This is a team of designers that is usually subordinate in responsibility to the corporate architects and deals with designs at the application implementation level. The placement of this organization is usually in close proximity to the database administrators whose responsibilities include implementing the architecture team's designs.

Design Team

This is another critical fundamental in the software development process that is part of the project structure. How the development team is built often foretells whether there will be optimum success in creating a project. All development methods and processes that are discussed here suggest that there should be a core team of empowered people to guide the project to successful completion. A core group remains that controls and develops the integrals of the application. The process should specify who the members of the core team are, as well as other members on call for the project. They should be empowered to develop by delegated authority of upper management. There should not be an up-the-ladder authorization process for everything in the application.

Develop the Project Structure

A project structure provides the framework within which the development effort will be accomplished. While simple and high level, it provides guidelines and flow that cover the topography of the local development landscape. It also highlights early on in the process a simple fact: projects that are ill-defined and fuzzy in requirements inevitably will miss deadlines and have budget overruns. It doesn't matter what the project structure or control mechanism is as long as there is one. It will take different forms for the different methods and these will be touched on to a small degree in that discussion.

Scope Definition

The process of defining a scope is also fundamental. It is a twofold concern, however. The first part of concern is the overall, higher-level scope of what is being architected. This scope must be defined and managed at a high level. The last thing desired is to deliver a rat trap, especially when the user asked for a mousetrap.

The second part of the concern is that of individual development component creep. If proper closure is not put on each level of the requirements analysis, no matter what the method, the scope of the development of that component may change (be expanded or decreased), in which case it will no longer integrate with the whole. Depending on which method of development is used, this has to be managed in different ways; the following is a discussion of those methods.

On the high level, scope can be contained by implementing strong project boundaries. This overall scope creep is avoided by defining goals, structure, use, and clarity of a project. This project must stress the importance of being able to deliver a piece of the project at every stage to ensure correctness of vision and a feeling that something is getting done!

Project Plan

There is an old saying about the difference between an amateur and a professional: a professional will plan everything out prior to the start of the job, while an amateur will spend more time and money redoing work because he is focused on doing one thing at a time with no view of the whole.

The project plan is one of the main components of the contract with the user that provides a timetable for that delivery. It is also sequenced in a way as to use resources in an efficient manner. As a tool, it is a mechanism that can be adjusted for unplanned activity. One caveat, though: it must remain dynamic. Unplanned events will take place, and as such they must be entered into the project plan if they have affected the schedule. The plan can also be used as a status tool for meetings with all concerned parties.

Data Architecture and Strategic Requirements Planning

In all methods of development there is also a need for a strategic requirements planning area that will focus on those steps necessary to create a high-level identification of the subject areas, the business entity types, the major functions, and the major processes identified. There is also a need for a corporate data policy. Although this will be covered in detail in a different section of this chapter, it needs to be stated here that there is no other method for getting and keeping management commitment than to have a corporate data policy that has been embraced by the senior management. Within data architecture and strategic requirements planning are the following areas.

Data Gathering and Classification

This effort establishes the basic boundary identification for the data-gathering effort. It defines the context of the effort in the sense that it defines the reason the corporation needs the data at this particular place and time. It also is the stage where the generic or topical areas of data use for the corporation are defined.

Business Area Data Modeling

This effort provides more understanding and linkage between some of the data utilized by the business area for the function being performed for the organization. The broad topical areas defined in the data gathering and classification steps are here further defined and annotated. Data relevant to the areas are formalized into entities and relationships between them. This modeling is done by the business area such that it will allow the different areas to be viewed for analysis of the processes and data that they use. These will be captured later in an automated tool when the model is created. But at this stage it is merely the assemblage of the data and establishment of the initial connections kept as documentation by a business area.

Current Data Inventory Analysis

This part of the information analysis is responsible for defining and capturing that data that are currently used to support the current business function. This is different from the data defined in the data gathering and classification and business area data modeling in that current data inventory analysis has to do with what data are used currently rather than what data will be needed to support the business area in the future. This step ensures that the data needed to run the current business are a subset of that data defined in the first two stages. Ways to do this include the capturing of data attributes from manual files, databases, source documents, and output reports. It should be captured in the same format as the data from the first two steps in order to facilitate the following step, which is the integration step.

Data and Function Integration

This is the final area of common functional practice and it integrates the entity and relationship lists that have been developed out of the business area data modeling efforts. Here, these data lists are combined, identifying those entities and relationships that are redundant or shared. This is a difficult step in that each business area may have a different name or description of the data, although it may be the same.

It is critical to define in this stage those that are true duplicates and those that are different. Those that are different must be renamed to ensure that all confusion will be removed for the future development of the models.

Event Identification

Event identification is also a fundamental step that must take place to define the activities that affect the data within the business problem area. As is well known, an event is an occurrence that sets in motion an activity that changes the state of an entity within the model.

In this effort, the events or processes in the functions are defined in terms of what adds, deletes, updates, or reads take place for each entity within the event occurrence. Each of these must be defined and documented for compilation in the next step. Events represent the triggering of processes and procedures and analysis of them often helps in the development of functional decompositions.

Procedure Definition via Functional Decomposition

Functional decomposition is another fundamental activity that must take place. It is the breakdown of activity requirements in terms of a hierarchical ordering. In order to cover this more fully, some terms and stages must be defined. A *function* is defined as a continuously occurring activity that exists to meet the needs of the corporation. Within each function are many *processes*. These processes have a start activity, a process activity, and a termination activity, which completes the process. Each process may or may not be broken down into subprocesses. Each subprocess, like its parent, also has an initiation, an activity state, and a termination, and it differs from the process in that it represents activity at the lowest level. That is, it is the activity or event that takes place at the entity level.

There are multiple ways to formally interpret the functional decomposition diagram. Since it is organized in a hierarchical structure with indentations for each lower level of activity, it is probably easiest to proceed from top to bottom and left to right.

Each function must be documented as to what requirement it fulfills for the corporation and in what business subject area the work is being done. Functions are composed of processes. Each process must also be documented to ensure that the start activity or initiation trigger is defined and under what conditions it happens. It must also be documented to also ensure that the actual activity is documented and what it comprises, and finally the completion or termination step of the process must be defined including the state of the data at the completion of the process.

Within each process are subprocesses, which provide the actual detail operational work on each business entity. The documentation for this must include the event or subprocess trigger, the activity description, and the termination state of the business entities involved. This decomposition is a necessary activity that will define what the data is being used for. The form that these decompositions take is specific to the method used, although they share the same common layouts just defined.

Process Use Identification

Process use identification is another fundamental action that is characterized by the compilation or integration of the identified events noted in the previous step. In this case, the events are integrated in order to eliminate redundancy and the resulting processes are optimized to ensure the business area's requirements are fully met. In order to facilitate the completion of process use identification, previous work must be done to examine the data and processes involved.

This work includes subactivities such as process dependency analysis and entity state transition analysis. Simply described, process dependency analysis is the identification of the sequence that multiple processes must be ordered in. A simple example of this would be that a frozen steak needs to be defrosted before it is put in the oven. A graphic example is demonstrated following.

It obviously is more complex than this, but you have the idea. Entity state transition analysis is a graphic manner in which all activities that can affect an entity can be viewed at the same time. While this is a detail level, it does contribute to the overall body of information that will be used to integrate the process uses. An example of this is also provided following.

When the process use identification is completed, then all integrated processes have been defined and sequenced in order to ensure that all activity is optimized for maximum logical efficiency.

New Function Creation

When the process for completely breaking down the functions, including processes and subprocesses, has been completed, they need to be reconstructed. They are rebuilt using an integration process that eliminates redundant processing and also defines shared processes. It is in this way that the current business process can be ensured of being supported and the new functionality requirements have been met. While this step may be embedded in the techniques of the various methods, and in some methods is not visible to the initial practitioner, the steps are there.

In the execution of the spiral conceptual method, for example, each stage within the spiral provides more detail and more integration with the iteration before it. Details of this will be covered in the methods section of this chapter.

Utilization Analysis via Process Use Mapping

In order to complete this appropriately the data must be complete and an accurate assemblage of the processes that are applied to the data must have been identified as noted in process identification. Note that this is still taking place at the logical level and that there are a few physical considerations at this time.

The subset of data that is used in the processes must be defined. They actually represent the different user views. Specifically, this needs to be done to the attribute level in order to ensure that the complete data complement is present. First, the entity referral chain is defined. This is the entity chain in sequence of call order. Second, the attribute set within each entity must be defined. These are identifier attributes as well as data attributes. When this is complete, these are then used as input into the next stage: access path mapping.

Access Path Mapping

This step is that of integration of the many process use maps that will show how the data are being accessed. The integration of these integrated process use maps produces a traversal path or access path that can be mapped against the model to show where access will be heaviest. The information this gives to the physical designer is invaluable. First, it will show where identifier maintenance will be required most. Second, it will show where activity volume will be heaviest, indicating a need for more frequent reorganization and distribution of the data. Last, it will show where tuning options must be put in place to ensure rapid access. These will be covered more in Chapter 15.

Entity Cluster Development and Logical Residence Planning

Cluster development and logical residence planning is the planning of the allocation and subsequent distribution analysis of where the data are and where they are needed in order to be processed. The following are some of the reasons for distribution:

- Network costs. It may be cheaper to keep multiple copies than to send a large amount of data over long distances.
- Availability. Access to local data may significantly increase the availability of the data.
- Security. The data that exist in multiple places can be used for recovery purposes.
- Data structure. The same data may be kept in two different structures or even platforms for maximum availability.
  The following problems are inherent in data distribution:
- Inconsistent reads by accessors when updates are occurring asynchronously.
- Excessive update cost for the multiple data sets.
- Recovery. When one data set goes down, how do you retain synchronicity with the others?

Based on these items, the cluster development of entities and the logical placement of the data can be done without too much effort. The only difficulty is, of course, deciding into which category it falls and then defining the residence plan of the data.

Application Development Templates

One of the easiest and most productive methods of leveraging any development methodology is using predefined templates for everything from project plans, documentation and milestone templates, the testing templates, and finally to the user documentation and training. When templates are used, then there is very little ramp-up time for the developer. She has merely to take the template and delete the unneeded information and insert the new material. It also provides consistency and uniformity. Unfortunately it requires that someone develop the initial templates. This is often the best use of consultants in a new environment or where there has been a change in the technical development process and there is little detail experience to be had. By providing the templates up front, all initial learning curves are started at an advanced point. Use templates whenever possible.

Quality Assurance Metrics

What good is a developmental process that speeds up the delivery of the application but results in inefficient code and performance? The answer is none. If speed were simply the answer, it would have solved the problem long ago. Unfortunately, when speed is the driver of the delivery of the application, it takes far longer in the end to reach a trouble-free application.

All the design issues overlooked in the analysis and design stages end up becoming iterations of change in the evolving application. Quality assurance needs to be a living process and attitude accepted and maintained within the application development methodology. In addition, it needs to be a gated process. That is, it must be a controlled process that has measured points for evaluation, progress, and quality checking. Without the metrics in place, there is no way of determining if the quality of the output product is consistent.

Maintenance Control Process

The maintenance control process is critical to the ongoing success and is partnered with a very strong quality assurance process. It should consist of three tiers of change control. The first is the architectural level, the second is the application model level, and the lowest level is the physical detail level.

The architectural level deals with new structures at the enterprise or subject area level that provide the data and process change control mechanism for new functionality or major changes to existing functionality. It is characterized by creation of new subject areas, new entities, and new activities and processes.

The second level is the application model level and deals with changes to entities and application business processes. It is characterized by the changes to entities, their keys, and the processes that affect them. The lowest-level change control is that of the detail change. It affects the detail process via a simple change to the data structure, such as the application of performance tuning and data characteristic changes.

The Software Development Methods

Up to this point, the discussion has been about basic business design functions that must be included in whatever development method is being used. There should be a brief discussion of the methods before continuing on.

Methods that are used in the software development practices can be categorized by level. The topmost level is the architectural level of detail, the next level is the working level of detail that is familiar to most programmers and managers, and the lowest is the atomic level. All of these are important, but it is important to understand that each is useful in its own way. Each of the architectural methods will be discussed in some detail.

Architectural Development Methods

The "waterfall" method was described by Royce in 1970. It is still the most widely used and most familiar method in the software development world. A template of this process is shown in Figure 9.1. It is called a "waterfall" for obvious reasons. All the effort of one stage needs to be completed before going on to the next stage. It is a fixed sequential process that has the work products of one level feeding as input to the next lower lever, much like water going down a stepped spillway.

A development project based on the waterfall method has the following characteristics:

1. You must carefully and completely define the output work product before proceeding to the next stage.
2. You must commit to a set of requirements that have been frozen at a fixed point in time.
3. Deviation from the defined requirements or the succeeding design is an indication that you failed in the requirements-gathering process.

While this waterfall process has been helpful in promulgating the understanding of some of the techniques and concerns that we have had earlier in this chapter, it still has some shortcomings. Figure 9.1 shows the basic process steps and provides some sequencing information. The shortcomings are the following:

1. It does not adequately allow response to changes in requirements; that is, there is no way to adjust for missed requirements or newly materialized requirements. There is simply no way to go up the waterfall.
2. It assumes a uniform and orderly sequence of development stages. It assumes that the stages are predictable in length and each is required.
3. It is rigid when it comes to rapid development techniques such as prototyping, in which some developed components might be kept and others thrown away.
4. There is no real risk assessment done until late in the process.

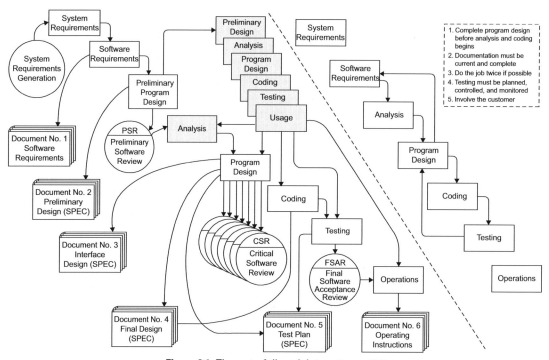

Figure 9.1 The waterfall model. From Royce, 1970.

Since the 1970s, developers and methodologists have been trying to address the inadequacies of the waterfall method. A solution that has worked with some degree of success is the "iterative waterfall" approach. The only difference between this approach and the traditional waterfall approach is that there are multiple iterations of analysis data gathering and design before going on to the next stage. Simply put, there are iterative data gathering/design presentation sessions, which are reviewed with the user before progressing on. It must be iterated until completion to ensure that all requirements have been gathered before moving on to the next stage. This altered approach has met with some success but still has some flaws. It has addressed the changing and materializing requirements but has not addressed the rigidity or the sequencing. All requirements still need to be completed before moving onward despite a staggered or layered approach, as shown in a primitive development diagram.

In 1988, B. W. Boehm developed the spiral development method shown in Figure 9.2. As one can see in its process, it addresses some of the problems associated with the waterfall method. Every stage of requirements analysis is accompanied/followed by a risk analysis phase. Also, the requirements go from simple (i.e., architectural) to more detailed as the spiral moves

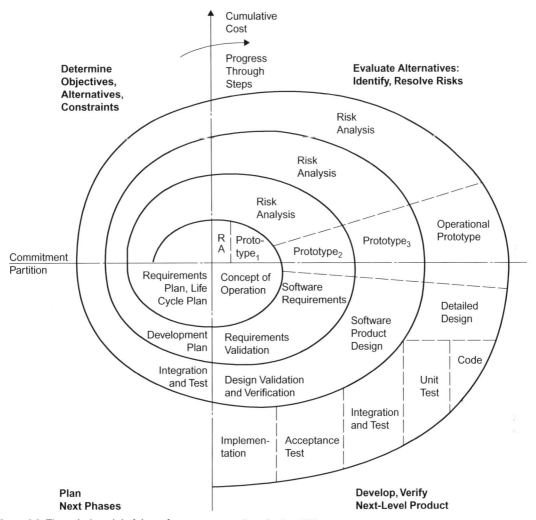

Figure 9.2 The spiral model of the software process. From Boehm, 1988.

outward. It also is a better predictor of expense, since the further analysis is done, the more expensive it gets.

But none of these methods truly represents the real work flow. As Watts Humphrey (1989) Managing the software process pp. 249–251, said, "Unfortunately, the real world of software development doesn't neatly conform to either of these models. While they represent the general work flow and provide overview understanding, they are not easily decomposed into progressively finer levels of detail that are needed to guide the work of the software professionals."

Additionally there are many more architectural models, such as the Agile method, the V method, and even the double

V method. All deal with how to best capture the requirements, interpret them, and implement them in the shortest period of time to give the users what they want.

The basic problem with architectural-level models or universal models, as they are called, is that they are, well, architectural. They are high-level flows that have been generalized to account for individual differences in detail processes. While this is a good method of communication and is necessary for the continued survival of the company, it is not what a software developer needs. To this point, it has been enough to speak about these as a common frame of reference. It does provide the understanding and communication basis for all involved. Unfortunately, the developer of the software referencing the data architectures needs something more specific.

Atomic Process Models

At the opposite end of the spectrum from architectural process models are atomic process models. These "elementary" process models are enormously detailed for an entire corporation. These have been covered in several places in the book and will be examined concerning their physical considerations in later chapters. They represent the compendium of all lowest-level tasks needed to complete the process. They exist for all of the processes in the company. One can see just how complex this compendium would become … and how useless it would be.

By the time the complete process compendium was defined to the level of detail required, it would be obsolete. These atomic or elementary process models are far more useful when the unique process is being used to develop the software code for a specific activity within an application. Precise definitions and information flows are important at this level. When these elementary processes are developed, they should be abstracted into a higher-level model to ensure integrity and ability to be shared if they were developed independently of a functional decomposition or reconciled with the other processes within the function defined within the functional decomposition of the application.

Entity Process Models

These application-specific models are more accurate than task-based process models because they deal with the real objects (the entities) that persist and evolve through defined states of sequences and transitions. Each entity must be defined to include the following:

1. All entity processes and their states
2. A definition of the triggers that cause the process to occur
3. A complete process model without limits or constraints
4. A constrained process model with those measures in place that control it

These can be and should be compiled and abstracted to the application level and from there reconciled and abstracted to the architectural level. In all cases, the information should be retained so that information navigation can take place up through levels of abstraction to the architectural level or down to the lowest level.

The Unified Method

Enter the unified method. This is a method based on the spiral method proposed by Boehm in 1988. It differs in that it has four basic states that are repeated and expanded outward by iteration:

- Inception – defining the approximate vision, business case, scope, and vague estimates
- Elaboration – refining the envisioned, iterative implementation of the core architecture, reconciliation of high risks, identification of most requirements and scope, and more realistic cost projections
- Construction – iterative implementation of the lower risk and easier elements with a focus toward deployment of the software
- Transition – testing and full deployment

These stages are iterated with short, fixed objectives that seldom last more than a few weeks. Its advantages over the waterfall are obvious. The subsequent iterations can pick up or further analyze something that was missed in the iterations before. It is ultimately flexible and does not keep a rigid design in place. Instead, the design is flexible and grows and expands as the data and process knowledge grow.

This method has been embraced fully by the object-oriented community and has proven to be an excellent method for working on these projects as they grow. Further experience will be necessary to fully understand whether this method is suitable for large-scale nonobject development, but the future looks promising.

References

Boehm, B. W. (1988). A spiral model of software development and enhancement. *IEEE Computer.*

Humphrey, W. (1989). *Managing the software process.* Reading, MA: Addison-Wesley, pp. 249–251.

Royce, W. W. (1970, August). Managing the development of large software systems. *Proceedings of IEEE WESCON.*

Additional Reading

Larman, C. (2002). *Applying UML and patterns.* Upper Saddle River, NJ: Prentice Hall.

10

MODELS AND MODEL REPOSITORIES

What Are Models and How Did They Come About?

A model is a symbolic or abstracted representation of something real or imagined. Building a model, such as a building or theme park, helps to visualize the design before the real thing is constructed. For a city architect, a computer simulation viewed from 1,000 feet above planned streets may reveal potential traffic and congestion areas.

It is in this manner that a data model helps visualize data structures to evaluate how completely and accurately they reflect the business problem. It is preferable to change a designed structure before any application system is built, since design changes generally cost significantly less than application code changes.

But just as important as this is the model's ability to present the designs revealingly. Data modeling concisely represents the endless body of dry material requirements that tend to obscure the more structural and powerful design facts of a complex business application. Skeletal structures can be more easily seen and other uses of a design understood when viewed as an integrated whole, rather than as voluminous text requirement listings.

The essence of a model lies in its efficient representation of the business problem area. This is achieved by eliminating unnecessary detail and substituting symbolic references for the actual components of the business subject. Therefore, a model need not be simply a smaller prototype of the real thing; it may use words, pictures, or any combination of media. In this way a data model drawn on a few pages can represent the structure of a database, which could occupy gigabytes of database storage.

Data Models Introduction

Many forms of symbolic notation have been developed that enable data models to represent various levels of abstraction. Some are lexical, others graphic; the better approaches are both. One of the earliest, Peter Chen's (1976) Entity Relationship model offers a set of shapes and lines that, much like musical notation, deliver a wealth of information with sparse economy of drawing. Entity relationship (ER) modeling was readily adopted outside academia, introducing the concepts of data modeling to a generation of information professionals.

Chen's ER spawned a number of variations and improvements, some of which have been embodied in computer-assisted software engineering (CASE) products employing ER methodology, in some it defines an entity as "a thing or object of significance, whether real or imagined, about which information needs to be known or held." Another source agrees that an entity is "something about which we store data." Chen's original ER technique made a firm (if not clear) distinction between entities, as just defined, and the relationships between them. To cope with inevitable complexities, Chen allowed relationships to have attributes of their own, making them look a lot like entities. This gave rise to heated debate over just what is an *entity* versus a *relationship*. Given the lack of clarity in definitions, it is not surprising that Edgar Codd said in 1990, "The major problem with the entity-relationship approach is that one person's entity is another person's relationship." Chris Date (1995) agreed, saying, "The ER approach is seriously flawed because the very same object can quite legitimately be regarded as an entity by some users and a relationship by others."

Information engineering (IE) is a streamlined refinement on the ER theme that discards the arbitrary notion of the complex "relationship" with an *n*-ary (i.e., the number of entities related) of two, three, four, or even more. IE models them as simply associated entities. Every relationship in IE is binary, involving two entities (or possibly only one if recursed). Information engineering also simplified the graphic notation in diagram style. It has become fundamental for a number of CASE products, including Powersoft's Data Architect and several others.

Another common modeling technique is IDEF, developed in the late 1970s and early 1980s. IDEF was later extended by various parties into a set of tools and standards that were adopted by the U.S. Air Force as the required methodology for government projects. IDEF is semantically weaker than ER and IE and forces its practitioners into arbitrary methods, which lack a sound foundation in theory. Nonetheless, it is a workable, easily learned methodology. It has been taken up either by choice or for government contracts by many modelers. The CASE tools Erwin, System Architect, and ER Studio offer IDEF1X data modeling products.

Entity relationship, IDEF1X, and information engineering all translate business requirements into formal symbols and statements, which can eventually be transformed into database structural code. Thus, the modeling process reduces undisciplined, nonmathematical narrative to algebraic regularity. Early practices, when data modeling techniques were not widely known, were to build on a bottom-up approach. Analysts harvested an inventory of raw data elements or statements and analyzed them. This examination was frequently conducted via data flow diagram (DFD) techniques, which were invented for the express purpose of discovering the data items so their structure could be considered. Expert analysis of this pool, including various forms of normalization, rendered aggregations of data elements into entities. Unfortunately, the number of entities in a database is typically an order of magnitude less than the number of data elements. In approaching this work and its inherent multitude of details, there is often the discouraging experience of watching the work funnel into a black hole of diagrams and documents, only sometimes allowing the escape of an illuminating ray of understanding.

Top-down, entity-based approaches (ER, IE, etc.) are more concise, more understandable, and far easier to use than those that build up from a multitude of details. Top-down techniques rapidly fan out through the power of abstraction to generate the multitude of implementation details. Current practice therefore leans toward capturing a much larger range of structural features toward modeling entities (e.g., "customer," "order") first, since most information systems professionals now understand the concept of entities or tables in a relational database. Entities are later related among one another and fleshed out with attributes; during these processes the modeler may choose to rearrange data items into different entity structures. While this delays the analysts' inevitable problem of populating the model's details, it has the correlated shortcoming of placing responsibility for critical structural decisions on the designers. This does not suggest that professional data analysts are incapable of making such decisions but rather that their time could be better spent if the CASE tool can make those decisions—swiftly, reliably, and consistently—for them.

Proponents of the object role modeling (ORM) schools represent that their methodologies accomplish precisely that, in addition to enabling and constraints better than in ER-based methods. In ORM it is the structure of relational mapping rather than the whim or experience of a designer that determines how data items ("objects") are assembled into entities. This does not remove all judgment and creativity from the designer. Rather, it allows them to rise to a symbolic level of discussion concerning business issues and implementation options.

Contrary to a frequent misconception, the academic foundations of ORM date back 20 years. This is the same era that gave birth to ER. Over the years, several CASE tools have employed this methodology, yet there still is no commercial product available. For a more comprehensive display of ORM, see Asymetrix's InfoModeler or read the works of Microsoft's Terry Halpan (2005). The modeling methodologies just discussed deal with conceptual and logical understanding of data but not necessarily the physical details of its storage. Additional techniques from the area of relational design are generally employed to represent tables, columns, indexes, constraints, and other storage structures from which to implement a data design.

What Does Modeling Do for Us?

Modeling reduces sets of complex requirements to a simplified and standardized format so people can work with them and have a common level of understanding of them. It allows the business information to be presented in an unambiguous and concise format that can serve as a mechanism of communication between the users of the system, the designers of the system, and the builders of the system. In addition, it allows a scaled version to be created without the investment of building the full-blown product. By virtue of this fact, the logistical as well as the planning problems that might arise during the design process can be detected and dealt with in a reasonable manner without the burden of a real stake. It ensures that the development infrastructure is in place for the real thing.

Finally, models allow us to map processes against the data and evaluate their behavior. If the model structure does not support the business processes, then knowledge is gained without expenditure of the time resource and impact on applications. Models allow us to evaluate the potential performance of the structure under varied conditions, giving us throughput and output capacity information that can be used to fine-tune or redesign the model if necessary.

Process Models Introduction

In the context of computing systems, the term "process modeling" has come to be associated with a number of ideas, all concerned with the dynamic activities of organizations, businesses, or systems. The basic idea is that such systems can be thought of as operating on multiple functions. The activity within each function exists as a number of interrelated processes. To study and understand systems, one constructs "process models" according to particular viewpoints and using modeling techniques. Further, models constructed from some viewpoints form the basis for computer systems used to support a particular behavior for an organization. Such computer systems are really themselves models of businesses or organizations. These ideas of forming different types of process models are described in a little more detail following.

Process Models—Why?

The members of the project team must understand what a process is essential for. Developers cannot code for a process they do not understand; they have to know the process in order to be able to effectively perform the process. Project managers need to have an understanding of the process if they are to make accurate assessments about the process status and take corrective actions. Customers of a software development organization need to understand the development process to be able to independently track progress, give advice, and consent to a process and subsequent changes. When different development teams cooperate on the same software project, they need to understand each other's processes to determine how the processes will fit together and what needs to be changed so they are able to integrate it. Developers working in different phases of a process (for example, quality assurance engineers, developers, and maintenance staff) have to communicate with each other. Process modeling can facilitate the interaction between the groups. Lastly, new employees can faster contribute their qualification if they get taught the process.

How Are Automated Models Developed?

In the days before automated design processes, all models were created manually. They followed a strict set of rules or behaviors as to placement, description, and retained information. These rules ensured that anyone using the method would be able to have repeatable results. These results consisted of a graphical diagram and detailed text information about the things desired to keep information about and the business rules that dictate the way these things interact with one another. The world is moving at a much faster pace nowadays than it was when things were done manually. Today, models are usually developed using a computer-assisted software engineering (CASE) tool that allows all of the modeling to take place in a user-friendly environment and captures and retains the results in a formal framework.

While the details of how the information gets into the tools is covered in the next chapter, it is simply entered and retained in structure within the tool. Many of the inherent rules and principles that provide the rigor for the model are embedded within the CASE tool, so it is more comfortable to use them rather than developing a model from scratch. The rules inherent in the tool adhere to the methodology that is embraced by the tool. After completion it should reflect the complete business requirements of the application under design.

How Are Models Retained?

Data models are retained via a model repository—that is, via a storage bank of data models. There are many different methods of maintaining a repository, both manual and through the use of software products that will retain the models. It would be oversimplifying it to say a model repository is just a simplified library for application models. Based on the architecture concepts discussed in Chapter 1, there is a need to find ways of defining architectures (and capturing their resulting models) at all levels, from the enterprise level down to the individual application level. Along the way there needs to be a method of integrating the redundant components of models and reusing these when appropriate by extracting the reusable construct out of the integrated whole. This will prevent us from getting out of synchrony when multiple people are using the same models as a source. Over and above all of this, there are the problem and probability of multiple versions of the same business area model being used for subsequent change releases, meaning sequenced changes. Repositories do this via versioning, integration, and a check in and out mechanism like Source Safe.

This will be discussed more in detail (how models are actually developed and what constructs they contain) in the next chapter. Some of the questions that will be answered include, What are the constructs of the data models that are brought to the repository? What are the constructs of a process model? Why keep data models in a formal repository and process models as artifacts (reports, indented lists, decomposition diagrams) and not in a repository?

Model Repository Policy and Approach

As brought up before, an enterprise's information architecture must be capable of containing multiple levels of information (i.e., conceptual/planning models, logical models, and physical design models). The capture of information can be from top-down, bottom-up, or middle-out, depending on the tools and methodologies being used.

The logical corporate repository providing an integrated model management strategy may be comprised of many different tools. Each of these tools has varying degrees of capability for supporting strategic, tactical, and operations business analysis methodologies; however, none of them effectively manages the complete information technology life cycle of conceptual business planning, logical and physical data analysis and design, logical to physical transformation, and implementation. To take advantage of the specific strengths of each, direct bridging, reconciliation, and reporting mechanisms between the tools must be in place to enable the business planning tool to feed the logical modeling tool that will feed the physical database design tool and at the same time leverage the investments already made in the corporation's stages of IT planning and systems development. The output of the physical design tool will be the translated, implementable model.

Figure 10.1 describes how the tools are used in the IT business systems development life cycle. Each tool maintains its own repository, and the shaded areas represent the shared objects within each of the repositories that are managed.

The architectural or business planning tool's specific strength must be its ability to provide and maintain enterprise models at the conceptual or information systems plan (ISP) level. It must provide the business analyst with the necessary tools and information to do high-level process/data analysis, process strength analysis, application area analysis, and various other options that facilitate the definition of IT systems and technology structures planned for development. These models are critical to maintain

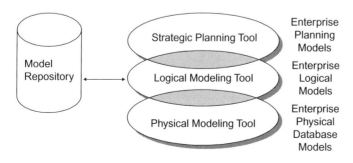

Figure 10.1 Shared repository objects.

because they represent the organization's software investment at the 50,000-foot level. With these models and this tool, business analysts can assess the impact of change at different levels of abstraction without necessarily impacting lower levels of analysis.

The logical modeling tool must support the data administration function of IT to perform application-level logical and physical data analysis and set up the corporate model repository. The logical modeling tool's specific strength must be in its management and maintenance of logical and physical data models. It must maintain a comprehensive data dictionary that allows the data administrator multiple views of the corporation's data, and data analysis at this level is the cornerstone of corporate data management. The models handled and retained by this tool represent the captured business requirements of a particular business function at a point in time. When changes are necessary, as they will be over the life of the application, this is the sourcing point for those changes.

The physical modeling tool will be used by the DBA group for physical data design and record management. Its strength must be its database design capabilities and its ability to reverse-engineer physical models. It must track evolving versions of DDL and interfaces with DDL repositories. The models handled and retained by this tool represent the physical structure and schema of the data stores that will exist to service the applications. The logical and physical modeling tool may be one in the same or two separate tools based on the delineation of the infrastructure responsibilities.

Shared Repository Objects

The use of multiple business process reengineering tools is a strategy supported by the Gartner Group's "Strategic Analysis Report," dated February 22, 1996. This report has been updated since then but still is applicable. This report states that "using direct bridges between multiple modeling tools that have been purchased over time will in effect build a best-of-breed solution for large-scale enterprise modeling and may be the best decision given the amount of investment an enterprise has in a given set of technologies."

The data administrator (DA) is responsible for the mechanism to synchronize the common objects in the architectural planning tool, the logical modeling tool, and the physical modeling tool. The DA participates in the enterprise planning (subject, business entity type, and entity) analysis in strategic planning tool in all areas where data objects are being created or changed.

The logical modeling tool is used to develop the enterprise business logical models. Models are developed without regard to the existing systems inventory, database management system (DBMS), technology platform, or communications facility. Application logical model (ALM) development is based on specifications from the project where the data administrator and the application team analyze and decompose data elements and work activities down to the elementary level of unit of work, and then capture and store the results in the logical modeling tool. ALMs are transformed into application database models (ADBM), and the DBA performs database design and converts them to physical databases.

In the case where physical models are reverse-engineered from physical models to logical models from legacy systems, a model repository management group identifies the processes and entities involved and then prepares a report for business requirements analysis.

The model repository management group maintains the integrity of the repository and any interfaces between the logical and strategic planning tools. To maintain continuing integrity between the strategic modeling tool and the logical modeling tool, the repository manager will ensure that any objects common to both repositories—whether discovered during architectural modeling tool business modeling or logical modeling data modeling—are first added to the architectural model and then transferred to the physical model. This will ensure that the appropriate enterprise business analysis is done prior to systems design. In addition, the repository administrator performs procedures on a weekly or other scheduled basis to report all changes of objects in the logical modeling tool and to report all inconsistencies of objects occurring in both the architectural modeling tool and the logical modeling tool. The conceptual/logical inconsistencies must be reviewed to ensure consistency and integrity.

Model-Driven Releases

The model management policy supports a "**R**elease-**r**elease"-based system development methodology. Release (capital **R**) means a group of business process changes representing many applications that are linked or integrated together via processing feeds. Release (small **r**) means that a set of business process changes within that can be delivered with a minimum of time and effort without compromising the options for the delivery of the rest of the business process changes.

Supporting an Application Release

The architectural model is the product of the process and information analysis that has occurred with the business sponsors and subject area owners. The organization of the architectural model is high-level service functions and processes, with the associated subject area clustering of business entity types. The information content of the architectural model is transferred to the enterprise logical model as a one-time starting point. From then on, business changes are transferred from the architectural model to a logical modeling tool staging model before being exported to the enterprise business logical model.

The staging model is a temporary logical modeling tool model where the new business requirements from the architectural model are analyzed to determine what the impacts might be to the enterprise logical model before applying them.

Model repository management, with the application teams, specifically selects or carves out entities from subject areas and subsubject areas (BETs) for all applications involved in a release. The subject area selection includes all the objects necessary to support entity relationship modeling for the application models in that release (Figure 10.2).

Application efforts that are overlapping are grouped into releases. This is an artificial construct that provides development synchronization points for the application teams involved. If there are no overlaps, then the application becomes its own release. If there are multiple efforts, the application teams work to meet a common database delivery date for the release. Multiple application models are permitted. However, detailed coordination across application models is required to control concurrent updates to the same processes or entities.

The application logical model is transformed after quality control review. The transformation process translates the ARM into physical structures and creates the application database model (ADBM), after which it is transferred to the physical modeling tool.

The DBMS-specific considerations provide the application database model with the objects required for the initial release of the database. The objects include the components of the design and the database objects (database, table spaces, data records, link records

Figure 10.2 Subsetting the application model out from the repository.

Enterprise Business Model
Organized by Subject Area

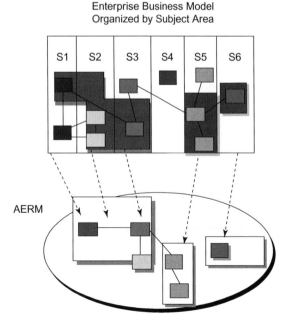

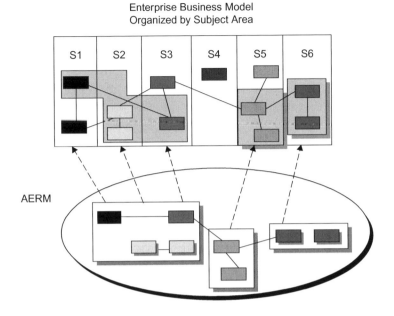

Figure 10.3 Reconciling the application model back into the repository.

and entry points). After all modeling is complete, each application model is reviewed before it is integrated back into the enterprise logical model (Figure 10.3).

The application logical model is transformed after quality control review. The transformation process translates the ALM into physical structures and creates the application database model (ADBM). The DBMS-specific considerations provide the application database model with the objects required for the initial release of the database. The objects include the components of the design and the database objects (database, table spaces, data records, link records, and entry points). The initial release number is set at 1.0 as specified in the model naming standards.

The work to create and complete an application database model is done in a modeling tool by the DBAs. Application database models for multiple application model releases will be gathered together and grouped according to a release synchronization mechanism that allows the applications to be implemented in an appropriate sequence. When the release is assembled, then the DDL can be generated and the physical database construction commenced.

Version Type: Participation

Participation in the model management process is denoted in Table 10.1, which refers to generic administration areas

Table 10.1   The Model Management Process

Model	Participant	Activity
Architectural Model	Corp. Architecture Data Administration	Bus. Req. Analysis Data Req. Analysis
Application ER Model (Logical Modeling Tool)	Data Administration	Data Modeling Process Modeling
Transformation within Logical Modeling Tool	Data Administration	ERD Denormalization Using Primitive Process Transformation
Denormalize Logical Model	Database Administration	Attribute Level Denormalization Based on Access Info. via Logical Modeling Tool
Transform Logical Model	Database Administration	Forward-Engineer Model via Logical Modeling Tool
Application Model	DBA/Model Repository Management	Perform Physical Modeling
Generate DDL from ADBM	DBA/Model Repository Management	Standard Relational DDL Generated
Implement Database	Database Administration	Construction of Data Structure by DBA
Reverse-Engineer from DDL to Physical Model	DBA/Model Repository Management	Reverse-Engineer via Physical Modeling Tool
Reverse-Engineer Physical Model to Logical Model	Data Administration	Capture R.E.'d Model in Logical Modeling Tool
Conduct Physical Modeling from Reverse-Engineered Physical Model	Database Administration	Perform Physical Modeling in Logical Modeling Tool
Generate DDL	Database Administration	Using Logical Modeling Tool
Implement Database	Database Administration	Construction of Data Structure by DBA

within the organization that are involved in the support of the infrastructure.

Seamless Development Control Process

A model management policy is not platform-specific. A platform is made up of physical components (operating system, DBMS subsystems, CICS regions, networks, servers). The presented model management provides a standard model structure that will support multiple platforms. Models are not tied to specific test environments or platforms. However, each production target platform and associated test environments have unique characteristics, which result from the particular technology of the production target platform. The output of each model process is a database. As such these are environment-specific as determined by the DBMS.

Test Environments, Releases, and Databases

A test environment is usually limited to a platform. It is made up of physical components that allow systems to be created, modified, and tested as distinctly separate from another occurrence of the same system.

For each system, one release per environment (development test, user test, production fix) is supported. Multiple system releases within the user test environment, system test environment, and production fix environment should not be allowed due to data overlay and program promotion problems.

The development database will support the development test environments. The development database is generated from the appropriate version of a physical database model. The model, database, table spaces, data records, link records, and entry points are migrated as appropriate.

The migration path through the test environments for database structures is development database to user test database, and user test database to production database. The data definition language (DDL) is generated once and then migrated through the test environments to production.

Release Stacking

Release stacking is a release management mechanism by which multiple releases for an application can be controlled; thereby allowing each release to be developed with overlapping time frames, but minimizes risk by tightly controlling the passage of releases through the test environments. The risk of running multiple, fully overlapping, releases is in direct proportion to the ability to control shared changes, fully integrate and fully test the overlapping releases prior to production implementation.

The migration of multiple releases through the test environments simply requires that one release must clear a test environment before the next release can be installed within that environment.

For example, system release 1.0 moves from the development test environment to the user test environment on 5/1. System release 2.0 can be installed in the development environment on 5/2. Release stacking allows an application development team to effectively run three releases: one in the development test environment, one in the user test environment, and one in the production fix environment. The source code representing each release is segregated via release-based libraries.

While it is possible to establish a release-stacking schedule that moves a release into a test environment immediately following the movement out of that environment by the prior release, this will limit the ability to freely move changes or corrections between test environments for a single release, specifically from development test to user test. When a single release occupies both the development and user test environments, the movement of corrections from development to user is straightforward. These corrections generally result from the discovery of errors during user testing.

It is recommended that the release prior to a release with database and dependent software changes is given sufficient time to fully stabilize in the user test environment by having access to both the development and user environments. It is strongly recommended that releases with database and dependent software changes are not stacked immediately upon the prior release.

Libraries associated with the models are release based—that is, the release code number of the model is appended to the library name. This builds a direct correspondence between the contents of a library and the model, which was the source for the contents of the library.

Emergency Corrections

An emergency fix is a production event, which results from the identification of a critical problem affecting production-implemented code and requiring immediate correction. The result of an emergency fix event is a production temporary fix (PTF), which must be applied to the production-implemented code. There are only two types of production changes: release-based changes and production temporary fixes. The incorporation of a PTF in the subsequent system release makes the PTF a permanent piece of the system software. Database changes are not initiated in the production fix environment.

Emergency Correction Procedures

The system release implemented in production is supported by a model within the server repository. During an emergency fix event, this model, reflecting the system release in production, will be the primary model for activities, which lead to the generation of the PTF. When analysis of the problem is completed, the following steps can be initiated.

PTF Implementation for Shared Batch and Online Objects

For systems that share objects between batch and online procedures, the implementation of a PTF that affects these objects must be coordinated to ensure that the correct load modules are available to both batch and online. If the PTF affects objects that are not shared between batches and online, the PTF may be implemented based on the needs of the batch or online portion of the system, whichever is affected. However, if the objects affected by the PTF are shared between batches and online, all factors must be considered in the implementation of the PTF.

References

Chen, P. (1976, March). The entity-relationship model—toward a unified view of data. *ACM Transactions on Database Systems, 1.*

Codd, E. F. (1990), The relational model for database management, Version 2, Addison-Wesley, ISBN 0-201-14192-2.

Codd, E. F. (1969, August 19). Derivability, redundancy, and consistency of relations stored in large data banks. *IBM Research Report.* San Jose, California

Date, C. (2005, September). An introduction to Database Systems. Addison Wesley. In T. Halpin (Ed.) *ORM 2 Graphical Notation.* ORM2-01.

Other Suggested Reading

Bobak, A. R. (1997). *Data Modeling and Design for Today's Architectures.* London: Artech Books.

Reingruber, M., & Gregory, W. W. (1994). *The Data Modeling Handbook: A best-practice approach to building quality data models.* John Wiley & Sons. New York, New York.

11

MODEL CONSTRUCTS AND MODEL TYPES

Data Model Constructs

The purpose of data modeling is to develop an accurate model, or graphical representation, of the client's information requirements and business processes. The data model acts as a framework for the development of the new or enhanced application. Over time, applications gather layers of change, just like an onion. These layers represent the adding of new functions and features, as well as the correction or adjustment of old features.

With all this accreted change we can see the original core of the application only with difficulty. Systems and applications often fall victim to this cobbling, accretive process. The essence of an application is then lost in the shuffle of paper and the compilation of day-to-day activity. Data modeling in an analysis session encourages both the developer and the client to remove the excess layers, to explore and revisit the original core of the application again. The new analysis determines what needs to feed into and what needs to feed from the core purpose.

Application Audience and Services

The analysis sessions suggested usually involve both the designers (project team) and the client. After the client and project team representatives agree on a scope and objectives statement, it is important to identify the true user of the application. Who uses the application? Who is affected by the application? Answers to these and similar questions help the participants stay in focus when searching for the desired application results.

After assembling the scope and objectives and an application user list, a list of major functions provided by the application is then developed. This list includes the functions of the existing application and any desired future functions in the new application. From this list, the information requirements of each function are modeled. Eventually all of the functions will be modeled. At this point it is important to be clear.

The functions to be modeled have been modeled, not the processes within them. Descending to the process level will bias the model. Process modeling will be covered separately. This analysis effort, as noted in previous chapters, should be done in an iterative manner, with each stage giving cleaner and more definitive requirements.

Entities

The next step in modeling a function is to identify the entities involved in that process. An *entity* is a thing or object of significance to the business, whether real or imagined, about which the business must collect and maintain data, or about which information needs to be known or held. An entity may be a tangible or real object like a person or a building; it may be an activity like an appointment or an operation; it may be conceptual as in a cost center or an organizational unit.

Whatever is chosen as an entity must be described in real terms. It must be uniquely identifiable. That is, each instance or occurrence in time of an entity must be separate and distinctly identifiable from all other instances of that type of entity. For example, if designing a computerized application for the care of animals in a zoo, one of its processes might be tracking animal feedings. Within that process, there are two entities: the Animal entity and the Feeding entity. An Animal has significance as a living thing. Each Animal is uniquely identified by its biological name or some other unique reference to it. Feeding has significance as a substance to feed things that eat. Each Feeding is uniquely identified by type of food, as well as date and time of its delivery.

Attributes

After you identify an entity, then you describe it in real terms or through its *descriptors or qualifiers*. An attribute is any detail that serves to identify, describe, classify, quantify, or otherwise qualify the state of an entity occurrence. Attributes are specific pieces of information that must be known or held.

An attribute is either required or optional. When it is required, there must be a value for it. When it is optional, there may be a value for it. For example, some attributes for Animal are description; date of acquisition; carnivore, herbivore, or omnivore; and animal weight. The description is required for every Animal. Again, some of the Feeding entity attributes are date and time of application, amount of food, and type of food. The date and time are required for every Feeding. The attributes reflect the need for the information they provide. In the analysis meeting, the participants should list as many attributes as possible. Later, they can weed out those that are not applicable to the application or those the client is not prepared to spend the resources on to collect and maintain. The participants agree on which attributes belong with an entity, as well as which attributes are required or optional. The smallest distinct sets of attributes that uniquely define an occurrence of an entity are called *primary keys*. These will be covered later in this chapter.

Relationships

After two or more entities are identified and defined with attributes, the participants in the sessions determine if a *relationship* exists between the entities. A relationship is any association, linkage, or connection between the entities of interest to the business; it is a two-directional, significant association between two entities or between an entity and itself. Each relationship has a name, optionality (*optional* or *mandatory*), and cardinality (how many). A relationship must be described in real terms.

Rarely will there be a relationship between every entity and every other entity in an application. If there are only two or three entities, then perhaps there will be relationships among them all. In a larger application, there will never be relationships between one entity and all of the others.

Assigning a name, optionality, and cardinality to a relationship helps confirm the validity of that relationship. If you cannot give a relationship all of these things, then maybe there really is no relationship at all. For example, there is a relationship between Animal and Feeding. Each Animal must be given one or more Feedings. Each Feeding must be for one and only one specific Animal.

Primary Identifiers

I would like to make a note here on the process of identifying a unique occurrence of a single entity. There needs to be a way of doing this because the primary basis of data processing has been based on processing unique rows, one at a time. With the advent of relational theory, it is possible to address a group of rows as a set of data. But the premise here is to discuss how to retrieve the one row back on a process call from a data store. In order to do this, there has to be an attribute or set of attributes within the entity that, when taken together, will allow a single row to be retrieved. This attribute or set of attributes is known as a primary key. This will have further ramifications when model transformation and physical models are discussed.

Entity Types

I would like to make another further note on entities. First, there are three forms that it may take in a model. These include kernel, dependent, and associative. The associative entity will be covered in a few paragraphs under the many-to-many relationship resolution, since it is the resolution or intersection object of the many-to-many relationship between two entities. A dependent entity is one that meets all the criteria of an entity but has an additional one of it being dependent on the presence of another, superior entity. By this I mean that a dependent entity is a child in a parent – child relationship. The primary key of a dependent entity is the key of the parent, along with any discriminatory attributes of the child that make it unique. By taking the key of the parent, it ensures inheritance of all the parent's characteristics and allows navigation up and down the hierarchy. A kernel entity is a central entity within all of the models. That means they exist in some form or shape from conceptual to physical. These are generally first defined in a high-level model and made more explicit as the models are made more explicit. Kernel entities represent the core of the business and are not dependent in any way. They are primary actors in the business functions and processes represented in all of the models.

Entity Relationship Diagrams

To visually record the entities and the relationships between them, an *entity relationship diagram*, or ERD, is drawn. As noted before, an ERD is a pictorial representation of the entities and the relationships between them. It allows the participants in the modeling meeting to easily see the information structure of the application. Later, the project team uses the ERD to design the database and tables. Knowing how to read an ERD is very important. If there are any mistakes or relationships missing, the application will fail in that respect.

Each entity is drawn in a box, and each relationship is drawn as a line between entities. The relationship between Instructor

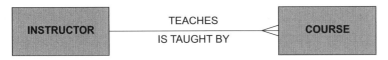

"TEACHES" and "IS TAUGHT BY" DEFINE HOW AN
INSTRUCTOR AND COURSE ARE RELATED

Figure 11.1 Relationship: example.

and Course is drawn on the ERD as follows. Since a relationship is between two entities, an ERD shows how one entity relates to the other, and vice versa. Reading an ERD relationship means you have to read it from one entity to the other, and then from the other to the first. Each style and mark on the relationship line has some significance to the relationship and its reading. Half the relationship line belongs to the entity on that side of the line. The other half belongs to the other entity on the other side of the line.

When you read a relationship, start with one entity and note the line style starting at that entity. Ignore the latter half of the line's style, since it's there for you to come back the other way. A solid line at an entity represents a mandatory relationship. In the preceding example, each Course *must* be taught by a single Instructor. However, one Instructor can teach many Courses. A dotted line at an entity represents an optional relationship.

The way in which the relationship line connects to an entity is significant. If it connects with a single line, it represents one and only one occurrence of that entity. If the relationship line connects with a crow's foot, it represents one or more of the occurrences of the entity. As long as both statements are true, then you know you have modeled the relationship properly. Figure 11.1 shows the parts of the ERD that the statement uses (notated by the broken line).

After some experience, you learn to ask the appropriate questions to determine if two entities are related to each other and the cardinality of that relationship. After agreeing on the entities and their relationships, the process of identifying more entities, describing them, and determining their relationships continues until all of the functions of the application have been examined.

Types of Relationships

There are many types of relationships, of which a few must be detailed for basic understanding (Figure 11.2). The first is a 1:1 relationship. This indicates that for every one occurrence of an entity, there exists one and only one occurrence of another entity. The second is a 1:M relationship. This relationship indicates that

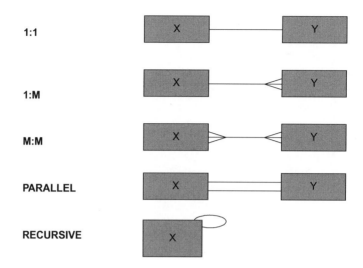

Figure 11.2 Types of relationships.

for each one occurrence of one entity, there are multiple occurrences of another entity. The third is an M:M relationship. This indicates that for all of the occurrences of entity X, there are multiple occurrences of Y. It also means that for each and every occurrence of Y, there are multiple occurrences of X. The fourth type of relationship is a parallel relationship. This is uncommon, but it does occur. It indicates that there are different subsets of X that relate to a subset of Y. These are called subset relationships and should be considered as one relationship for practical purposes. The last type of relationship is a recursive relationship. This is a relationship that relates to another occurrence of itself. An example of this would be a company table where one company owned another company as a subsidiary. How these relationships will be handled will be covered in later chapters.

This process of analysis continues until all the entities in the business problem area have been made explicit and related to one another. Each entity and relationship has been detailed to the exhaustion of the working knowledge of those present in the meeting. When this data analysis has been completed, it is time to look at how the processes relate.

Model Types

Conceptual Business Model

Explained simply, a conceptual data model (CDM) shows (in graphic and text form) how the business world sees information it uses. It often suppresses or blurs details in order to emphasize on the big picture. Conceptual data modeling is one of the most powerful and effective analytical techniques for understanding and organizing the information required to support any organization. This form of model focuses on the big picture, and the really important strategic objectives that will ensure prosperity for the organization. Data are shared across both functional and organizational boundaries in the business. As a result, this is critical for removing redundant data and process in the conduct of the organization's processes by increasing shared data use and encouraging process reuse.

There are a number of basic steps involved in conceptual business modeling. It is, of course, an exercise in the gathering of requirements from a user environment. The difference between conceptual models and lower-level models is detail. To put it simply, conceptual models are highly abstracted, architectural-type views of the business area. At their level they capture the major entities and how they might be related together. The conceptual data model is not specific in nature but is generic. The relationships within it are not made explicit as to type or cardinality. They are just present. Domain constraint data (that set of limits placed upon reference domain data or validation data) are not included. This model is only intended to capture the highest level of business use so there is an understanding of what the process is. It is accompanied by a high-level activity hierarchy or functional decomposition diagram that depicts the major functionality that is accomplished in the business problem area.

The functional decomposition diagram is a hierarchical structure that identifies, defines, and logically groups the business functions that are performed by the current system. It isolates the processes; it shows no data inputs, outputs, data stores, or sources of information. The principal objective of the FDD is to show the primitive functions of the system for which logic is to be specified. It will be further examined and analyzed in much greater detail in the next phase of this project: logical model development.

Logical Model

The logical data model or information systems model is a more structured interpretation of the conceptual business model. It exists as a communications mechanism within the more technical environments that are populated by database analysts and designers, as well as systems analysts and designers. It is more explicit in nature than the conceptual model and focuses on the detail level of entities and their relationships.

However, the same concerns exist in logical models as they did in conceptual. The model should be impartial to the way the data is used and arranged in the manner in which is naturally associated and that semantics (to a lesser degree in logical modeling) is important.

- The first step is to place the conceptual model into entity normal form. This means that the model is optimized with respect to consistency of treatment of entities: entities defined in simple and standard manner, elimination of redundancy in entity content (no overlapping entities), and stability of entities as defined by the concerned business problem area.

- The next step in the process is to resolve any many-to-many relationships by defining an association entity. This entity should be attributed with all data items that are associated uniquely with the entity interface. An additional step must be taken here for all association entities. It is to review, with an eye toward normalization, all newly attributed data items. Particular care must be given to the removal of repeating groups.

- The next step is to determine those data items that uniquely identify an occurrence of the entity. There can be many of these identifiers, called candidate identifiers. All should be documented as to content and structure.

- Immediately after the candidate identifiers have been defined, a selection of the primary identifiers must be made from the candidate list. These are the specific identifiers that uniquely identify a single occurrence of the entity. The other candidates should not be discarded as they are viable identifiers that may be used for other purposes. These primary identifiers can be referred to as primary keys.

- The next sequential step is to attribute the entities that have been defined and keyed. The process of attribution is to find the single, most appropriate home for a data item on one of the entities present. If no home is found, it is a possibility that a new entity has been found. If this occurs, the item must be researched and resolved before continuing. Attribution is heavily dependent on the semantic definition of a data item as well as its characteristics. These have to be correct, or misattribution can occur (it would be discovered later, but why waste the time?).

- Primary keys should then be propagated downward to all dependent entities (characteristic and association entities) as foreign keys. Large (many columns) keys should be noted for evaluation in the physical translation. Concatenation of keys will be necessary in association entities. All unique attributes from the parent entities (super-types) are propagated to the category entities (sub-types) of the generalization hierarchies. This should also be done for any aggregations involved in the model. This is critical to perform as further analysis in the business problem area may indicate that only the parent entity should be kept or that only the category entities should be kept. This is a decision made in physical interpretation, but it cannot be properly done if the information is not present at that time.

- Finally, the domains of all attributes should be defined, and any constraint rules governing these domains should be defined. Domain information can be defined as the execution of special business rules within the business problem area. Examples of this are edit rules, valid values for content of the domain, valid ranges for content of the domain, and derivable data algorithms for content of the domain. However, these are not specific to the logical model but are critical in verifying that all domain constraint information has been defined and that it has not been mistakenly attributed to entities as data.

Along with the logical data model should be a process model of the same level of specification. It should contain information about the processes that affects the entities in the logical data model. It can be in the form of hierarchically defined decomposition diagrams or a graphically depicted process in a detailed data flow.

Physical Model

The physical model is an even more detailed and structured interpretation of the logical business model. It exists as a definition mechanism within the technical environments that elaborates what changes have been made to the logical model in order to adapt it to the environment that it is targeted to exist in. Along with the physical data model should be access path diagrams that show in detail what transit paths will actually be taken through the model as each process is executed. By tracking and accumulating these paths, key structures within the model and the subsequent database will be highlighted that will have an effect on performance.

Chapters 14 and 15 cover the options available in this translation in greater detail. Suffice it to say that up to the point of development of the physical model, the target environment is not critical or needs to be identified. When the target environment is identified, then the changes necessary to facilitate its maximal efficiency in that environment can be made and the physical model created.

Dimensional Model

Dimensional models are the physical implementation of a denormalized entity relationship structure. They are most often used in data marts and data warehouses and are treated as such under the specialty databases section of this book.

Physical-Level Design

For a given conceptual schema, there are a large number of physical design alternatives in a given DBMS. The following must be analyzed:

- The DBMS queries and applications
- The expected frequencies of invocation of queries and transactions
- The time constraints of queries and transactions
- The expected frequencies of update operations

More on these will be discussed in later chapters on physical design.

Primary Keys

The primary key is the physical manifestation of the primary identifier in a physical table. The rules and definition are analogous with the entity being a table and the attribute(s) being peerable with columns. The formal definition is also transferable. These and their specific details will be covered in Chapter 16.

In order to fully understand all the ramifications of primary keys on the design, it is necessary to digress into two classifications of relationship types: identifying and nonidentifying. In identifying relationships, the primary key attributes of the parent or source entity become components of the primary key of the child or target entity. This means that the child is characteristic or existence dependent on the parent.

In nonidentifying relationships the primary key attributes of the parent entity become nonkey attributes of the child. This means that the child entity is not dependent on the parent and is not existence dependent on it.

During this phase one of the most important things to do is to create the relations/tables: each entity that was rendered in the logical model representation becomes a relation or table in the physical design. This includes the entire attribute load as well as the identifiers. Particular attention needs to be paid to the attribute data characteristics when the translation takes place because they may vary by the implementation DBMS.

The second step or phase is to implement the primary keys. As discussed previously, these represent the identifiers that were selected that would allow the data to be addressed as a set or a single tuple or row. In actuality, an index must be created for each primary key. In most relational DBMSs, these indexes are the primary means or retrieval, projection and navigation. Enforcement for the primary keys will be listed in the set of restrictions and constraints that must be encoded by programmers and or inherent in the DBMS.

Implement the foreign keys: for each foreign key, an index will be created; the key will be listed in the set of restrictions that must be enforced by programmers and/or the DBMS.

Implement the nulls: for all practical purposes in commercial applications, there are no fields for which nulls are allowed.

Implement the special restrictions: these must be included in the list of restrictions to be enforced by programmers.

Normalization

Normalization is the arrangement of data items according to their association with one another within a given framework of reference. It is a process that has been used over many years to arrange data in an unbiased framework so that it could be referenced for design decisions. Normalization allows the data to remain independent of its use. This independence from use extends through to independence from change. To clarify this, it must be said that the predominance of evolutionary change within the business environment has to do with the processes involved and not the data. In the relatively few instances of evolving data needs, change is more easily effected with normalized data than with unnormalized. Another advantage to normalized information is that it maximizes share ability in that the data is not specifically oriented to any application. And finally, it allows nontechnical users to understand the graphic representation of the data.

Normalization occurs in stages. Once the normalization activity has taken place within a stage, the data is said to be in a "normal form." There are several normal forms. The first three are of concern in most commercial data models. A brief description of these might be helpful in explaining the effects of denormalization:

First normal form. All of the repeating groups of data columns have been removed from the table and made into other tables.

Second normal form. All attributes not dependent on the complete primary key are removed and attributed to more appropriate tables.

Third normal form. All attributes that depend on columns other than those contained in the primary key have been removed and attributed to a more appropriate table.

Fourth normal form. All attributes that depend on not only the primary key but also on the value of the primary key are moved to third normal form entities.

Fifth normal form. An entity is in fifth normal form if its dependencies on occurrences of the same entity have been moved into a structure entity. Simply put, every attribute has a key.

Denormalization

It is into this world of normalization with its order and useful arrangement of data that the issue of denormalization is raised. Denormalization is the evaluated introduction of instability into the stabilized (normalized) data structure.

If one went to such great lengths to arrange the data in normal form, why would one change it? In order to improve performance is almost always the answer. In the relational database environment, denormalization can mean fewer objects, fewer joins, and faster access paths. These are all very valid reasons for considering it. It is an evaluative decision however and should be based on the knowledge that the normalized model shows no bias to either update or retrieval but gives advantage to neither.

Overall, denormalization should be justified and documented so future additions to the database or increased data sharing can address the denormalization issues. If necessary, the database might have to be renormalized and then denormalized with new information.

Overnormalization

Overnormalization produces numerous tables with greater interdependency, which results in frequent joins affecting query response. Overnormalization is a process that can be described as a condition that may occur when normally grouped items such as Address or Phone Number are broken into normalized components which leave the intelligence behind (the commonly recognized level of the data).

It is also inherent in "overloaded" attributes, in which parts of the attribute really represent a separate data item. An example of this would be zip code, where the first three characters of the zip code represent the state code of the state of residence. The zip code therefore contains two data items in its group. Overnormalization of this might lose the original intelligence of the zip code and require a join operation to reunite it. Some investigations into multifact data items which fall victim to overnormalization was done by Dan Tasker (1989).

Domains

A domain is a valid set of values for an attribute that ensure that values from an insert or update make sense. Each attribute in the model should be assigned domain information, which includes the following:

- Data type—Basic data types are integer, decimal, or character. Most databases support variants of these plus special data types for date and time.
- Length—This is the number of digits or characters in the value—for example, a value of 5 digits or 40 characters.
- Date format—The format for date values such as dd/mm/yyyy or yyyy/mm/dd.
- Range—The range specifies the lower and upper boundaries of the values the attribute may legally have.
- Constraints—Special restrictions on allowable values. For example, the Beginning_Pay_Date for a new employee must always be the first workday of the month of hire.
- Null support—Indicates whether the attribute can have null values.
- Default value (if any)—The value an attribute instance will have if a value is not entered.

Domain Constraints

Domain constraint information is that information that is associated with the domains of the attributes or data items. These constraints consist of physical translation of the business rules that apply to the content of the data item. They represent an attribute value relationship, not an entity occurrence relationship, and therefore should not have any keyed activity. There should be no key propagation. The reason for this is that domain constraint tables by definition are independent reference tables used by many different other entities for validation. If each propagated a key to the domain constraint table, the foreign key structure would be enormous. Although many DBMSs and case tools use this as a way of instilling referential integrity, it overly complicates the process unnecessarily.

The occurrence of limited set values to domain data represent what is called the permitted value set for the domain. It represents metadata for that domain. Here are some examples of domain constraints:

- *Valid value sets.* These are valid translation values for a particular data item. These include code tables, translation tables, and existence check tables. For example, CT might be a valid value for state code 21 in a valid state code table.
- *Valid range table.* These are valid ranges for a particular data item. These can be numeric/alphanumeric range edit tables or reasonability range tables. An example of this would be state code must be a value between 01 and 52.
- *Algorithmic derived data.* This is data that is derivable by computational activity, such as adding, subtracting, multiplying or dividing a data item. An example of this would be review date = hire date + 180.
- *Translation.* These are in effect valid value set tables that are not used for validation but as a print translation table that allows processing to be completed on the codified data and translated only when it has to be presented to the outside world, such as on a transaction screen or on a print.

Reference Data

These are a new class of table that may or may not be utilized in the modeling infrastructure group. These tables represent data that are unchanged by the application that they are being used by. They may represent complex data that are beyond the simple lookup tables described. It is clear, however, that although these data may not be created or updated during the application business process, they must be updated or created externally by some other process that has definable currency and integrity.

Generic Domain Constraint Constructs

It is possible to create an aggregation construct (dissimilar objects being treated the same for a specific purpose) to house many varied types of limited-set, domain constraint data within one entity. It falls into the designer added entity category and is constructed with a "type" attribute to distinguish what type of domain constraint it is, as well as a code for the different values.

Reference

Tasker, D. (1989). *Fourth generation data*. Sydney, Australia: Prentice Hall.

Suggested Reading

Muller, R. J. (March 8, 1999). *Database Design for Smarties: Using UML for data modeling*. San Francisco: Morgan Kaufmann.

12

TIME AS A DIMENSION OF THE DATABASE

What Is to Be Done with Historical Data?

The scope of this problem is growing just as historical data stores on large database servers are swelling with data. It is not a trivial issue; modeling historical data, doing the logical design of database components, and creating the physical implementations are tough tasks. However, the problem is often overlooked because in the initial phases of system design, there isn't any historical data, and so the *real* problems haven't arisen.

But with today's capability (and need) to access, retrieve, and process this data—both in production and in ad hoc query systems—historical data issues are gaining attention. The access mechanism for both processing and retrieval is primarily SQL, but what about the peculiarities of historical SQL queries? What are the performance issues for large databases? More difficult still is archiving this data. The data must be archived according to the underlying object's structure at the time of archival, which may or may not represent the object's structure today. This approach presents difficult design and access issues if the archived data must be retrieved at a later date.

These issues will be covered in this chapter. In the first part of the chapter the focus will be on data modeling. In the second part the focus will be on the physical implementation and access strategies required from the standpoint of large systems. Although the material in this chapter applies to any large relational database, DB2 or Oracle will be used for specific examples.

Application History

A primary problem facing the information technology world today is the implementation of history within the business application. Business applications must often follow a trail of recorded activity from the beginning of a process to the end. The specific data needed for such processes is the connected sequence of occurrences, which is associated with finite functions and specific points in time. Connecting this sequence of events, the entity occurrence's activation (or "birth") can be recorded, document the occurrence's state changes and aging activities can be recorded, and finally, mark the occurrence's inactivation or termination can be recorded.

Thus, from a data professional's perspective, history is a significant design issue that must be considered from conceptual architecture, though logical and physical models, to physical implementation, and finally, to access definition and tuning. The issue must be raised in each phase:

- In the architecture phase: What's the best way to deal with the application's historical needs? What information must be retained in order to facilitate the business process?
- In the logical modeling phase: How can history be specified in the manner that will capture the business requirements and present a basis for a clean translation to a physical model?
- In the physical modeling phase: How can it be ensured that history is treated in accordance with technical specifications for the DBMS target environment as well as the application architecture?
- In the implementation phase: What specifically can be done to take advantage of the options given by a selected DBMS?
- In the access and tuning phase: What impact do the characteristics of the history, as well as the application's access frequency distribution and answer set volumes, have on physical placement and indexing?

The application's restart/recovery, disaster backup and recovery, and security and audit considerations should not be overlooked. However, these concerns are outside this chapter's scope, where the focus will be on retrieval and update concerns. Archiving will be touched on, but only in the light of its relationship to history.

How do we describe time? Throughout this chapter, the expressions *time-sensitive* (time-dependent) and *non-time-sensitive* (non-time-dependent) will be used. These terms describe the entity occurrence's attributes within the business problem area. What is being defined is the continuous flow of the occurrence sequence as measured and structured by calendar dates. Time sensitivity is merely a measure of how susceptible an attribute's (or entire entity occurrences) value or content is to change. When discussing modeling issues in later chapters, it will be seen that time sensitivity is inherent in any discussion of history.

Some information on databases today is not considered time-sensitive and, therefore, does not contain a date attribute. While undated, it represents a static image of the information being retained on the database. But what if the information was to become time-sensitive? With no date attribute, it would be impossible to tell when the information was effective, or when it was recorded in the database. Luckily, this situation is not encountered often, but when it does occur, the information in the database's current view must be upgraded with a date.

Where the business function requires a record or image in time to be accessible, a date must be contained as an attribute on the occurrence. This attribute may be what distinguishes the occurrence from any other; thus, it must be defined as part of the occurrence key to ensure uniqueness.

Classes and Characteristics

Information required for the business function may be classified historically in a variety of ways. In this chapter the following will be discussed: current occurrence, simple history occurrence, bounded simple history, and complex history. *Current occurrence* is a static snapshot view of an entity occurrence's attribute content. *Simple history* is the signing or tagging of a date to the attribute contents of the entity occurrence. (Based on the date tagged to the occurrence, the attribute's contents are valid for the date defined.)

Bounded simple history is the limiting or bounding of the attribute values' effectivity by an effective (begin) date and expiration (closing date). It provides a definitive time interval when the attribute values were in effect. Many occurrences provide a continuous timeline of effectivity periods. *Complex history* is also bounded by begin and end dates, but supports more complex functions for the business and data. For example, these functions include: out-of-sequence change activity, out-of-sequence change activity with forward propagation, functions that separate processing date and effective date of data as well as future date processing.

The dates used to define the entity occurrence's historical characteristics selectively are Effective Date; Expiry Date; Posting Date; Prior Effective Date; Prior Expiry Date; and Close Date. Definitions follow:

- Effective Date records the specific date the entity occurrence attribute values became usable for the business function.
- Expiry Date records the last specific date on which the entity occurrence attribute value set is usable.

- Prior Effective Date is the Effective Date of the previous effectivity period during which the entity occurrence attribute values became usable.
- Posting Date is the date the change was applied to the record. It is also referred to as the Last Change Date.
- Prior Expiry Date is the Expiry Date of the previous effectivity period when the entity occurrence attribute values became unusable for the business function.
- Close Date records when information is closed off or logically deleted by the incidence of new or superseding information that renders the occurrence unusable except for audit trail purposes.

Current Occurrence

With current occurrence, a date is not needed because a change event causes a new occurrence to be inserted and the old one deleted; or, the information's occurrence is overlaid with the new version. The advantages to this type of information from a historical perspective are that it represents the entity occurrence's latest image. Only one occurrence exists for the attribute value set that comprises the key of the occurrence.

Here are some basic rules for this type of history:

- Not more than one set of attribute key values may exist at one time.
- If any dates are present on the record, they are not part of the key.
- If new information is added with the same attribute key values, it either updates the current record or deletes the old and adds the new occurrence.

Simple History

As defined earlier, simple history describes situations when a simple date is used to tag or mark an occurrence with a Posting Date. This date is used to tag or mark an occurrence with a Posting Date. This tag is just for the purpose of defining when the activity that initiated the entity occurrence happened, and becomes part of the attribute values that make up the key to the entity occurrence. The advantage to this type of history is that although multiple occurrences of the key set attribute values exist, a specific occurrence can be retrieved by specifying a particular Posting Date as the retrieval argument. A basic rule for this type of history is that the Posting Date must be part of the entity occurrence's attribute key values.

Bounded Simple History

This type of history is characterized by the need to look at previous occurrences of the same data group to find which characteristics were in force during a particular date window. By far, this requirement is the most common one. It can be easily and simply achieved by having an Effective Date and an Expiry Date.

Two viewpoints exist as to whether both dates have to be in the attribute key values. The first says that both Effective and Expiry dates should be present in the key for calculation purposes. The second viewpoint is that only the Effective Date in the key—and by default the next occurrence's Effective Date—should become the Expiry Date. Either way, the overall result is a continuous timeline of effective periods. This type of history provides an existence continuum of what attribute values were in effect and when. This type of history is also appropriate for future effective processing, meaning the ability to add the occurrence to the physical environment prior to the Effective Date and letting it be triggered on the Effective Date by date-driven processing.

In applications that allow change to entity occurrence attributes during effectivity periods:
- A change to an occurrence is made only if the change's Effective Date is equal to the entity occurrence's Effective Date.
- If an update occurs, the Posting Date should be changed to reflect the change's date.

In applications that do not allow entity occurrence values to change during an effectivity period:
- A new occurrence of the entity must be created and use the current date or the Posting Date as the Effective Date.
- The prior entity occurrence must be updated with the Posting Date as the Expiry Date.

Complex History

This third type of history (also called historical logging) requires that all previous occurrences of the historical data be available for retrieval in such a state that these occurrences can be reapplied as necessary. This third type of history (also called historical logging) exists to process out-of-sequence changes, such as early terminations and retroactive changes. Two types of complex history exist:

Type 1. This type allows processing of the out-of-sequence change or termination after the original occurrence has been logically deleted or marked closed as of a specific Close Date.

This method is used when the out-of-sequence change or termination has no effect on subsequent occurrences.

Type 2. Complex history (the most complex of all) occurs when an out-of-sequence change or termination affects all succeeding or preceding occurrences. In this case, a chain must be developed that lets the business process follow the sequence of occurrences by their Effective and Expiry Dates. This chain is accomplished by having the prior Effective and Expiry Dates retained on each occurrence to facilitate retrieval and updating.

Here are some basic rules for Type 1 complex history:

- Always use Effective, Expiry, and Posting Dates as part of the entity occurrence key.
- When processing the out-of-sequence change, it is critical that the previous occurrence be closed out as of the out-of-sequence transaction's effective date.

And for Type 2 complex history:

- First, this type of history activity should be discouraged; it is extremely resource-consumptive. It must, after all, read each occurrence precedent or subsequent to the out-of-sequence change and update each until the business process reaches the desired state of stasis. The second reason for discouragement is that it causes problems with transaction audit trails. It rewrites history in fact and in effect. Previously recorded audit trails become invalid. And new audit trails must be generated. It can and will cause audit exposure problems.
- If it is used, always use Effective, Expiry, and Posting Dates as part of the entity occurrence key.

Logically Modeling History

In the early days of logical modeling, history was not reflected; most people felt that multiple occurrences found in the entity's history were the result of cyclical or triggered events driven by the business process. It was deemed desirable to keep the model somewhat pure from the possible influences of process orientation. History—the perceived result of a process—was ignored or at best, treated as a physical modeling concern. History is indeed the result of a process, but the process involves just the entity of concern. In modern terms, it could be described as an entity's multiple life change states.

Now, if history is viewed as another dimension of an entity—the time dimension—how is it modeled? Building on much work by senior people in the field, a more definitive specification can be made that still leaves the logical mode relatively intact and pure. The specification is that historical detail is the associative entity that results from the resolution of the many-to-many relationship between the finite set of the entity's occurrences and the infinite set of occurrences of time. Each occurrence can be associated with one or more points in time, and each point in time can be associated with one or more occurrences. Following the rules for resolution of many-to-many provides an associative object whose primary key is the concatenation of the primary keys of the two associated entities. Put more simply, the result of the association is an entity whose primary key is the primary key of the original entity plus a date.

The process for attribution of these entities is based on a simple question of time dependency. Time dependency exists where there is the possibility of attribute content change over time. If a time dependency exists, then the attribute should reside with the historical detail specified by date. If no time dependency exists, then the attribute can remain on the primary entity that has no date. The result of the modeling effort is two entities with the same basic primary key, with the exception that the time-sensitive one has a date as part of the key.

Relationships from other parts of the model to the affected entities should primarily be made to the non-time-dependent entity, rather than to the time-dependent one. Completing this step lets the relationships exist without reference to time. Relationships to the non-time-sensitive entity also prevent a date in the key from being propagated to all the dependent entities in the model. When the date is propagated throughout the model, the unit of work is expanded tremendously. This expansion occurs because the referential integrity within a relational database is paramount. Without it, the database could contain inconsistent data. The expansion of the unit of work would exist for all activity involving inserts and updates to the time-sensitive entity.

Physical Design of History

If the time (no pun intended) has been taken to model history properly in the logical model, the option to decide how best to implement it physically can be easily made. Remember, both time-sensitive and non-time-sensitive data have been modeled: The time-sensitive data is the *association object* between the entity and time. This association object is the historical detail table that must be implemented. The non-time-sensitive entity becomes the root table.

To implement any physical database from a logical model, data use patterns and access traversal paths must be defined; these will lead us to an understanding of the integrated access load that will exist on the database. These patterns and traversal paths must be defined for access to history as well. As noted previously, the logical model contains primary, non-time-dependent and time-dependent entities. Access patterns and traversal paths will reflect the call pattern for the data in the database. If the data calls are predominantly to the non-time-dependent-entity—and then immediately to the time-dependent one—you can save an access by denormalizing the two entities back together. Of course, you should exercise caution in denormalizing, particularly if dependent entities are involved that carry the propagated key from the non-time-dependent entity. (Of consideration, too, is the referentially constrained group containing the propagated key. If "collapse" denormalization has taken place, the key including the date would be propagated down the chain. The net effect would be a cascade update to all the dependent entities.)

If most of the calls are to the entity's current occurrence, denormalization (here, creating redundancy) of the time-dependent characteristics from the time-dependent entity to the non-time-dependent entity would provide the latest occurrence's logical image. Upon implementation of this construct, a table containing the data's most recent image manifests. The $n-1$ and previous versions would be retained on an associative history detail table.

Physical Implementation of History

Translating the physical model into implementation involves the selection of options and variables; the goal is an optimal information structure that will address the business user's need. For simplicity, relational references will be used as the basis of the examples (simpler because of the commonality of the models in all stages of the relational design process).

One option that could be entertained during physical modeling of the access process has to do with the addition or insertion of an occurrence; this is to partition or segment the table by date. Partitioning may resolve some potential access problems, such as retrieving a group of occurrences from the same history period. However, it may also introduce hot spots (areas of high activity that invoke channel and physical read-access contention) in the database if the additions are all on the same or near the same dates. Thus, evaluate partitioning *very* carefully. The negative side of the impact can be difficult to adjust for during performance tuning.

Partitioning may be performed vertically as well but only in the case where you have extremely long rows in the time-dependent physical model table. For vertical partitioning, the whole key must be replicated for the second table—including the time-dependent keys.

Physical placement of the time-dependent and non-time-dependent tables may be done on different DASD devices, thereby reducing contention. Indexes facilitate access by allowing the query predicate to be as specific as possible with keyed and nonkeyed discriminators. When building indexing for the physical model tables, you should at a minimum address an index on the primary identifier to include the time-dependent keys. These keys will become the discriminators, which let us retrieve (that is, access) the smallest set of history occurrences, and for updates, these keys let us retrieve only a specific historical occurrence. Additional indexes—on part of the key or on non-key attributes—should also be implemented based on access traversal paths defined for the business activity.

Performance Tuning

As noted earlier, each entity in a business environment has a life cycle of its own. The entity cycle (creation, multiple-state changes, and termination) represents the business process information accumulation over time. This history, and the cumulative effect on the volume of occurrences on the physical table, is variable based on the entity's characteristics.

Thus the impact on the physical database of decisions regarding physical model denormalization, as well as those regarding the implementation option, must be reviewed frequently. Simply put, the physical database characteristics will change over time based on the acquisition and storage of history. Redesign and reimplementation of some physical model tables are par for the course once you have experienced performance decreases due to history accumulation.

Finding Patterns

Another way you can address performance problems due to history accumulation is archiving. As noted at the beginning of this chapter, history should be a design consideration from the earliest stages of the application's development. As an adjunct putting history into the design process, archiving should be a factor in the conceptual and logical phases, not just a tuning tool for the physical database.

Archiving concerns retiring data from a database as specified by criteria determined by the data user. Specifically, the user must detail the format and at what level both history and archived history must be retained. This goal is most often achieved by developing a time and frequency graph of the information's access activity on the database. Generally, data retrieval frequency diminishes along the activity timeline. Usually for a simple processing relationship, within three to six months, access activity tapers off. A good example is the mail-order business.

In certain other industries, however, such activity has a different pattern. For example, an airline reservation application would start slowly and build rapidly, right up until flight time. Activity would then drop off to a minimum after the flight left.

The frequency of updates and deletes has a different time pattern than data retrieval activity, and therefore must be mapped separately. For example, the window of change activity might stretch over a long period of time for an airline reservation system, whereas there would most likely be a smaller window in a mail-order business. The separate activity graphs (data retrieval, update, and deletion), when integrated, should display a curve that will define an archival point best suited to the data concerned (that is, to the industry's data). Such knowledge will tell us when to remove occurrences from the primary data store and place them elsewhere.

By tracking and evaluating all these patterns, you will come up with an archive plan, which may be developed side by side with other history implementations. As for the physical implementation choices for archive data, these choices range from storing it in tables on slower speed devices, to storing the data as sequential records on tape. These will not be covered in detail here, because they are often less a database structure concern and more an issue of the environment's technical structure. In the second part of the chapter, changes in this strategy will be discussed; however, as new techniques are under development by the DBMS vendors, what can be said is that an archiving strategy should be defined shortly after making decisions about the application's history strategy. To minimize the data that must be retained online—an effort that will pay off in lower overhead costs and better performance—archive efforts should parallel the history efforts as much as possible.

Tips and Techniques for Implementing History

How to store and access historical data is a complex issue. Performance and maintenance of historical data are trivial in newly installed applications: Every system runs beautifully with minimal amounts of data. But data volumes will rise and expand until the stress exposes the inherent weaknesses of the original design template. The response to these stresses and the performance changes that are made to adjust to them not only will change the design but will also often affect the program code itself.

One way to respond to the stress of decreasing performance is to look at the amount of data being retained. When the performance goes beyond a specified negative threshold, it is time to look at either purging or archiving the oldest data. Archiving does create a new set of problems. For one, the data when needed is no longer online and a special mechanism has to be executed in order to recall it or make it available. Second, data structures change over time, albeit slowly, and therefore the archived data's structure may not match the current data structure.

In the first part of this chapter, the logical side of implementing historical data stores was reviewed. Now the physical implementation and query access can be reviewed. These techniques could be applied to any large database, but the frame of reference will be relational because most of the larger historical data stores are maintained in relational environments. Two primary areas for review exist: The type of history in systems, and the physical database structuring of historical data and SQL accessing. SQL accessing will be generic because the implementations of SQL on the different vendors' platforms each have idiosyncrasies.

Types of Systems

Historical data is a generic term and means different things to different people. In previous paragraphs, historical information was reviewed in these respective classes: current occurrence, simple history occurrence, bounded simple history, and complex history. With regard to these types of history, the underlying physical structure will be sympathetic or associative to the data. By this is meant that the physical table structure is dependent on the volume, access characteristics, and total longevity of the historical data. Data access in these stores is also dependent on the type of information being stored.

Everyone wants all of the necessary data instantly accessible all of the time. In the real world, this is simply not possible. Not all data need to be retained forever; some data are used once and thrown away, some data are updated in its historical state, and still other data evolve from access to infrequently used data. These dependencies emanate from data's underlying operational nature.

In a personnel system, the goal is to capture the data facts of an employee's life within a corporate entity accurately: from simple changes in salary, to changes in occupational position, through changes in name changes and dependency caused by marital changes, to location changes. Over time, these changes alter the historical image represented by historical data; for example, organizations change, departments come and go, salaries get restructured, and employee benefits packages and options get replaced. The query to capture the life cycle of an employee over time is complex. Imagine the history within the organization. What is the salary history throughout the last five years? Were you even employed for the company that long? Where were you employed before? Is the benefit plan in use today that was in existence when the employment began? Did you get married and have children during the time frame?

This is an example of bounded complex history that can have an unended life cycle, meaning that it cannot or should not ever be deleted, only archived after some significant event (such as changing jobs internally or being terminated).

There are major differences between personnel systems and other application systems. An example of another kind of system is one that stores financial data for a fixed period such as maintaining financial data by day, within month, within year, for seven years. While it has a fixed life cycle, the data itself can vary in its access patterns; it is not subject to change.

The most difficult historical data to store are data that are kept in certain service industries. This data is subject to out-of-sequence change (a correction or adjustment of a past event), or needs to be kept for inquiry purposes because of legal contract reasons. In most instances, it can have a fixed life cycle, but sometimes change to the data must be maintained forever to handle certain types of inquiries. An example is a utility bill from a company that supplies services to a home. Line items appear on the monthly bill for each type of service delivered. It is possible that a mistake can be made that may not get noticed for months or years. Corrections and adjustments must be made at the point of discovery retroactive to its inception. In order to do, that history must be examined.

Let us analyze this further: several charges on a phone bill were found to be erroneous due to poorly routed traffic from one country to another country after a year had elapsed. The business need for inquiry existed; therefore, each line item had to be examined by the customer and the service rep. As a result of this, prior phone bills were also called into question. In the past, in a poorly designed data environment this situation would have required long periods of correspondence through the mail to determine and correct the errors. However, with access to historical data, the items in question could be examined and proper adjustments could be made immediately.

In one example of this type of application, rather than an adjustment being posted, a correction entry is added to the data with a different set of effective dates. In another example of this type of system, the original line items are corrected with a transaction date, a new record is then inserted, and the effect rolled forward.

In all of these systems and applications discussed, the data's life cycle and access types are defined not only on the types of systems but also on the business requirements. Different corporations in the same industry do not store or maintain data in the same way and may have very different ways of approaching their customers. In corporations controlled or regulated by some external body or organization, historical data are maintained according to a set of predefined rules, and an auditing requirement is also present. This becomes even more difficult to handle when the data must be maintained for a historical period and the audit trail changes must be maintained separately for the same period.

Physical Structure

While examining the various types of physical structures for historical data, some tenets and premises should be defined. First, it must be assumed that maximum data availability is a goal. Second, a generalized approach to the problem can be taken. Third, the data can be structured in either a vertical stack or a horizontal plane. Lastly, it may also have to be partitioned, either by the means available in the DBMS or by user partitioning.

In most application systems, data must be partitioned. This partitioning requirement is generally driven by the small batch window for utility maintenance or by the need for archiving data. Archiving data is the example for discussion. It is a requirement to archive or purge a period of historical data at a certain age. The physical problem is how to eliminate this data without having to release and recreate the underlying physical structure. Since most historical data is stored in date sequence, the clustering index will be by date and identifier (identifier in the generic sense). The classic example is data stored on a 13-month cycle, where the oldest month is dropped as a new month begins.

Assuming a large amount of data exist, it is inefficient to drop the structure, remove the old data, and recreate the table based on partitioning by a new date range. The proper method is to define another table that effectively maps the ranges in the partitioned table. When it comes time to drop a period of data, the partition holding the data can be offloaded to archival storage and replaced with rows for the new period. A control table can be set up to record the change, completing the process. This method works best to control fixed cycles of historical data.

Some applications require data to be accessed within a specific historical window; others require access to individual components of that window. Depending on the application's requirements, historical data's horizontal distribution can produce much better performance. This type of structure allows all data subperiods for a particular ID to be stored in repeating columns within a full window—for example, having all of the months of the year) on each row of a financial history table.

In many financial systems, data are accessed only within a specific period, and in these cases, data can be structured across a row rather than in individual rows. Systems that roll up financial data for a period can achieve a great performance boost if the data can be stored horizontally within that specific period as just noted. A second benefit for large quantities of data is for the horizontal groups to be further partitioned by specific ranges within the identifier. By horizontal structuring, the number of I/Os can be significantly reduced and DASD requirements are generally lower, since the identifier is not repeated for the data within each period.

Whenever this structure is considered, it is always best to model it both ways to prove the worthiness of the denormalization. The alternative to this horizontal placement is the creation of an individual row for each Identifier date-period combination. Although it does waste more DASD, it allows each specific period to be operated on separately. Obviously, other methods can be used.

Date effective processing, required by most systems that record and store historical data (bounded complex history especially), is at best difficult to define properly for all access. Because data are date- and perhaps time-sensitive and can change over time (as with the personnel system), two dominant access requirements exist: the need to change the data while retaining the old and the ability to reconstruct what the data looked like at any point in time. The issues become more complex where a parent table is bounded by effective dates and changes must be made to a child table also bounded by effective dates. Since data integrity must be maintained and a change can come to a child between the dates in the parent, defined referential integrity (RI) within DBMSs cannot be used, and the RI defined via DBMS rules becomes more complex and affects performance.

A final problem is the ability to restore archive data to respond to queries or business needs. Two major problems need to be addressed: to what area do we restore the data and what format are the data in (is the table's structure archived the same as the table's current structure)? These issues are often overlooked until it is time to answer the query. This question has no simple answer, but the most common approach is to restore the data from the archive by the period required into a separate data structure that is named logically so programs can process it (if required) without change. If the archived data's structure is different from the current structure, either a translation program is required to extract from the archive to the corrected format or the data must be returned to the same structure using dynamic SQL to extract the queried data from it. Obviously, many other methods can be used. The primary point is that the data and its underlying structure must be archived with a potential mapping that must be maintained throughout the archived data's life cycle, mapping it to whatever the data structure is today.

Historical data have a tendency to grow far beyond the initial design's scope. The issues for a comprehensive initial design must address the data's structuring and archival, the related data's archival, tracking the archived data by period and storage medium, and the procedures for archive data restoration. If these issues are not completed at the outset, difficult and sometimes insurmountable problems will occur at a later time.

Dimensional History

Historical data as far as dimensional models and databases will be covered as part of the specialty database section of the book under data warehousing.

Reference

Tupper, C., & Yevich, R. (Nov. 1993). Gone but not forgotten. *Database Programming & Design, San Francisco*, 12(6), 33–40.

Other Suggested Reading

Bobak, A. R. (1997). *Data modeling and design for today's architectures*. London: Artech Books.

Fleming, C. C., & von Halle, B. (1989). *Handbook of relational database design*. Reading, MA: Addison-Wesley.

Reingruber, M., & Gregory, W. W. (1994). *The data modeling handbook: A best-practice approach to building quality data models*. John Wiley & Sons, New York, New York.

4

THE PRODUCT

13

CONCEPTS OF CLUSTERING, INDEXING, AND STRUCTURES

Cluster Analysis

Cluster analysis is a generic term applied to a large number of varied processes used in the classification of objects. For the last 30 years, cluster analysis has been used in a large number of fields. For the purposes of this discussion, we will restrict interaction with clustering primarily to data. Although it is on these principles that some of the foundation of relational theory was based, the concept of clusters is pervasive through all types of data structure theories. We will have a generic discussion on clusters and segue into how this applies to data.

What Is a Cluster?

Everitt (1980) studied the definitions of a cluster and found that the most common feature of the definitions was their vagueness and circular nature (terms such as *similarity, distance, alike,* and *placement* are used in the definition but are themselves undefined). For present purposes, let us agree that a *cluster* is a region of high density within or surrounded by regions of a lower density. This definition, by the way, allows the cluster to be semantically referred to as a natural cluster.

Cluster Properties

It is clear that clusters have unique properties compared to nonclusters. Cormack (1971) found that clusters had the properties of external isolation and internal cohesion. External isolation refers to the separation of the entities in one cluster from those in another cluster by some dimension of empty space. Internal cohesion refers to the entities within a cluster being similar to each other.

Data Architecture.

Sneath and Sokol (1973) described a number of properties of clusters. We will discuss these briefly before moving on. They are as follows:

1. Density – this is the property of a cluster to have high occurrence content in a local area as opposed to areas of low concentration.
2. Variance – this is a property of looseness or concentration of entities or points within the cluster itself.
3. Dimension – despite a cluster being amorphous in shape, it does have external dimension. It has external boundaries; therefore, it must have a "radius."
4. Shape – this is a purely subjective evaluation of the cluster—what does it look like: a sphere, an ellipsoid, and so forth?
5. Separation – the degree to which clusters overlap or remain separated in the space in which they reside.

Cluster Theory Applied

How, then, can these conceptual categories and definitions be applied to the data problems? Data are clustered as a result of the natural processes that affect it. What impact will clustering have on data, and how can we use it for our purposes? Well, there are two components to this clustering. The first has to do with the data characteristics such as date, time of date, reason for identification, and common mode of reference. The second has to do with how those characteristics can be leveraged to provide information retrieval and update capabilities.

The first part of clustering has to do with the intrinsic characteristics of the data. What are the data clusters? How is data variance defined within the data cluster? What are the data cluster's dimensions? How are the data clusters related, and how far apart are the clusters? In the beginnings of data processing, these clusters were virtual materializations of the file cabinet contents they were replacing. Just as in the file cabinets, some folders of the files were thicker than others (clusters), and some folders were empty. As data processing became more sophisticated, symbolic representation and distribution of data left the virtual materialization behind, and the direct analogy to filing cabinets did not apply any more.

Instead, file handlers were developed that interfaced with the data, and the evolution of data processing moved forward. Finally, as more and more data became usable, the file systems evolved into DBMSs. It is a tremendous boon to commercial applications that the development of data processing has advanced beyond the state where physical location on a disk was paramount in the retrieval and processing of it.

It is hard to tell which forced which. Did the need to store more information force the growth of new methods of storage, or did the advancements in storage technology allow more data to be kept? It appears that it may have been both at one time or another, or possibly a synergistic effect between the two.

Many of the solutions to the clustering of the data are embedded in the types of DBMSs that have been developed. For example, hierarchical clustering is when data are clustered by all the occurrences within a specific level of the hierarchy, with each subordinated level being chained to the level above it. Therefore, to process an individual that has subordinates within multiple levels, one simply identified the individual within each cluster as the process descended through the hierarchy.

For example, relational clustering is when the data are clustered in sets that are based on like characteristics, and these sets (clusters) are linked or related to one another by some of the inherent characteristics of each cluster. Therefore, to process an individual member of a cluster (set) that had corresponding or related members in another cluster, one simply threaded through the sets to create the data chain.

As you can see, the DBMSs have evolved to handle the physical placement of the data and some of the clustering of the data. These collections of the clustered and arranged data are called databases. These databases are created within and managed by the DBMSs that have evolved. They handle the recovery, processing, and data interface with the database, as well as handling some of the base data issues. They also have been expanded to handle other issues, such as how to allow for growth, shrinkage, and creep. Let us examine these issues briefly.

Growth is that process of accretion of members to a cluster of data. Simply put, it is the process of gathering more members of clusters than you currently have and retaining them. It involves the DBMS having a mechanism that will locate space for the new member of the cluster and the insertion of the member into that space.

Shrinkage is simply that: the shrinking of a cluster of data via divestiture of some members of the clusters that you are currently retaining. It involves the DBMS having a mechanism that will locate, delete (or mark for deletion) a cluster member, and then open up the space for reuse.

Creep is the slow but inexorable growth of a cluster within a group of clusters that when left unchecked will influence the performance of the data access. Simply put, if one cluster becomes too big, then the process spends more time working with members of that cluster than it does all the other clusters. This can be caused by not understanding the nature of the clusters to begin with or because the reasons for the cluster have changed (business changes) or were unplanned for (product mixes or promotional programs that cause an influx of members to the cluster). There are no automated mechanisms within DBMSs to handle creep. There are tools that tell the monitoring individuals that creep is happening, but it must be handled by human intervention, as the solution requires analysis and prudent decisions.

These are the phenomena that affect databases and the clusters within them. They are the direct result of the insert, update, and delete functions that are part of any given process. But if these actions are examined in detail, it becomes evident how actions interact with data clusters. This will have a profound influence on the understanding of keys covered later in this chapter.

Inserts

An insert is the addition of a member data to a cluster or clusters by accretion; that is, the entire data complement of the member is placed in the cluster with its like kind. But in order to do this, there are some basic premises that need to be explored to avoid error. The primary error that could take place is trying to add something that is already there in the first place! This predicates that the member content of the cluster be read and matched against certain data characteristics and content to ascertain that the member is not there before the insert or add is attempted. How often is this done? The easiest way is to read the actual member information out in the cluster to do an item-by-item comparison to see if anything is different. This way might become cumbersome if the number of the members in the cluster were in the thousands or even millions. Another way would be to select some abbreviated form of the data for comparison. These abbreviations of the member content will be called *keys* from this point forward in the book.

Once the comparison is made, then a search for a free position is instigated in order to place the new member. When it is found, the insert is easily accomplished, or a guard is put in place to ensure that the processor is notified of the error. The placement of the inserted member in relation to the cluster is not material now. Its position will have an effect on efficiency, since it may not be in juxtaposition to the other members of the cluster, but it is certainly in closer position to this cluster as opposed to another cluster. Wherever the location is, it will be marked in such a way as to have its abbreviated data key indicate which cluster it is a member of and where the bulk of the cluster or center of the cluster can be located.

Updates

What, then, is an update? It is simply the changing of some member information and leaving the remainder of the data unchanged. How is this accomplished? Much like the insert, the cluster needs to be read to find if it is a member of the cluster. Comparing the abbreviated set of data characteristics, when a match is found, the member information in the cluster is overlain where it stands. Everything is fine. But what if the new data do not fit in the same position as the old data? In the insert, the effort was to find a location for a brand new member. In the case where the update will no longer fit, the same option is true. So the current member's place in the cluster is marked as closed, and a new place is located for the member, just as in the insert. Also, just as in the insert, the abbreviated data information is set, depending on which cluster the member belongs to and where it can be located.

Deletes

A delete is just that: the removal (or the marking for removal) of a member of a cluster. Just as in the insert and update, the location of the member within the cluster must be defined in order to be removed. We again have to use the abbreviated member data content in the key to identify the matching member. Once that is done, then it is simply a matter of marking the location where the member once was as an empty space or marking it as a "logical delete," which means that a pointer is set within the record indicating it is not viable anymore.

Physical Structure

To this point the discussion has been about the logical concepts of what clusters are and how they are interfaced within a computing environment. The discussion was also about their content and characteristics and how a member of a cluster can be identified and even related to other members of other clusters via an abbreviated characteristic list or key. Let us examine in more detail how the physical structures manifest from these concepts. These clusters, when materialized, become tables. Going back to the original discussion on abbreviated data characteristic sets, it was shown that by examining them in situ, it saved us the effort of reading the rest of the data elements. It still required work to go to the data cluster to read them. Somewhere along the evolutionary line in database technology it was decided to separate these abbreviated data characteristics out and to keep them as a separate physical cluster to themselves.

Clusters in the real world of relational and networked databases are called tables. A group of related tables is called a database. With this in mind, let us look at keys and how we can deal with them to make the tables more accessible.

Key History and Development

A primary key is a value or set of concatenated values that, when projected against the database in a search argument, yields "n" returned records. Since data processing began there has been a need to operate on one record at a time. This is a limit of the human interface, since ergonomics usually involves bringing up an image of the one record and operating on it before returning it to disk. In order to accomplish this, certain characteristics that varied frequently within the record were selected that allowed for discrimination from other records. Sometimes one characteristic was not enough and they had to go to a second and third characteristic. Sometimes it was only through the concatenation or chaining of the multiple values that allowed discrimination, however. As evolution continued in the data processing industry, the file systems, which used the key or key chain approach, were being converted to DBMSs (database management systems), which used the keys more efficiently and provided more automated methods of backup and recovery as well as performance tuning options.

Beginning with the first databases, the use of keys began to have an effect on how the data were stored on the physical devices retaining it. Prior to this time, the data tended to be serialized, and the entire set of information was read past a magnetic device read head and compared against the discrimination criteria or sorted internally for a record location to be done. With the advent of the DBMSs and the use of disks and data drums, the criteria were actively put in the read head and the read head moved over the data. This applied the criteria as a moving search on the device.

Innovative research continued while DBMSs were developing faster and faster methods of retrieving data. The concept of the index was initiated during this development, and a reduced set of the identifying keys was kept separate and apart from the data. The index had the key values and an address where the associated data could be located. These were known as key sequence data sets (KSDSs). VSAM functioned in this way.

Hierarchical and network databases took keys to a newer level in the sense that they allowed data traversal pathways within the databases by way of keeping physical addresses of the components of the database stored. These physical addresses allowed the data chains to be walked up and down, and in the network's case across the top of the chains. This maneuverability within the data structure was a tremendous asset because the data could be kept in its natural cluster order and yet be linked to all of the other data associated with it.

With the advent of relational design, the data components with similar characteristics and common keys would be grouped into sets. The rationale was that set operations could be applied to the resulting groups or sets. Thus, relational processing became a possibility.

Let us examine this in a little more detail. Up until this time, the only way to process data was one record at a time. It had to be selected, examined, operated on, and then returned from whence it had been retrieved. It was slow and labor intensive when the record count was in the millions. It was, in fact, millions of reads. With the advent of the relational concepts and the resulting gathering of like data into tabular sets called tables, operations applicable to all members of a set could be executed at the same time. Instead of a million database reads, updates, and database writes, it could simply be done as one update statement against a complete set of a million rows. This was very powerful indeed, and the resources saved and the processing efficiencies advanced the cause of relational tremendously. But let us return to keys.

To repeat, the keys represented a unique set of data values that were representative of the whole and could be used as retrieval criteria, but in this new relational language and database there were no navigation addresses in the data record. The only addressing was to be found in keys that were designed for retrieval. Navigation around the database was accomplished by the use of propagated keys between the tabular constructs. By creating foreign keys (keys that were the primary keys of a foreign object), a navigation path was always available. In this way the data were freed up from a predetermined chaining method and could be retrieved top to bottom, sideways, and bottom to top.

The path to the data could be threaded rather than reading all the linked chains necessary to get the data.

Primary Keys

The primary key is the physical manifestation of the primary identifier in a physical table. It is that unique set of concatenated values that when presented as the argument will return one row from the physical table queried. The rules and definition are analogous with the entity being a table and the attribute(s) being peerable with columns. The formal definition is also transferable.

In order to fully understand all the ramifications of primary keys, there is a need to digress into two classifications of relationship types: identifying and nonidentifying. In identifying relationships, the primary key attributes of the parent or source entity become components of the primary key of the child or target entity. This means that the child is characteristic or existence dependent on the parent and therefore must use its parent's identity as part of its own. The relationship between them carries this identity and so is referred to as an identifying relationship.

In nonidentifying relationships, the primary key attributes of the parent entity become non-key attributes of the child. This means that the child entity is not dependent on the parent and is not existence dependent on it. The relationship between them does not carry this identity and so is referred to as a nonidentifying relationship.

Foreign Keys

A foreign key is a column or column combination of one table whose values are required to match those of the primary key of some other table to facilitate navigation and facilitate occurrence pairing. A formal definition can be stated as follows:

> If T is a table whose primary key is key1, key2, key3, ..., key n, and in another table Q there is a set of columns C1, C2, C3, ..., Can that satisfy the time-independent constraint that for every row of Q there exists a row of T with values key1 = C1, key2 = C2, key3 = C3, and key n = Can. It can therefore be stated that the combination C1 through Can is a foreign key that refers to the primary key of T.

This is all well and good when the columns naturally fall into the tables. What happens when they don't fall into the table, which is what happens most of the time? How does one navigate and facilitate the action of traversal during retrieval? The answer is propagation.

Foreign Key Propagation

Foreign key attributes must automatically migrate from entity to entity based on the flow of the connecting relationship. In a one-to-one relationship, the primary keys of each participant are migrated to the other based on their equal participation. For example, if entity X has a primary key of A, and entity Y has a primary key of B, then the foreign key in A would be B and vice versa. In a one-to-many relationship, the primary key of the one participant is migrated to the many participant to ensure backward navigation capability. For example (using the same naming characteristics), if entity X has a 1:M relationship to entity Y, then the primary key of A would be migrated to Y as a foreign key.

Problems arise in foreign key propagation when a relationship has optionality. In this case, if X (primary key A) may or may not participate in a relationship with Y (primary key B), then the foreign key in Y may or may not be populated all the time. When there are no values, then the foreign key is null.

Let us discuss a null for a moment. A null is a state of nonexistence. It represents the capability of something to be present but that is not present. Because of some of the rules initially developed to deal with the SQL implementation of relational algebra and relational calculus, a state was necessary that would indicate the capacity for presence where presence was not achievable. Simply put, they invented a placeholder when there was no surety of the ability to populate the attribute. While nulls are a distasteful, but acceptable, reality, they were never intended to be used as the possible definition of keys—in particular, the propagated key that was to represent the foreign key in the target table.

Null foreign keys create navigation and selection problems. How can one find a match for navigation when there is nothing in the column to compare? Most of the time with investigation it is easy to find a modeling solution that does not embrace the null or optional value, such as by making the relationship nonidentifying, which would allow the keys to be considered simple attributes.

Candidate Keys

These keys represent the number of all possible key combinations that could be used to access the data on the tables or data stores. These include partial key combinations or a secondary group of the attributes that, used in combination with each other, provide a retrieval path into the data. The primary key is a member of (and the most important of) the candidate keys that provide unique access or singleton select capability. Other examples of candidate keys are keys for reporting or group set retrieval for cursor access. All other candidate keys represent alternate pathways to get at the full or partial data.

Natural Keys

Natural keys represent that concatenation of actual data values that together represent a unique key identifier to access or retrieve one single row or "singleton" record. The emphasis is on the natural component. It is a naturally occurring value like the "blue" in blue car or the "tall" in tall men's shop. It is not the name of the column or attribute, but it is the content value that provides the uniqueness. As data processing evolved, the natural keys became lengthy and cumbersome. It would only seem practical, then, that as things became more efficient in data processing, it would become more efficient at identifying occurrences of records. To accomplish that end, engineered keys were created.

Engineered Keys

Engineered keys represent the abbreviated values the outside world has encoded things with in order to save time and processing money. So instead of saying, "the 1998 gold Buick Riviera with wire rims and the 300hp engine" (wishful thinking), it has been encoded as "VIN #" (Vehicle Identification No). Instead of saying, "Malvern Willie Wagglethorp III," he is encoded in the data as "Employee #23135343." A value has been assigned to a set of natural keys that can be related to something in the real world, such as a badge number. These are representative and have become ingrained in the data processing culture and even everyday culture—for example, Social Security numbers.

Surrogate Keys

Surrogate keys represent a purely arbitrary number that is often computer generated and is unknown outside the application system. They occur in two flavors. The first is an artificial key and the second is an identity column. We will cover these two in the following paragraphs.

As noted before, artificial keys are arbitrary numbers generated to represent the value of a natural key or key string. In order to maintain integrity, the value of these artificial keys must be correlated to a natural key or key string. This is because when output is produced from the actual application, there is no way to identify what the individual record had to do with because an arbitrary number was generated as a representation. The problem is with the transience of the artificial key. Whenever artificial keys are used there has to be an association table to resolve it. That is, there has to be a table that contains the natural key in conjunction with the artificial key in order to resolve it.

The second type of surrogate key is that of the identity. This, again, is a system-generated key. It is different in that the DBMS maintains the internal registry of the identity value. This identity column then becomes the key and the natural key becomes part of the attribute load of the entity. In some ways the identity column has enhanced processing, since unwieldy keys do not have to be dealt with, and the large keys do not have to be propagated to a subordinate table to maintain referential integrity. In other ways it has compromised the rigor of the normalization process in that it is allowed on any table whether it is normalized or not. In effect, the identity column allows a cluster of attributes that have nothing to do with one another to be clustered and treated like an entity when in fact it is an aggregation.

As a further evolution the concept of a unity development. This is a system-generated key that is internally kept by the DBMS. It is created by whatever means necessary within the DBMS, such as by hashing or otherwise, and maintained by the DBMS when used for propagation. In the case of a unity, no external reference to a natural key is necessary, although it is good business analysis to identify them.

High Water Keys

The first of these is the so-called high water key (highest key value yet recorded) and the closely related next sequential number key. These represent the next available key value in an ascending key sequence. Neither of these allows for the reuse of keys that may have belonged to a deleted record. But they are useful in an application where there is a high level of insert activity. The high water or maximum value to date key is retrieved, incremented, stored back in the key hold, and used in the identifier of the new insert and so on.

One of a Kind Keys

A variation on the theme of this is the one of a kind (OOK) number. This is a key value that is generated from a random number generator and compared to known key values. It is used for insert of a unique value as well. The high water mark key and one of a kind key are often used as a logical locking mechanism that prevents interruptive access during long units of work.

Let us examine this logical locking mechanism in action briefly. A table is set up with a single row resident in it. This represents the highest value attained to present. The row is read into the process and kept while the unit of work process is being performed. A lock is kept on the row and any subsequent actions that try to retrieve the row are told it is locked. When the unit of work is complete and the row is ready to be written out, the lock is released so the next transaction can get at it. This logical locking mechanism acts as a gatekeeper that channels many transactions into a single file access.

The high water mark also represents a quick method to get to the maximum or next number without searching the entire table. It functions merely by getting the current value for the process, temporarily storing it for yourself in the process and then immediately going back to the Single row table and updating the value to be self + 1. Thus, in milliseconds the next number is available.

As stated before, these are great time savers, but they make no effort to reuse key values that have been deleted in the process. They are therefore one-way encoding or upward marking mechanisms that might run to the physical limit of the sequence of the attribute before the process obsolesces. You may just run out of numbers. Reuse is a good saver of the number sequences but involves complexity that may not be desirable in the process you are building. It is best to make this decision early in the design of the database and process.

Other Specialized Keys

Get range keys and key banding are another method of dealing with keys. This is a mechanism that separates key values into bands. A band represents a value range of the keys. In this scenario, a band is allocated to a particular process, and all the numbers in that range are used up before another range is allocated. This is useful where a number of different processes may be adding records at the same time and need to be kept separate. Also, it is useful where that unit of work may generate more than one record and this allows more freedom and less interaction with a key generator. Key ranges are managed outside the system but can be referred to inside the application via program logic that references the ranges.

References

Cormack, R. M. (1971). A review of classification. *Journal of the Royal Statistical Society,* Series A, Edelbrock, UK, 321–367.

Everitt, B. (1980). *Cluster analysis.* New York: Halstead Press.

Sneath, P., & Sokol, R. (1973). *Numerical taxonomy: The principles and practices of numerical classification.* San Francisco: W. F. Freeman.

Suggested Reading

Aldenderfer, M. S., & Blashfield, R. K. (1984). *Cluster analysis.* Sage Publications Inc., Newbury Park, CA.

Boyd, L., Jr., & Iverson, G. R. (1979). *Contextual analysis: Concepts and statistical techniques.* Belmont, CA: Wadsworth Publishing.

14

BASIC REQUIREMENTS FOR PHYSICAL DESIGN

Requirements for Physical Design

At this point in the development life cycle the logical model exists and there is an application architecture design. Hopefully (and unfortunately this is not always the case), the majority of requirements will have been defined and physical database design can begin. It is this author's belief that there is a direct proportion between time spent in the previous analysis and design phases and the success of the project. It is truly a case of "pay me now or pay me later."

This chapter focuses on all the input necessary to create a good physical design that will stand the test of time in terms of flexibility, availability, and performance. In the previous chapter, the considerations in choosing a DBMS were reviewed, as well as the environment that the database and application will be running in. This is a review of the same considerations but from a different aspect, that of the application database.

How Much Data?

It is important to determine as early as possible how much data will need to be kept and how it will be maintained, archived, and/or purged. These are frequently the hardest questions to get answers to. The retention requirements as to how long to retain data on a specific table or even for the entire database in the end must be answered by the user of the application. Retention often has to do with legal considerations, as well as recovery and restart concerns. This is a more detailed review of the different areas of application in the physical design and the best ways to handle them.

History

Although this was covered in detail in Chapter 12, it is good to understand how it, along with the other factors involved, affects the physical implementation of the model. History is a process that produces multiple occurrences of the characteristics that comprise a row of information. Since it is somewhat physical in nature, it should be addressed either at the end of the logical design or at the beginning of the translation to physical design. In either case, the type of history will affect the data volume and processing load on the database. If addressed as part of the logical model, the many-to-many relationship resulting from the intersection of the time entity and the data entity is resolved into an association entity. This association entity can be implemented as a separate table by propagating the key as defined in the normal logical modeling procedure and then adding the specific date attribute to the key that will distinguish the row as unique. (It can also be collapsed back into the nonhistorical component if the attribute load is not significant.) If history has not been addressed as part of the logical model but is instead regarded as a physical data design problem, then different date attributes must be created and added to the entity being translated. Because history has a significant impact on the database and is complex by itself, there is an entire chapter dedicated to its implementation.

Population Quantification of Application Data

In the previous chapter the concern was what the footprint size of the database would be in the choosing of a DBMS. Here, the concern is with the actual processing of the data. This is where the question is developed and answered. Where is the best source for the data and how do we get into the database? In most scenarios the effort is converting the data from an older, slower system to a newer, faster one. The process is relatively simple then. It is merely to write conversion programs that change the structure of the data into the format needed for the new application structure. It is then simply a minor problem to run a utility, usually supplied by the DBMS vendor to load the data into the table. Unfortunately, sometimes the data must be separated and normalized before it can be put into the format necessary to be loaded. This adds an extra step into the conversion process but a necessary one.

In either case, the most important things to be concerned about are the quality and integrity of the data. Some things to consider when defining the best source of the data are: (1) use the most current data possible and (2) use the data with the most integrity. These rules should be used together and interdependently. It is best never to use the newest data if it is from the least reliable source. Conversely, never use the data with the most integrity if it is so old that it is of little use. Work with the user client to define what is the best of both worlds. Document the conversion process and sources. This will help in future references and conversions.

Concurrency

Concurrency is that concern when two or more things are being done simultaneously or near simultaneously. The concurrent processes may or may not be using the exact same resources. Concurrency issues fall into two subcategories. The first issue is that of the concurrency of user traffic. It is important to quantify the number of users that will be using the application at the same time and in what manner (i.e., what kind of transaction or reporting activity is taking place). Is it 300 users per day or per hour? Are they doing simple queries or complex ones? Are they doing reporting with queries that produce bulk result sets that will be subreported on?

This is tangential input that is gathered when the access path information that has been gathered is being considered. The concurrency of the number of users will have an impact on the number of physical entry ports into the database. It will also have an effect on the number of processes that the DBMS can run at the same time, which may or may not be regulated. The number of users and their transaction type and volume per time period are a critical physical consideration that the systems programmers and DBAs will need to be aware of.

The second issue of concurrency is how many internal types of accesses will be using the same set of database objects at the same time. While these two are related, the second has to do with managing the integrity of data within the objects. This is of immense concern with the management of data when online transactions are performed. In most DBMSs there is something called "locking" that manages who has access to what data at what time. This locking by a lock manager ensures that data being written are not overwritten. Two users trying to get the same object from the database will not end up having the same data and both will try to change it to something different.

There are some provisions in some DBMSs that allow for "dirty" reads that allow someone to read an object that has been detected as being updated by someone else. There is software help in these cases that will allow the status of the object to be reread and checked to see if it has been updated, which might invalidate the other work done on the record. At the very worst, a reread must take place, and at the very least, the data read and sequence of the process have been saved.

There was and still is, to a degree, a consideration for application-level control of concurrency. It is called "logical locking" and is a manner of controlling the flow of update access to the database object by way of a keyed gateway. It ensures that only one person at a time is allowed complete access to a specific piece of data on a table without depending on the DBMS. It is useful in those situations where the unit of work is a long one that would certainly be beyond the boundaries of the internals of the DBMS. In this logical locking process, a value is entered into a gate key and is stored there. The unit of work captures the value that is in the gate key field. It then goes about its work. When the unit of work is completed, it checks to see if the gate key has changed. If the key has changed, then a reread is done and reprocessing takes place to ensure that the update is done to the most recent data. If it has changed, then the unit of work is written, confident that nothing has been overlain.

Logical locking can also put inserts in sequence by reading the current value in the gate key field and incrementing it by 1 to store the next sequential value in the gate key field. This ensures that no overlays can take place and the field will have a constantly ascending value. These are application-specific mechanisms to be used when the physical DBMS cannot handle the locking considerations to keep concurrency active.

Security/Audit

Security in the database design process concerns the intended reliance on a structure (either in the DBMS or developed by the application) that ensures protection from unauthorized access. Audit, in this same process, is concerned with the ability to detect and report invalid, unauthorized, or incorrect use of the data (either implemented in the DBMS or by the application).

Security must be established at the level of granularity that supports the protection requirement. If protection from unauthorized access is at the transaction level, then the security should be at this level. If it is at the table level, then views should be used. If it is necessary at the column level, then special encryption routines should be used. Caution should be used when implementing security, since the finer the level of granularity, the more overhead associated with the process. After all, the most secure room is a room with no windows or doors. Unfortunately, one cannot get things into it or out of it. An acceptable level of risk must be established by the user in conjunction with the data processing community in order to ensure secure and efficient system and database development.

Another concern is whether you should have an open shop or a closed shop. An open security shop allows all data to be read unless otherwise defined as secure. This minimizes the number and structure of the controls in order to protect the data. A closed shop, on the other hand, has all the access defined to specific authorization groups with specific privileges to each group.

The overall areas of concern with security should be the following:

Unauthorized access from external users

Inadvertent

Deliberate

Unauthorized access from support personnel

Recovery

Maintenance

Initial load

In order to establish unauthorized access from external users, a security framework must be in place. It should consist of multiple tiers of increasingly difficult gating mechanisms:

- Level 1, physical access exists for read-only non-application data, such as morning status, bulletins, and news.
- Level 2, access to applications outside the gate, might be access to the application main menu.
- Level 3 might be access to restricted transactions on the menu.
- Level 4 could be restricted access to the business view on the tables being accessed.
- Level 5 can be the restriction of view by encryption of specific columns.

All of these levels of gating allow the granularity to be established for the application. At each level a mapping can be made for particular criteria that allow passage within. This is usually comprised of a privileges table and a personnel table matrix.

Critical to the entire structure is the need to be embraced at each level. In other words, once you have made it through a gateway, there is only one way out: the way you came in. Normally, the gateway is controlled by the use of closed menu envelopes that will allow you access within the envelope you are in. If you have access to the envelope or envelopes within the main envelope, you may progress; otherwise, you can stay where you are or leave. The concept of envelopes is critical to security. There should never be a situation that an accessor is not within an envelope of some sort. Additionally important is the need to record anyone who comes in or out of the envelope. Access logs may be critical in solving data destruction events.

In truth, most people do not deliberately try to destroy data (although this is on the rise). In reality, most data destruction by people is by inadvertent means. It is in these cases that the access logs can be useful. If it is a program that is doing the destruction, it can be pinpointed and corrected rapidly.

But what about the other side of security exposure? What of the side of security away from the public? This consists of the exposure to the maintainers of the physical infrastructure. These are the people who support the integrity mechanisms for backup and recovery and utilities for reconstruction. These people are usually controlled by the mechanisms that are embodied in the utilities that they have power over. Also, the windows of undetected opportunities to corrupt data are few and far between. In most cases this type of access is more tightly controlled than the application access.

Audit

Audit must be established to produce proper documentation to support the granularity of the security. For example, the establishment of accountability (who, when, where, how, and, to a small degree, what) is generally adequate in a simple recording system that does not disburse or maintain funds. In others, the establishment of responsibility (the who and the what are necessarily more specific here) is critical due to the sensitivity of the application or the financial profile of the company. Implementation of audit requirements should be done so as to minimize the impact on physical hardware resources.

Archive/Purge

As part of the normal design a separate task concerning archiving takes place. Archiving considers the retirement of data from the database on the retention and retrieval requirements of the user. Specifically, time and frequency studies should be done in coordination with the user to ensure that data are retained in the format and at the level where it is most needed. Generally, data retrieval frequency diminishes along the timeline of activity.

Usually, for a simple processing relationship, access activity drops off within three to six months. An example of this would be a mail-order business. Other complex processing relationships such as airline reservations start slowly and then build rapidly until flight time and then are archivable. In the airline example, the time period may be one year for advanced booked flights. Other complex processing relationships may have archivable information along a timeline, such as order/invoice processing.

It is prudent to define these data retrieval needs and points of archivability with the user and make these definitions part of the design documentation. Implementation of these definitions ensures that only necessary data are retained online. In addition, it is also prudent to establish those points of time when the data are no longer needed for any reason and can be purged from all files. These points of time may involve legal as well as business constraints.

Recovery/Restart

Generally, recovery can be defined as the need to rebuild a database due to hardware failure or other nonsoftware failure. Restart, on the other hand, is the need to reset a database to a prior point due to program error. These are loose terms and arguable definitions, but restart and recovery are separate and distinct in both scope and impact to the user.

Restart is the resetting of the database and the rerunning of update information transactions to achieve currency of data due to program failure. In the DB2 world, data are not written to the database until a commit point is initiated. As a general rule of thumb, a commit point should be issued either by a certain number of records or by time. If done by time in batch, the commit should be done at least once per half-hour of run time. As the commit is done, the committed key to the row should be saved. If a software error occurs, a rollback to the last valid commit can be done and a restart initiated on the last committed key. Online transactions automatically have a commit written when a sync point occurs, so commits are not needed within the transactions.

Recovery is the rebuilding of the database after destruction or other form of integrity compromise. It is done from image copy tapes that restore the database to a particular point of time and then either log forward or remain at the recovery point and the activity subsequent to the recovery point but prior to the destruction is redone. Recovery takes careful planning to ensure that the appropriate level of backup is present. All files participating in the recovery must be available at the time of the recovery. Of additional concern is the impact of referential integrity on the recovery process. As noted before, all referentially constrained tables must be recovered at the same time to avoid integrity errors.

Sort/Search Requirements

Candidate qualifiers (alternate keys) identified during the logical modeling process should be reviewed at this time for use as inversion lists that can be implemented as alternate indexes. Care should be taken not to create these on partial key lists of the primary identifiers (primary keys), since this would be superfluous in most cases and the DBMS would probably not utilize it. These usually tend to be index requirements that are in a different order than the primary key and exist to support an alternate access path. They increase performance for these accesses.

Reorganization and Restructuring

Data will fill the database and grow with time. When this happens, the controls over the structure of the database will be taxed to maintain good performance because the volumes and size no longer reflect the original design. The way that growth and insert activity are handled by most DBMSs is to store the new record as close to the rest of its like data as possible. After months and even years, this distance from the original data may become significant. In fact, it has become disorganized in the sense that like data are not contiguous anymore. In order to respond to this, most DBMSs have developed utility routines that will reorganize and restructure the physical data to resemble the original layout and physical data clustering that was designed. These are often called reconstruct or REORG jobs and must be done on a frequent enough basis to ensure good performance.

Data Integrity

As mentioned previously, relational database vendors are pushing more and more functionality into the database engine. As a result, enforcement of database integrity can be pushed into the definition of the database objects. But should it be? The following topics discuss how the database can be used to enforce data integrity and the wisdom in doing so.

Referential Integrity

In the process of design, it is common for association and characteristic entities to have identifiers that are concatenations of the original kernel entity. There is a natural dependency enforced by the keys of these associations and characteristic entities. It is prudent to implement a mechanism that verifies the presence in the parent entity of a unique set of identifiers that would be inserted in the dependent entity. This mechanism is, in fact, what referential integrity is. It can be placed in the database during the design process, or it can be coded into the application logic as the programs are developed. The database approach is what is normally recommended because the data are easier to change and the relationship is, in fact, data oriented. There will be performance implications whether the referential integrity is put in the application code or in the DBMS. There are considerations that must be made if the constraints are being placed in the application. A few of these are as follows:

- On INSERT activity the following steps must be done
- On DELETE activity the following steps must be done
- On UPDATE activity the following steps must be done

Application referential integrity can be placed in individual programs or in callable modules that all application programs can refer to. To reduce the overall size of the load version of the programs, it is recommended that callable modules be used. On the other hand, if constraints are not desired in the application, then the DBMS is the appropriate choice. However, there are a few things of note in the DBMS:

- A delete with the restrict option will not be allowed to operate if there are rows in referentially dependent tables.
- A delete or update must acquire locks on the parent table, as well as on all dependent tables or their indexes in order to perform the referential integrity check.
- The recovery process is very specific for all referentially constrained tables. All tables that are referentially constrained must be recovered at the same time, even if only one has changed.

Despite these concerns, there are reasons for implementing referential integrity in the database rather than implementing it in the application program:

- If referential integrity exists in the database, it does not have to be coded many times within the application programs.
- Referential integrity changes are more easily implemented within the database than when in application code.

Overall, the need is to define the level of commitment to the implementation of referential integrity and then decide whether it should be implemented in the application (education of programmers) or in the DBMS (education of the DBA).

Data Access

In order to do a proper physical database design, it is important to understand how and how frequently data will be accessed. Where does this information come from? Ideally, process models should contain references to business functions that will indicate how frequently a business process should be followed. This can be translated to pseudo-SQL (pseudo-code that does not need to parse but needs to contain access and ordering information). The criticality and concurrency of transactions are also important. This section will cover the following subparts of information vital to physical design of a high-performance database system.

- Access implications: Data gathering and analysis must be done in the manner in which the user accesses the data. Additionally, the tools used for the access must be taken into consideration. For example, reporting tools often are broad spectrum—that is, they will work with many different DBMSs, and as such they use very generic methods for access. Unless they have a pass-through option, like WebFocus does for Microsoft Access and SQLServer, the passed through query will have poor access performance. If the access method is through a GUI front end that invokes DBMS stored procedure triggers or functions, then it is far more tunable for performance.

- Concurrent access: Concurrent access is of concern for two considerations: network load and locking contention. Network load is not discussed here. Locking implications are dependent on the required access. If the data are required to be held static—that is, unchanged—an exclusive lock must be secured by the program executing the action. This exclusive lock prevents others from accessing the data while it is in use. There is an option to allow a read of the information while it is locked, knowing it will be changed. This is known as a dirty read and is done when the data needed are not those being updated. When too many programs are trying to access the same data, locking contention develops and a lock protocol is invoked, depending on the DBMS involved. In some cases the lock is escalated to the next higher object level in order to prevent a buildup of processes waiting to execute.

Privacy Requirements

Security controls for the data depend on its confidentiality. Payroll systems are notoriously tightly controlled, even to the point that test data are kept confidential from the programmers working on the system. Unfortunately, security is frequently over- or underimplemented, causing security problems or performance problems. This section will cover the following topics to help the designer understand how to implement database security and how it interacts with operating system security systems such as RACF or Top Secret.

- Operating system security: Operating system security is usually relegated to an external security product that has direct user exit relationship with the operating system. This ensures that security attacks against the operating environment are thwarted and recorded for review and analysis. They normally function by setting up a profile of a group and/or individual that specifies the privileges allowed for that particular group or individual. Because each operating system has different requirements, they won't be specified in detail here.
- Audit trails: Audit trails exist to provide a historical trace of activity from the unchanged state of the data to the changed state reflecting the differences. It is necessary to capture the identity of the changer, the time, and the date of the change, and lastly the location and agent used in order to make the change. This information will allow researchers to follow the audit trail backward should the need arise. It also provides a record of accountability for those making the changes.
- Database security: Database security is a third tier of defense against unauthorized access. Most DBMSs require user ID access for all database users. This ID is set up individually or as a group to allow a set of privileges to be performed on database objects. The privileges can be Read, Insert, Delete, Update, and Execute. There are also several group levels such as Data Reader, Data Writer, Systems Admin, and Data Base Owner. All of these can be implemented in a menued approach to ensure maximum security coverage without impacting database performance.

All of these layers of security need to be implemented in overlapping and dovetailed fashion in order to maximize defense against unauthorized intrusion or security compromise. Work between the data administration, database administration, the security, and audit functions will provide the best solution for the least cost with the least performance impact. In turn, it will address the security needs from both a legal (Sarbanes-Oxley) and a corporate security perspective.

Suggested Reading

Elmasri, R., Navathe, S. B. (1999, August). *Fundamentals of Database Systems*. Reading, MA: Addison-Wesley Publishing.

Fleming, C. C., & von Halle, B. (1989). *Handbook of relational database design*. Reading, MA: Addison-Wesley.

Martin, J. (1973). *Security, accuracy, and privacy in computer systems*. Englewood Cliffs, NJ: Prentice Hall.

Reingruber, M., & Gregory, W. W. (1994). *The data modeling handbook: A best-practice approach to building quality data models*. John Wiley & Sons, New York, NY.

15

PHYSICAL DATABASE CONSIDERATIONS

Three-Level Architecture

There are three very distinct and important rules or tenets about databases that are critical to keep in mind. These are separation/insulation of the program and data, multiple user access activity support, and usage of a repository to store the database schema. The purpose of the three-level architecture is to separate the user from the physical database. As one can see from Figure 15.1, the three levels consist of the following:

1. An internal level or schema, which describes the physical storage requirements and structure of the database. This will describe the complete details of the data storage requirements in terms of files and space needed for data stores, as well as indexing or hashing.

2. The conceptual level or schema, which describes the structure of the whole database for all users. This level hides the details of the physical database and focuses more on describing the data content and its use in understandably named database objects. It is a high-level data model that reflects all the entities and attributes that can be used at this level to fulfill this

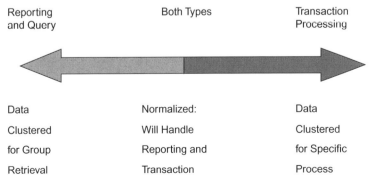

Reporting and Query	Both Types	Transaction Processing
Data	Normalized:	Data
Clustered	Will Handle	Clustered
for Group	Reporting and	for Specific
Retrieval	Transaction	Process

Figure 15.1

need. Relationships are also reflected here and are in user-understandable terms.

3. Last is the external level or schema. This level consists of the integrated user views of the client base. Each external view will describe the information needed for each business area, eliminating that view from others. These user views often take the form of visual basic screens or graphic user interface (GUI) front ends that provide the user access to the data they are authorized to see and present it in a user-friendly manner.

A lot of DBMSs don't keep them as three different layers, but some combine the top two and others the bottom two. In any case, the premise of these layers is to show and define the boundaries of the three types of requirements. What is important is that these separate three layers are abstracted up and away from one layer: the physical layer. These layers are really the descriptions of the data needed at that level.

In order to allow these layers to talk to one another, it is essential that the mappings of the data carried at each level map to the one it communicates with. Thus, there is a mapping layer between the internal layer and the conceptual layer, and another mapping between the conceptual layer and the external layer. Therefore, when a query comes in from the external user through the GUI front end (which is in fact the external layer), it must go through the external conceptual mapping to the conceptual layer. From the conceptual layer it must go through a mapping to the physical layer. Each layer represents a reformatting of the data to make it useful at that level. But with the use of models, then all three can be related through the mapping software tool and the relationships between the levels maintained. This is also called the ANSI/SPARC database model, and if the models used in traditional and object-oriented design are examined, the similarities can be seen.

Architecture Layer	Entity Relationship Model Level	Object Model Level
User View Layer	Business Model Level	Presentation Level
Conceptual View Layer	Logical Model Level	Business Level
Physical View Layer	Physical Model Level	Physical Level

Let us examine each of these architectural layers and some of their characteristics.

The User View Layer

This layer allows the user to manipulate and use the data. In the entity relationship world, it consists of data entry screens, reports, and the panels that make up the application. In the object world, this represents the presentation objects that the user must interact with each day.

This layer is highly denormalized. That is, the data may be redundantly carried on many screens, reports, and panels. Examples of user views might be the customer order screen, the item description query screen, and a customer invoice report.

The Conceptual Layer

It is in this layer that the main entities, relationships, attributes, and keys in the business domain are initially identified. It is important to remember, as said many times before, that this layer is platform and implementation independent. From this layer one could derive a network, hierarchical, relational, or object database model. At this point, all that is important is that the underlying structure of the database is being defined, no matter where the final database will reside. The underlying structure of the conceptual model will contain duplicate information, but it is most often in the form of access keys. A small amount of denormalization occurs as a result of defining primary keys and propagating foreign keys by the implementation of relationships. In the network database it allows the side and downward navigation without performance implications when this model is translated to the physical. In the relational model this is necessary for proper navigation and allows the up and down and left and right traversals to take place in the database without ever suffering performance implication.

The main difference between the user view and the conceptual view is that the user view sees the database as a series of data entry screens and reports that contain redundant data that exists purely for the convenience of the user or users. (Two separate users may have almost the same information, but they each need it their own way.)

The conceptual view contains redundant data only when required to identify a row or in order to enforce business rules embodied in a relationship between two entities—that is, in the aforementioned keys that are defined within the entities to facilitate navigation.

The Physical Layer

This last layer describes the true physical structure of the database. Specifically, it describes the physical structure of the database down to the detail level. This physical layer describes the database in terms of table or file layouts, data column names and characteristics, and indexes. If clustering indexes or physical partitioning mechanisms are supported by the DBMS, these are also defined here. Also, primitive sizing numbers can be derived from this data by multiplying the number of bytes per row times the number of rows expected in the table structure. This size should be added to by the length of the keys times the numbers of rows, which will give the size of the indexes that will be needed to maintain this table.

So it is easy to see that by starting with the external layer and capturing those requirements, the users' needs have been met. Those requirements can then be analyzed to find out what in the next level needs to be defined. This analysis provides a basis for the designers and developers to work from. And then, finally, the analysis of the actual physical structure can be used to support all three layers that the operations and DBA personnel need to accomplish their work. The project team can now relate how all of the views discussed to this point focus on the physical database. This is where the rubber meets the road, as it were.

Data Independence

Before continuing much further, the concept of data independence (touched on earlier in the discussion of information engineering and structured analysis) needs to be discussed. Data independence is simply an easier way of saying that due to the separation and isolation properties of the three layers, it is possible to make changes to one level of the architecture without it affecting other layers. The basic principle of abstraction applies. The further one is abstracted from the absolute detail, the more that can be done without affecting the physical construct of the detail. This data independence between layers can be defined in two different modes.

Logical Data Independence

This is simply the ability to change the conceptual layer without changing the external layer. For example, columns can be added to any entity that allows additional processes to be written against the database objects without having to redefine the external layer. Changes can also be made to integrity constraints in the conceptual model without affecting the external layer design. By the process of mapping, the change has prevented any impact on the user while activity goes on. Eventually when the new data are needed, a new user view will be created.

Physical Data Independence

This is simply the ability to change the internal layer without having to change the conceptual layer. This can include such things as moving table structures to different devices, separating the indexes from the tables, or logging transaction activity differently. An example of this can be illustrated as simply as being able to change the data characteristics of an individual index or reorganizing them for faster performance, or the change can be as sweeping and forceful as moving the entire database structure to a new DBMS platform. (Remember that the conceptual layer is platform and DBMS independent and can easily be picked up and moved to a different DBMS as long as it is in the same family.)

Database Languages

When a design is complete for a database and a DBMS is selected for the database, the conceptual and internal schema need to be defined so the mappings and other activity are understandable. In DBMSs where there is no strict delineation between the two layers, a single specification is used to provide the mappings. This specification, known as data definition language (DDL), is used by the DBA and designers to define both conceptual and internal schema. In DBMSs where there is a strict separation between the two, then the DDL is used for the conceptual layer schema only, and a separate specification storage definition language (SDL) is used for the internal layer schema.

Once a database is created and populated with data, users must have a manner in which to manipulate the data. A specification called data manipulation language (DML) is used for this purpose. There are two subtypes of DML: a high-level or nonprocedural DML and a low-level procedural DML. The high-level DML can be entered interactively through terminals and other mechanisms (including programs) to manipulate the data for transactional purposes. These high-level DMLs are called set-at-a-time DMLs because they deal with the set of data on the database that has particular characteristics. The low-level or procedural DMLs have to be embedded within application code. This type of DML is subject to retrieving a single row or small subgroups within sets of data. Because it cannot be operated on as a set and each record must be looked at singly, it is called record-at-a-time DML. This type of DML must be used in conjunction with such program constructs as loops in order to process the data as needed. DBMSs of all kinds implement these specifications separately. It is just important to know that these specifications exist and that they must be examined and learned separately for each DBMS.

Classification of Database Management Systems

We will now examine all the primary types of database management systems and use an example to show the differences For the simplicity of it, we will call the first entity the Employee entity, the second the Work Project entity, and the third the Employee Benefits entity. These entities appear as they are implemented in the different DBMSs. Copies of the attributes of these entities are described in Table 15.1.

The first type of system for review is the hierarchical structure of databases. This database model arrived in the early 1970s as a way of addressing the need to process information in faster modes than via file system mechanism. It has the visual appearance of an inverted tree root or dendrite pattern. At the topmost point is what is referred to as the root structure. This root record has physical pointers to other dependent and nondependent records called segments. Figure 15.2 shows the model for a hierarchical system.

Table 15.1   Entity Attributes

Employee Record	Work Project	Employee Benefits
Employee ID	Employee ID	Employee ID
Last Name	Project ID	Salary
First Name	Project Desc.	Title
Social Security Number		Bonus
Department		
Employee Deductions		
Federal		
State		
City		
Elective A		
Elective B		

The characteristics of this model are that the physical pointers must be maintained in order to navigate around through the root and segments. Parent–child relationships are allowed, and parents can have multiple child segments. Children could not, however, have multiple parents. This was the limitation because in order to navigate, sometimes it would require going all the way back up the navigation call chain of pointers to the root before going to another root and then down in a new call chain. It was stiff and caused unnecessary overhead in the less structured processes like the reporting aspect of business. Special segments were often created as workarounds that would contain pointers to other segments to avoid the upward travel in the call chains, but they didn't completely solve the problem.

COMPILATION OF PROCESS LOGIC DIAGRAMS
Event procesess Yellow, Green, Blue and Purple

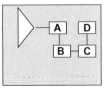
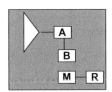
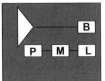
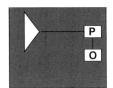

Figure 15.2

The next type of DBMS was the network database. The term *network* does not refer to the electronic network but to the visual graphic that allows interconnection between physical segments in a nonhierarchical manner. Yes, it uses most of the same structure of the hierarchical DBMS, including pointers. The major difference is that the network model allowed children to have multiple parents rather than a single parent. This facilitated navigation tremendously throughout the databases, increasing efficiency. The shortcoming to this database was that the pointers still allowed only navigation to what they were related to. Each relationship was tied to a physical pointer that had an address associated with it. When the database content changed, pointers had to be recalculated, leaving room for error and having to do a lot of work. Figure 15.3 shows the model for a network system.

The third type of DBMS was the relational. From the previous paragraphs, it is obvious that hierarchical and network database models had problems, specifically between parent–child and child–parent relationships. These limitations prevented application developers from solving real-world problems in the database and forced them to put some of the business rules in the programs. This forced maintenance cycles to occur for each time a business change came in that affected the database. Worse yet, both of these models suffered from the limitation that when a new relationship was required, physical coding and restructuring (pointer recalculation) had to be done. Enter into this arena the relational DBMS model.

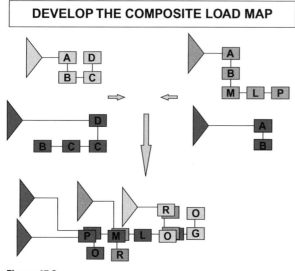

DEVELOP THE COMPOSITE LOAD MAP

Figure 15.3

Developed by Edgar "Ted" Codd in 1972, the relational DBMS model (originally called System R) had a unique strength in that it was based on the combined mathematical principles of set theory and frequency distribution. This was unlike the other DBMS models, which were based on the processing needs of the program using the data. They were not centered on the characteristics of the data, and as we have discussed previously, processes that affect the content of the data structure change much more frequently than data structure does.

In the relational DBMS model, entities are called *relations* and consist of collections of attributes. Each relation is labeled with a primary identifier, which allows the unique identification of each tuple or occurrence. Relations also contain special attributes called foreign keys that allow navigation to be completed. The beauty of the primary and foreign keys is that they do not contain physical pointer information. They contain business information that links the entities together, making navigation completely open to wherever it needs to go. Although this method is slightly slower than the previous methods, it is much more flexible and application report friendly.

The next type of DBMS is the object database model. This last type of DBMS has been touched on in several places and will be covered in the last section of this book because it has limited uses as a commercially viable volume processing DBMS.

Factors Impacting Physical Database Design

When the physical design is completed, not only is the most appropriate structure to house the data desired but also a design that guarantees the best performance. This twofold desire is attainable; it is not a pipe dream. For any given conceptual-level design, there are many different possible physical implementations. It is not possible to choose the best implementation without looking at all of the actions that will be taking place against the physical database.

Analysis of Queries, Reporting, and Transactions

The activity against the database is critical. A reporting database has a different physical structure than a transaction database. The reporting one is denormalized to get the most data in the most usable structure with each database call. The transaction database is denormalized to put all of the pieces together that are needed for the process of transaction being served. The normalization process gone through for the conceptual level leaves the data in a neutral position not favoring reporting or transactions. Here by choosing whether the database is a reporting (or query response) database, a transaction database, or both, the direction for the necessary denormalization is defined. If building a reporting database, then the clustering and collapse of long-dependency chains to retrieve more data with each call can be undertaken. If building a transaction database that needs to run very rapidly, the data should be in smaller clusters and gathered by how the process will use the data. A simple analogy is that selecting a reporting database denormalization is like selecting a workhorse for an effort. It can carry a heavier weight, but it moves a little more slowly. Transaction database denormalization is like selecting a sleek racehorse. It has very little to carry, but it moves very fast. But what of the databases that need to be used for both?

Neutral-type databases that need to do both reporting and transaction processing must stay unclustered or in normalized form. This allows SQL joins and relational algebra to be applied to the structure for maximum efficiency for both, without physically changing the database for a specific workload.

Queries, Reports, and Transactions

Part of the consideration for physical database design is the activity being passed against it. The transaction, query, or report creates a unit of work that threads its way through the database in a traversal route that can be mapped. Some of the process mapping has been covered in Chapters 9 and 10, but a small recap would not hurt here. Functional decomposition in those chapters was defined as the breakdown of activity requirements in terms of a hierarchical ordering and is the tool for analysis of activity. The function is at the top of the hierarchy and is defined as a continuously occurring activity within the corporation. Within each function are many processes. Processes have a start activity, a process activity, and a termination activity, which completes the process. Each process may or may not be broken down into subprocesses. Each subprocess or event also has an initiation, an activity state, and a termination and differs from the process in that it represents activity at the lowest level.

Interpreting the Functional Decomposition

Since the functional decomposition is organized in a hierarchical structure, it is easiest to proceed from top to bottom and left to right. Each function is documented as to what requirement it fulfills. Functions are composed of processes. Each process is documented to ensure that the start activity or initiation trigger is defined, its process is defined, and finally the completion or termination step of the process must be defined. Within each process are subprocesses, which provide the actual detail operational work on each potential table involved.

Event Identification

A separate but related task is called event identification. An event is an occurrence that sets in motion an activity that changes the state of a potential table within the database. This event is really what triggers a process. These processes are what end up adding, creating, deleting, or updating the potential tables involved. In this stage the events or processes within functions are defined in terms of what adds, deletes, updates, or reads take place for each entity within the event occurrence. Each of these must be defined and documented for compilation in the next step. What these represent is the unit of work that the transaction, query, or report that the application is requiring of the database.

Process Use Identification Reviewed

Process use identification is characterized by the compilation of the identified events noted in the previous step. In this case the events are mapped and integrated in order to eliminate replication and the resulting processes are optimized to ensure the business areas requirements are fully met. When completed they represent the canonical result or nonredundant set of events that cause access to the database.

Utilization Analysis via Process Use Mapping

This is a big word for the complete and an accurate assemblage of the event/processes that are applied to the database. In order to do this properly, the subset of data that is used in the process must be defined. First, the database traversal chain is defined for each event or process. This is the potential table navigation chain in sequence of call order. Simply put, it is a sequential list of the potential tables that will be accessed and what keys will be used in the navigation. When this is complete for each event/process, these are then used as input into the next stage: access path mapping.

Time Constraints of Queries and Transactions

To this point there is an understanding of what type of activity is going to come to the potential database. There is even knowledge of what potential tables. What is not known is, do two critical things both have to do with time? The first question is, what is the frequency of the transactions, queries, and reports? Often transactions are expressed in terms of arrival rate for processing. Without getting into the details of queuing theory and the like, it is just important to understand how many of what accesses are expected. This information with the access map will also point out future hot spots in the potential database, even before it is built.

The second critical thing is, what is the time constraint of the activity? Simply put, what is the service-level agreement for the activity? If it is a report, is it within hours or overnight? If it is a transaction or query, is it subsecond or is longer acceptable? Is the transaction or query synchronous or asynchronous? This information along with the frequency of the activity and the access use map will allow the physical designer to choose equipment, platforms, and network configurations that will support the application needs.

Analysis of Expected Frequency of Insert, Delete, Update

The expected frequencies of these particular types of activities reflect the potential load on the DBMS. It may influence the choice of DBMS or platform. Inserts also have a consideration on free space available and index reorganization. Deletes have an impact on data reorganizations to reclaim fragmented space. Updates also have a consideration, particularly if they vary the length of the row. Reads are minimal in load on the DBMS. The number of each type of each of these activities will help the designer make physical choices.

Other Physical Database Design Considerations

There are three other references that are used that aid in the choice of implementation DBMS and platform. These have to do with the DBMS itself and not necessarily with the data it is trying to push or pull. While it may seem to be a somewhat shortsighted approach to look at these DBMS-specific issues, it is a pragmatic designer that does it. The best-designed systems and databases can fail if placed on the wrong devices, running under the wrong DBMS, or having a poor match between the DBMS and the operating system of the machine that it is running on. The following are some of the factors that can affect the success or failure of the database:

1. Response time. This is the end-to-end time for the transaction from when the Send key was hit until the results occur. It is easy to see that what is being retrieved can affect the time spent by the DBMS, but what is not known is what other factors the DBMS might encounter such as the system load, operating system schedule, or network delays. What needs to be done here is to analyze the unit of work with the systems people at a high level to ensure that there is nothing intrinsic about the transaction that will affect the response time.

2. Space utilization. Again, this has little to do with what the application is trying to store in the database, but it applies more to the way the DBMS stores the data. This is critical from a work-in-progress perspective. Typically, if a lot of sort/merge activity is being done and there isn't enough free system storage, then the sorts will just run slower and slow everything down. The space taken up by the DBMS is also critical. If the software takes up too much room, then you need more storage just to process. This is what happened in the PC world with the difference between the Microsoft Windows and IBM's OS/2. Many people bought Windows for its convenience factors, only to find they needed a bigger machine in order to run real work.

3. Transaction throughput. This is the average number of transactions that can be processed by the database system within a given period of time. A benchmark can and should be run on varying DBMSs on the same type of system with the same type of workload in order to get unbiased results. These benchmarks can be purchased or arranged with unbiased testing organizations, whose sole business is to evaluate DBMSs. It is critical though that this benchmark for throughput must

be measured under peak conditions. Again this transaction throughput has very little to do with the application or the specific database structure but much more to do with the DBMS and its ability to service the transactions in the environment that it will be running in.

Population on the Database

Quantification of the amount of data on the database is critical in making decisions about the choice of platform and DBMS. Three factors will affect the population of the database after its initial installation and population: growth, purge, and archive.

Growth is affected by two things. The first is the number of inserts or "adds" being done within a calendar period. These account for the steady increase in size of a normal database that is keeping track of its data over time. The second way growth is affected is the number of bytes changed with the update of the variable-length fields. The first can have a profound impact on the database if there are many tables with long rows. While the second of these two effects of growth seems trivial, let me remind you of the 4,000-byte variable fields seen so commonly nowadays that will be used for comments on the database once the history starts rolling in. These Text and Comments fields tend to be landmines that can cause explosions when least expected. Allow for them, because they *will* happen.

Delete/purge is that set of rows or population that will be removed via some criteria at periodic intervals. While this is a desirable thing, remember that the population has to be at maximum before the purge or archive will resize the database population. This does not apply to logically deleted rows, where the row is marked but never removed. These logically deleted rows are just status marked and have no effect on the population of the database. In fact, they may sometimes inhibit active efficient processing from taking place due to the exception logic that must be put into the application programs to bypass them. Logical deletes and purging will be covered in the next chapter.

Data archive is another way in which the database population is affected. If an archive sweep based on data is run, then the diminishment counts of the database should be applied to the annual calculation of the database population. If it is a single-point archive, such as every third year, this should be documented as a cyclical data archive of the database so proper DASD can be allocated as the cycle continues.

References

Bobak, A. R. (1997). *Data modeling and design for today's architectures.* London: Artech Books.

Codd, E. F. (1970). A relational model of data for large shared data banks. *Communications of the ACM, 13*(6), 377–387.

Suggested Reading

Fleming, C. C., & von Halle, B. (1989). *Handbook of relational database design.* Reading, MA: Addison-Wesley.

Reingruber, M., & Gregory, W. W. (1994). *The data modeling handbook: A best-practice approach to building quality data models.* John Wiley & Sons, San Francisco, CA.

16

INTERPRETING MODELS

Physical Design Philosophy

The object of the design process is to provide a physical structure that is flexible enough to provide rapid response to access activity and yet be reflective of the true business use that it is being designed for. In the early design stages, the DBMS selection is independent of the model. A model is translated to the physical model after a choice of DBMS has been made. It is here that the model is adjusted to the particulars of the environment it will run in. It is also here that choices will be made concerning technology platforms, as well as data placement decisions.

Objectives

The following basic objectives of relational or object relational database design should be prioritized during the initial points of the design cycle:

- Integrity
- Flexibility
- Performance
- Accessibility

Design alternatives will often support conflicting objectives. It is when this happens that the prioritized objectives list will help the decision process. Each of these is examined in the following paragraphs.

Integrity is the characteristic that ensures that the database will have the appropriate rules and mechanisms in place to ensure that the data are not easily compromised and the inserted data contents are subject to rigorous processes. Integrity is addressable at two levels: structure and validity. *Structural* integrity means that every database table object in a database must be understandable in a business context. Components should not be implemented solely for technical or performance reasons. Operational data components do not reflect any real business object. Referential integrity of all relationships between entities must be maintained, either in the database structure or in the application code. Data redundancy must be minimized.

The column types and attributes available in a DBMS must be used to optimize the data validity and usability. If user-defined attributes or characteristics are used, the business user should be aware of their use and purpose.

It is critical that the initial database design provide *flexibility* through the use of normalization techniques. Normalized data structures provide a design that requires minimal modification to handle changes to the existing business model. Additions or changes to entities or relationships must be documented to ensure that all functional dependencies have been identified and referential integrity is ensured. Flexibility is maximally insured by the neutral bias of the model. It should not tend toward a reporting structure, nor should it tend to an operationally efficient structure. By being neutral it allows better indexing opportunities to be used to tune the database.

Performance issues are normally at odds with both integrity and flexibility. The trade-offs must be carefully considered. Typically, a flexible design requires potentially expensive join processing, whereas a performance-oriented design would denormalize data structures to reduce joins. The denormalized design would then have to maintain data redundancy and inherit potential integrity problems. Best performance for an operational database that is used for reporting is usually attained by indexing and prejoining tables. This allows flexibility and integrity to coexist with the performance mode.

The nature of relational databases is to allow the physical structure to be closely relatable to the logical business model. This allows all users to interpret the data structures more easily and thereby make the contained information a more valuable asset. The relational database allows access from a number of different routes such as CICS, TSO, and Batch activity. In addition, many reporting packages, such as Webfocus, Forest and Trees, and Crystal Reports, allow *access* to the data through ODBC connections. When the physical structure is understandable by the business, their use of these tools enhances their productivity.

In summary, these four objectives must be defined and prioritized during the initial project effort. Additionally, they must be monitored throughout the application development cycle in order to ensure that consistent results can be guaranteed.

Most successful data processing projects manipulate these objectives to ensure that the priority order maximizes the projected efficiency in the selected processing environment. This is validated with the business user at every stage of the development cycle.

The Entity Relationship Model

Models as they come from the logical modelers represent the compilation and interpretation of the business requirements of a specific area by the modelers. This embodiment of the business requirements allows a common object to be viewed by all those dealing with it to minimize gray areas and to maximize understanding.

While the known entities represent the areas of business focus and the attributes represent the compiled facts about them, many do not understand more than this. For example, the relationships between the entities represent the business rules as to how each entity behaves in participation with the other. Additionally, many do not realize how critical a key or identifier is to not only the design process but to what the key becomes on model translation as well.

This chapter covers some of the basic components of models, their characteristics, and, more specifically, the actions that can be taken to adjust and transform the model for maximum performance while still maintaining the same characteristics as the original business model. By maintaining the original characteristics, the business user is ensured that his or her requirements will be met when the model is implemented as a database. The maximum design efficiency is achieved through the use of data model and process model interaction. The rigor produced allows flexibility, as well as comprehensiveness.

Interaction Analysis

All interaction analysis and mapping exercises depend on the development of a process or activity decomposition diagram. This is a breakdown of all of the activities of the business area in the enterprise that are being worked on. It is normally created in a top-to-bottom listing with a left-to-right expansion. A natural sequence is assumed but not necessary in the top-to-bottom arrangement of the activities listing. At the far left top of the diagram are the initial processes of the businesses. These follow down on the left side at the highest level of the process. After this is defined, all direct subprocesses are defined by adding an indented list under each major process on the left. When these are completed, they then are broken down into their subprocesses and added to the diagram by further indenting and adding under each subprocess. This continues until all processes' activities are defined down to the elementary level. Two examples

Figure 16.1

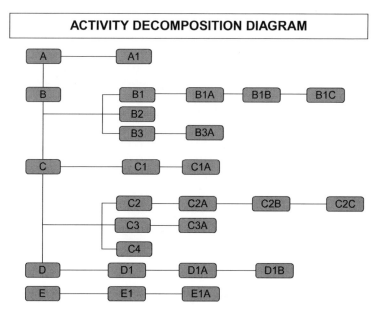

Figure 16.2

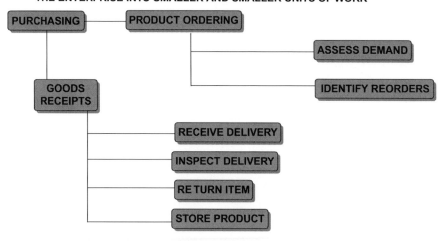

appear in Figures 16.1 and 16.2. One shows the pictorial representation of the activity decomposition, and the other shows a small detail section for explanatory purposes.

Interaction analysis is the process of evaluating each process and determining the data requirements of each and developing

	Customer	Customer Order	Customer Account	Customer Invoice	Vendor Invoice	Product
Customer Order	R	C	CR			
Customer Order	CRU		RU			R
Customer Order	U		U		RU	
Customer Order	U		U		RU	
Customer Order	RU		RU			RU
Customer Order			U		C	
Vendor Invoice					R	
Vendor Invoice					RU	
Customer	RU		RU	C		
Inventory						CRUD

Figure 16.3 A CRUD matrix.

a matrix of what data are used by what process. By mapping the data to the processes through interaction, all processes that do not have data either are invalid processes or represent missing data from valid processes.

Conversely, by reverse mapping all processes to the data, the data that have no associated processes are either extraneous data items or are missing the valid processes that need them. This mapping can take many forms. Several will be covered here.

The CRUD Matrix

The first and simplest is the C-R-U-D matrix. This is a visual array that is developed on paper or in computer text. The array has two vectors: a vertical and a horizontal. The horizontal vector, normally put across the top of the matrix, is a list of entities that exist in the logical model. The vertical vector, normally run down the left side of the matrix, is a list of all of the processes that exist in the business area being mapped. At each point where the two vectors meet there is a box that should be filled out. Into this box should be entered whether the action is a *C*reate, *R*ead, *U*pdate, or *D*elete. This provides the mapping that validates what processes use what data and the reverse. CRUD matrices also show where incipient hot spots may exist in the resulting database even before the logical model is physicalized. Figure 16.3 shows an example of a CRUD matrix.

Entity Life Cycle Analysis/Entity State Transition Diagrams

Entity life cycle analysis, although time consuming, is an excellent way to determine if there are any elementary processes that remain undefined or if additional attributes are needed to ensure validity of the entities and processes associated with the

Figure 16.4

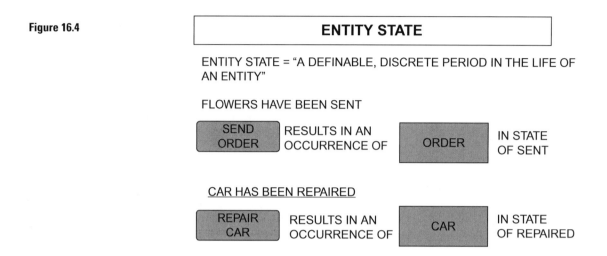

ENTITY STATE

ENTITY STATE = "A DEFINABLE, DISCRETE PERIOD IN THE LIFE OF AN ENTITY"

FLOWERS HAVE BEEN SENT

SEND ORDER — RESULTS IN AN OCCURRENCE OF — ORDER — IN STATE OF SENT

CAR HAS BEEN REPAIRED

REPAIR CAR — RESULTS IN AN OCCURRENCE OF — CAR — IN STATE OF REPAIRED

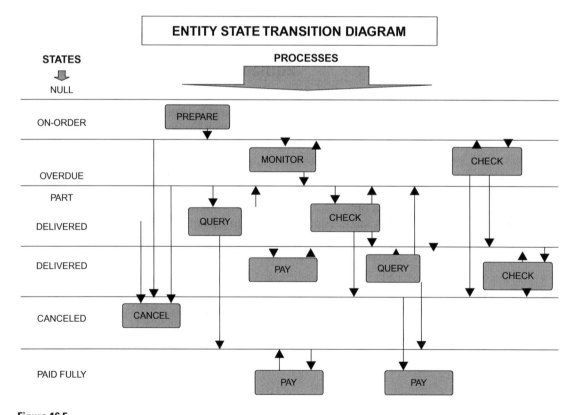

ENTITY STATE TRANSITION DIAGRAM

STATES → PROCESSES

NULL

ON-ORDER — PREPARE

MONITOR — CHECK

OVERDUE

PART

DELIVERED — QUERY — CHECK

DELIVERED — PAY — QUERY — CHECK

CANCELED — CANCEL

PAID FULLY — PAY — PAY

Figure 16.5

data and process models. This life cycle analysis has basic rules that specify the following:
1. Each entity has a life cycle.
2. The entity must be in an entity state.
3. It must pass through the null and creation states.
4. It may exist in only one state at a time.
5. It changes states due to an elementary process.
6. It can change into any of several states (it is not sequentially linked).

Figure 16.4 shows an example of an entity state.

Figure 16.5 shows an entity state transition. Note how the prepare order state can go directly to the cancel order state. Also note how the monitor order can lead to a delivery state or back to a prepare order state if items had been missed on the original order. While this mapping may seem complex, it is a simple but accurate rendition of the business process in a text and graphical package.

Process Dependency Scope and Process Dependency Diagram

Process dependency interaction analysis also depends on the process decomposition having been done. A process dependency scope is a further delineation of the activity decomposition diagram. It groups activities into structured sets that are in dependency order, which the activity decomposition may or may not

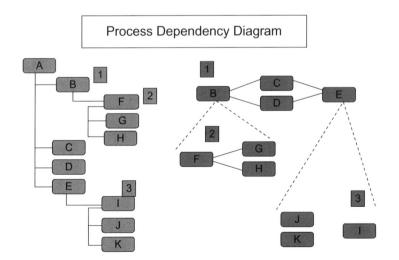

THE SCOPE IS DONE ON ONE LEG OF THE DECOMPOSITION AT A TIME USING THE OUTPUT OF THE DECOMPOSITION DIAGRAM

Figure 16.6

Figure 16.7

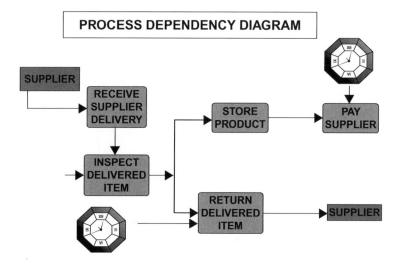

PROCESS DEPENDENCY DIAGRAM

Figure 16.8

EVENT ANALYSIS

SPECIFY THE EXACT EVENT OR SET OF EVENTS THAT TRIGGERS AN ELEMENTARY PROCESS

IDENTIFY BUSINESS STIMULI / DEPENDENCIES BETWEEN ELEMENTARY PROCESSES COMPRISING THE RESPONSE

be. In some cases several activities and their subprocesses may take place simultaneously. See Figure 16.6. This allows the overall dependency sequence to be defined in a graphic manner. Figure 16.7 shows an overly simplified example with clocks as a gating mechanism showing time triggers.

Event Analysis

An event is a happening of interest to a process. See Figure 16.8. Event analysis involves three categories of event control mechanisms: preconditions, triggers, and guards. Preconditions

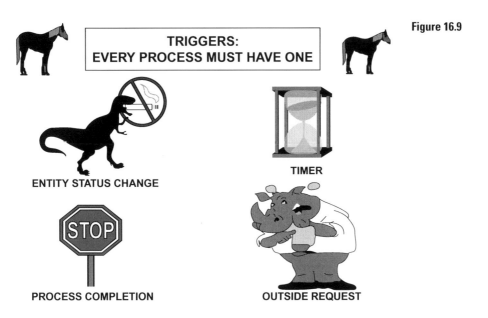

Figure 16.9

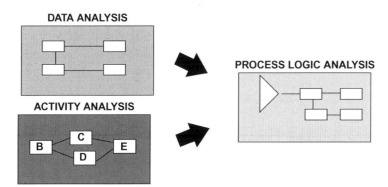

Figure 16.10

are those event control mechanisms that enable the process to execute. Triggers initiate a process to execute. A guard prevents a trigger from executing. We want to record temporal or timed, externally requested, data change, and process status change events. Figure 16.9 shows another way of determining sequencing and entity/process interaction.

Process Logic Diagrams

Process logic diagrams are the result of the interaction analysis between data and process. All other interaction analysis methods should be translated to a process logic diagram. The process logic analysis diagrams become very critical in the denormalization and performance tuning of the model as it is physicalized. Figure 16.10 shows the method for creating a PLD.

Interaction Analysis Summary

Good model transformation requires that all of the interactive activity between the data model and the process model has taken place within the scope of the business context being implemented to ensure that the business requirements have been completely captured. This interaction activity must include a step of review, which includes the business user of the model. See Figure 16.10.

Changes to ER Models

Many different changes can be made to models to increase performance. These will be covered in more detail in the succeeding paragraphs. All of these considerations are based upon common principles:

- All DBMSs function on a file basis. In the case of the relational DBMSs, the files represent the tables that contain the data. Each file (or table) that the DBMS must keep open or keep a pointer in is overhead to the using application. Therefore, the fewer the tables present (generically speaking), the better the performance.

- All data that are retrieved by the DBMS must be evaluated in some manner in order to decide which processing path it must take. Depending on the complexity of the physical structure of data that has to be evaluated, it may have to be moved to different portions of the DBMS to be evaluated. In other words, if the data structure is not simplified or made efficient, then the DBMS has to move a lot of data to a more complex evaluation mechanism within itself, which involves a lot of I/O, and this takes the form of slower throughput.

- Full-function DBMSs have automated recovery mechanisms for units of work. Most of them function through the use of logging for the units of work being applied. Good design of a model can significantly affect the referential sets involved in the units of work. The more complex and larger the unit of work, the longer it takes for logging, and subsequently the longer it takes to recover these units of work.

- DBMSs are engines, and the better the quality of the fuel that is put in, the more efficient they are. Even though some manufacturers have tuned their DBMSs' engines to partially or completely detect sequential input to take advantage of read-ahead buffering, the fewer data that have poor quality or are out of sequence, the more efficiently it will run.

A small note is inserted here to explain some of the acronyms used in this chapter. DA stands for data administrator, the person or group of people responsible for capturing business requirements in a logical model. DBA stands for database administrator, the person responsible for translating the model into a form that can be converted to data definition language (DDL). Specifically, the DBA is responsible for designing and building the structure of the database in the target environment.

Based on these simple principles, some forms of change to the model can be made that will allow it to have a smaller "footprint" on the direct access storage device (DASD) device, while still retaining the characteristics of the model that the business signed off on. The denormalizations that are acceptable in this framework fall into two categories: entity relationship diagram (ERD) denormalization and access-level denormalization. Each of these will be covered in turn and discussed in non-tool-specific language that can be used within or outside the use of a CASE design tool.

ERD Denormalization

The Collapse of 1:1 Relationships

One-to-one relationships reflect that for each A there is one and only one B. While the key attributes of the entities may or may not be the same, their equal participation in a relationship indicates that they can be treated as one by any unit of work being applied to the data. Only the attribute loads are different. Combining the attribute loads does not change the business view and decreases the access time by having one fewer physical object (table) and associated overhead (indexes). See Figure 16.11.

Figure 16.11

COLLAPSE 1:1 RELATIONSHIPS

Resolution of Many-to-Many Relationships

This means that for every A there are many Bs, and for every B there are many As. While this

1) Combine attribute loads on 1:1 relationships

2) This excludes GH parent–child relationships

Figure 16.12

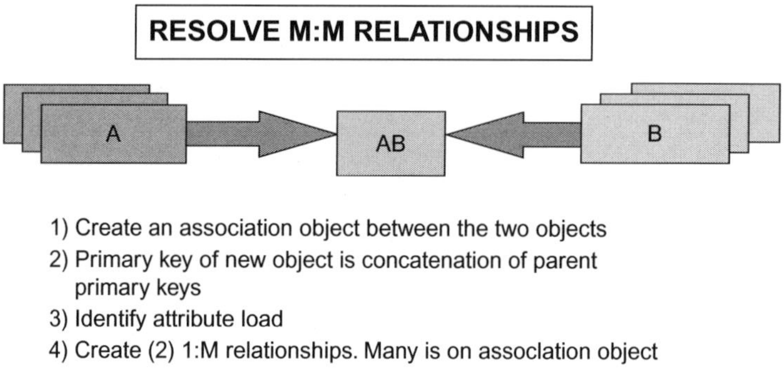

RESOLVE M:M RELATIONSHIPS

1) Create an association object between the two objects
2) Primary key of new object is concatenation of parent primary keys
3) Identify attribute load
4) Create (2) 1:M relationships. Many is on association object

makes for a complex interaction (the real amount of the occurrences is the Cartesian product of both numbers of occurrences), many-to-many relationships reflect the intersection of separate keyed occurrences.

Manually this can be handled by creating a mutual entity between the two entities, which is called an associative entity. The key to this entity is the concatenated primary keys of the participating entities. For example, if the key of A was 1 and the key of B was 2, then the key of the associative entity AB would be 1, 2. CASE tools automatically resolve this by creating an associative entity during model transformation. However, tool manufacturers generate nonstandard names for the associative entity and the keys identifying it.

In order to produce standardized names, many DAs resolve the many-to-many problem by creating the associative entity and properly naming the keys. With the associative being developed, it often becomes obvious when processes are mapped against the entities that the intersection entity (the associative) is the real focus of interest. In the rare case that an associative has no attribute load, then the one valid attribute is the date of the relationship. In many cases the associative table is the only one implemented, and the salient attributes of the participants are migrated to the associative for implementation. See Figure 16.12.

Resolution of Recursive Relationships

Recursive relationships represent self-referencing or involuting relationships. While this may sound complex, it merely indicates that there is a parent–child (possibly multilevel) hierarchy involved. In the case of a single-level recursive, its behavior is similar to a one-to-many relationship, with the key being propagated as a foreign key to the other participant. The upshot is that the recursed entity has a foreign key that is really another image of the primary key. CASE tool transformations generate a nonstandard foreign key name. The DA would resolve the recursive relationship and properly name the foreign key. In the case of a multiple-level recursive, CASE tools resolve the relationship as it did in the single level as stated before. The DA must then manually create a foreign key (renaming it uniquely) for each level of recursion. For example, if a recursive relationship had three levels to its hierarchy, there would be three foreign keys that were associated to the primary key. See Figure 16.13.

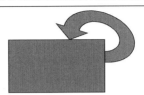

RESOLVE RECURSIVE RELATIONSHIPS

1) Determine the number of levels of recursion
2) Choose
   a) Multiple entities - one for each level or
   b) Foreign key propagation for each level
Note: History is not a valid use for recursion

Figure 16.13

Actions on Super Type–Subtype Constructs

Super type–subtype relationships represent a type of parent–child relationship. The child entities are dependent on the parent, and each child specifies a particular type of the parent. Normally they are mutually exclusive. Subtypes are promoted by DAs into separate entity types, with the attendant primary keys being propagated to the new entities. While this may seem contradictory to the basic rules set up in the initial paragraphs, upon review and access mapping, it becomes clear that activity most often happens to the child entities and not the parent. In many cases the parent can be discarded because the points of interest may only be the children.

Based on access requirements, attribute loads of the child entities, and volume statistics, the collapse of the children upward into the parent may be justifiable. This is done by creating a type column in the parent and migrating all attributes of the children up to the parent occurrence row. This will create null fields, but this may be acceptable.

Based on other requirements, lateral collapse may be affected between surviving children where the parent has been removed. This is only justifiable where one of the children has most of the accesses and the others have almost none. It is accomplished by entering a type column in one of the sibling entities and moving all of the attributes of all the selected children to it. Again, it will result in null fields, but this should only be done in cases of negligible access and negligible volume.

Many tools implement the subtypes and super type as separate entities upon transformation, but as in the case of the many-to-many, where naming conventions of the entity and the keys are manufactured by the CASE tools, the results of the transformation

Figure 16.14

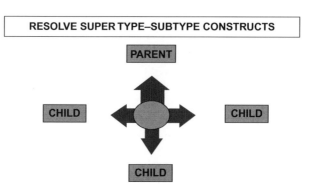

RESOLVE SUPER TYPE–SUBTYPE CONSTRUCTS

PARENT

CHILD

CHILD

CHILD

1) Promote children to entities and discard parent
2) Implement parent and all children
3) Collapse children into parent and implement
4) Combine smaller children if one is large

are nonstandard entity and attribute names. Additionally, many CASE tools bring down all inherited attributes to each subtype. The DA must promote the subtypes and correct the names to ensure compliance to naming standards prior to transformation. See Figure 16.14.

Actions on Multiple Relationships

Multiple relationships represent different business relationships between the entities involved. These are called subset relationships because they represent unique relationships between subsets of the data on each of the entities. Subset relationships represent different business views of the partial sets of entity occurrences on the two entities—for example, half of A is related to half of B in one specific manner, and the remainder of A is related to the remainder of B in another specific manner. An example of this would be a multiple relationship scenario between sales and invoice. Sales can be related to an open invoice, a back-ordered invoice, or a closed invoice. The business area may want to model them this way. In most cases they represent different life cycle states of one of the participating entities. As in normal relationships, foreign keys are propagated to the many entity. In model translation this can be treated as a single relationship or as multiple single relationships. It is easier and does no harm to consider it one relationship and thereby save implementation of many objects. Additionally, it saves the expense of determining which occurrences go on which tables when they all have the same primary key.

Another way of handling it is by creating an associative entity type between the two original entity types. The associative entity type (in this case an aggregation) would include a code or type

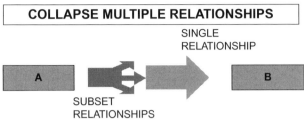

Figure 16.15

COLLAPSE MULTIPLE RELATIONSHIPS

SINGLE
RELATIONSHIP

A   B

SUBSET
RELATIONSHIPS

1) Assure that these are <u>subset</u> relationships
2) Often represent life cycle states of entity

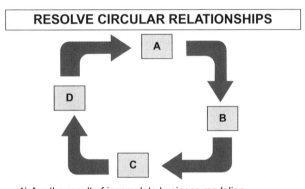

Figure 16.16

RESOLVE CIRCULAR RELATIONSHIPS

A

D

B

C

1) Are the result of incomplete business modeling
2) Are fine if all relationships are mandatory
3) If no simple solution, remodel to fourth normal form to
   remove possible null foreign key

attribute, which would be used as a discriminator to indicate which subset was being associated. Either can be done in the logical model as it is understandable to and approved by the business owner. CASE tools individualize one of the relationships by changing or adding a character to make the foreign key unique during transformation. The result when DDL is generated for multiple indexes (depending on the number of subsets) is that duplicate indexes result (the foreign key of one has a modifier added to its name). This is not acceptable or efficient and should be handled by the DBA prior to translation. See Figure 16.15.

Resolution of Circular References

This is not a frequent occurrence, since it represents a logical modeling error. As such, it needs to be corrected before any translation or transformation takes place. This correction must be completed prior to the logical model being accepted. Circular relationships exist in certain situations where third normal form does not adequately define the business requirements. It manifests itself as a dependency relationship loop that exists containing a partial dependency of one entity on another in the loop. Simply put, a series of entities in a circular relationship would end up in an endless loop if one were trying to navigate an access path by the keys involved. An example of this is the employee-manager-office-business entities. The problem occurs where the employee may optionally be a manager. As one can see, the navigational aspect of this construct leaves the accessor in a quandary. The resolution to this is to create a fourth normal form entity that resolves any optionality issues and populate it with the appropriate attributes. This entity is a 1 to optional 1 relationship but allows specification to remove the circular nature of the relationship. See Figure 16.16.

Resolution of Duplicate Propagated Keys

Certain relationships are regarded as identifying because they require the key of the participating parent to be included as part of their own key. Because identifying relationships propagate keys to receiving entities and those in turn could be identifying to other entities, keys are propagated downward through the dependency chains. In most businesses these dependency chains are short, and there is little complexity involved; in other businesses these dependency chains can become quite long—up to 10–12 entities. This leads to a primary key of 10 to 20 attributes. When these long keys are involved in relationships with other entities, it could cause a situation where the dependency chain loops back to reconnect to a previous entity (circular-type relationship) or a situation where two dependent chains are resolved by an association object. The identifying nature of the relationship forces multiple keys of the same name into the association object, thereby causing duplicate keys.

CASE tools automatically add a discriminator to prevent a duplicate name, but this does not meet naming standards. In a manual mode this is easily handled by naming the duplicated keys differently or by eliminating one of them because they represent the same data content value. In a CASE tool, several actions are possible in order to resolve this: The first is to selectively remove the identifying nature from the relationships before transformation. The second way is to remove the redundant relationship in a circular relationship. The third way consists of renaming the duplicate keys to a new name that meets naming standards after transformation and allows the duplication to continue. In all cases these should be resolved in order to minimize key length and confusion at the same time. See Figure 16.17.

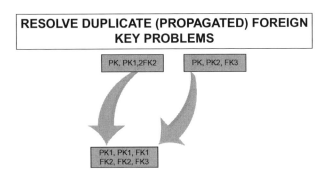

Figure 16.17

1) These are the result of propagated dependencies or characteristic entities
2) Result when two dependency chains have an M:M at lowest level
3) Delete one set of foreign key information from the entity

Access-Level Denormalization

Access-level denormalization falls into several categories. These encompass the movement or change of structure within the physical model based on the characteristics of the accesses that will be using the data. Under no condition should denormalization be done without access path justification. Some of the physical techniques are noted in the following. Again, let me state that these are based on performance need rather than arbitrary whim.

Movement of Attributes

Movement of an attribute from one entity to another entity is strictly based on access path justification by the project team that includes the application personnel, as well as modeling personnel. DAs should not perform this without supporting documentation. In order to accomplish this form of denormalization, the attribute is copied to the new entity and deleted from the old entity. This is done in the physical model and represents an attribute-level change that results in a change to the DDL and the physical database structure. Changes of this type must be communicated to all involved personnel in order to minimize rework.

Consolidation of Entities

Consolidation of entities is not done very often. It represents the task of physically combining the attributes of two tables into

Figure 16.18

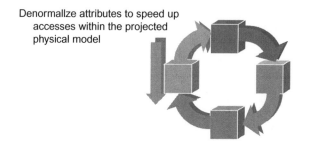

ACCESS DENORMALIZATION OF ATTRIBUTES

Denormalize attributes to speed up
accesses within the projected
physical model

Figure 16.19

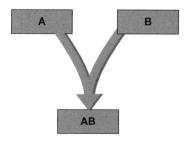

CONSOLIDATION OF ENTITIES

1) Collapse all 1:1 relationships into one entity
2) Consider collapse of all 1x:1 relationships

one. The result may end up being the combined key of both or
the most detail-level key in a collapsed hierarchy. It is primarily
done to consolidate lookup or domain constraint data entities
into the parent entity. This may look to be counterproductive
from the logical views, but in reality it may be very logical if the
target entities have been the result of overnormalization (breakdown of complex group items to their atomic level). This is not
only done for DASD space conservation but for access reasons
(doing one read on a collapsed entity rather than three reads or a
join of three entities). Consolidation of entities must be justified
by the access paths provided.

Derived Attributes and Summary Data

This is the creation of entities or attributes to facilitate multiple
or special request views for the project team. This activity is strictly
based on access path justification by the project team, which
includes the application personnel as well as modeling personnel.

DERIVED ATTRIBUTES

Figure 16.20

1) Derived attributes exist for three purposes:
   a) Used for operational purposes (switches)
   b) Used for processing or accessing purposes (flags)
   c) Used to hold external data (parameters)

SUMMARY DATA

Figure 16.21

1) Summary data is retained when:
   a) Reporting or MIS data
   b) Results of intermediate calculations
   c) Cost of redundant recalculation is wasteful

Entities are created as normal entities would be. No relationships are defined connecting the entity to the rest of the entities in the model. Attributes are created as normal attributes would be in the entity where they will reside. Designer entities are normally for summary data purposes where they are used as holders for partial calculations or totals. Designer attributes are for totals, operational data such as switches, and next sequential number storage.

Implement Repeating Groups

Introduction of repeating groups is strictly based on access path justification by the project team that includes the application personnel as well as infrastructure personnel (DA and DBA). Additionally, the repeating group would have to be a small volume fixed group that cannot grow. Based on these criteria, DBAs do not perform a lot of this denormalization. In order to accomplish it when it is desired, attributes have to be created in the occurrence

Figure 16.22

| INTRODUCE REPEATING GROUPS |

1) Introduce only fixed numbered groups
2) Do not introduce variable-length columns
3) Be wary of the maintenance factor

Figure 16.23

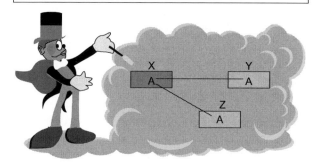

| INTRODUCE REDUNDANCY |

1) Selectively introduce redundancy based on:
   a) Frequency of maintenance of the redundant columns
   b) Access path justification only
   c) No key redundancy is allowed

description just as they are for a normal attribute. This is done until there is a column for each member of the repeating groups.

Introduce Redundancy

Introduction of redundancy is strictly based on access path justification by the project team, which includes the application personnel as well as infrastructure personnel. Introducing redundancy is the redundant placement of an attribute on another entity in order to facilitate faster performance. In most cases the DBA copies the attribute to the new entity or creates it as a new attribute in that entity because there is no relationship between the entities. The important thing is to remember that for each redundancy introduced there is a penalty as well. Each redundant attribute needs to be updated at the same time as the original in order to be kept in synchronization for referential integrity. See Figure 16.23.

DENORMALIZATION SURROGATE OR SYNTHETIC KEYS

Figure 16.24

1) Use when natural key is too long
2) Must have a natural key behind it
3) Model must contain synthetic key resolution rules or
   algorithms

TABLE SEGMENTATION

Figure 16.25

1) Vertical segment table when row is too long
2) Horizontal segment based on volume or access

Introduce Surrogate or Synthetic Keys

Introduction of surrogate keys is based on the conservation of space as well as faster access. It is investigated as a solution for the cases where propagated key strings are too long or violate implementation DBMS limitations. In those cases where it is deemed viable, a surrogate key is created and the natural key is either removed to a separate entity or placed as attributes within the occurrence definition of the entity being operated on. In those cases where the natural key is moved to a separate entity, it is matched with the surrogate identifier, thereby creating an association table upon implementation. See Figure 16.24.

Vertical or Horizontal Segmentation

In those cases where an entity occurrence exceeds the implementable row length of the target DBMS, vertical segmentation must be accomplished. A new entity is created with the same key

Figure 16.26

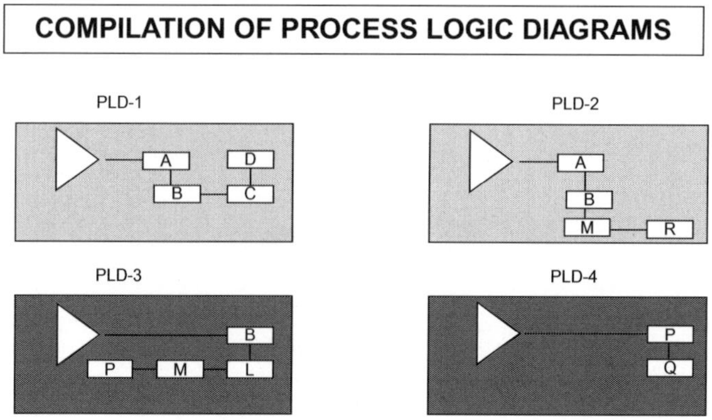

COMPILATION OF PROCESS LOGIC DIAGRAMS

as the original (made unique, of course) and the attributes of the original row are separated in half and each half is attributed to one of the entities. The result is two tables that can be joined into a single entry based on occurrence key values. See Figure 16.25.

Access Path Mapping

This step is that of recording of the many event/process use maps that will show how the data is being accessed. The assemblage of the process logic diagrams defined previously now will be utilized. The access path defined in the PLD is recorded on a physical model diagram of what the potential database tables will be. Each PLD is recorded in a different color and aligned in parallel. When this is done, it produces a combined set of overlay traversal paths or access paths that can be mapped against the model to show where access will be heaviest. This supplies the following information to the physical designer:

1. It shows where identifier or index maintenance will be required most.
2. It shows where activity volume will be heaviest, indicating a need for more free space for insertion and frequent reorganization and distribution of the data.
3. It shows where tuning options must be put in place to ensure rapid access.

Figure 16.27 shows the result of the integration of PLD1, PLD2, PLD3, and PLD4. Figure 16.28 shows how, when they are combined, they produce the composite load map.

The composite load map allows the designer to see the areas for the final stages of physical model translation. He may choose to ignore these but will have them available if and when the need

DEVELOPMENT OF THE COMPOSITE LOAD MAP

Figure 16.27

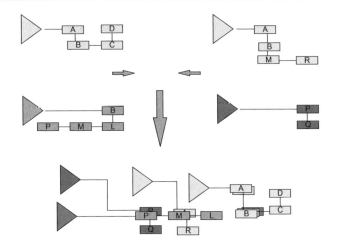

THE COMPOSITE LOAD MAP OF ACCESSES

Figure 16.28

arises for performance tuning. The first of these is the identification of potential "hot spots" in the new database that will be created. See Figure 16.29.

The next area is the identification of referential groups. That is, these are groups of entities that are updated as a group by the processes that have been identified.

Finally, the composite load map identifies the unit of work constraints. Similar to the referential groups in concept, this

Figure 16.29

IDENTIFY HOT SPOTS

• Where do the accesses overlay
each other on the ERD?

1) High overlay paths indicate
   a) frequent index maintenance
   b) multiple indexes
   c) freespace considerations

2) Frequent access to entities
   indicate:
   a) need for frequert REORGs
   b) possible higher-speed device

Figure 16.30

IDENTIFY REFERENTIAL GROUPS

Referential groups represent
those interrelated entities that
must be updated as a group.
These then become referential
sets that must be considered
when planning backup
recoveries and unit of work
scenarios

Figure 16.31

UNIT OF WORK CONSTRAINTS

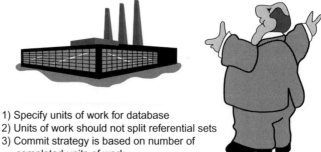

1) Specify units of work for database
2) Units of work should not split referential sets
3) Commit strategy is based on number of
   completed units of work

identifies a unit of work that must be completed for the entities to be in a completed state. It may or may not involve multiple access paths within the composite load map. See figure 16.30 and 16.31.

Conclusion

When all of the interaction analysis, denormalizations, and composite load map definitions are completed, the performance of the physical model can be determined before any physical structure is created. It also provides a basis for future change assessment when new business processes are added to the current workload.

These techniques and methods will also minimize the actual database "footprint" or space allocation on DASD, while at the same time allowing the model to represent the business and be flexible to those predictable business changes that might occur. When significant business changes occur, these steps can be applied again in the top-down process after the requirements have been captured and integrated. Overall these represent things that can be done at different stages in the design process that will maximize efficiencies of the model.

Reference

Tupper, C. (1998, September). The physics of logical modeling. *Article DBPD*.
    Copyright © 1998 Miller Freeman Inc.

5

SPECIALIZED DATABASES

17

DATA WAREHOUSES I

Early Analysis in this Area

Since the beginning of the organization of business processes into functions that optimized record keeping and thereby the ability to compete successfully in the marketplace, there has been a need to display or report on the basic information that was used by the direct functional processes. The business processes were distilled and encoded in programming languages that provided a concise set of actions to be performed on the data. The data used for the processes were arranged in the most optimal structure possible to ensure rapid movement through the programs that represented the captured business processes.

Unfortunately, the structure of the data for optimal processing for the business did not represent some of the information (interpreted data) necessary to monitor or project trends in the business. The very structure that allowed rapid processing of transaction-type activity impeded the process of interpreting the information and arranging it in a format that allowed business decisions to be based on it. The early DBMSs (database management systems) did not help the situation, since they tended to be inflexible and required that the data be arrayed in a pattern that the processing requirements for a specific business process needed. If other business processes needed that same data, then their business need was captured in a separate data structure.

During this time frame there were many people in the industry trying to assess the risks involved with the burgeoning new field of data processing. Among others, Richard Nolan (1979) documented his views of the problem. He identified six stages in data processing as part of a classic article published in the *Harvard Business Review* in 1979. His article, "Managing the Crises in Data Processing," explored the characteristics of the evolution that occurs in organizations as they become aware of the value and cost of the data they use.

As Nolan pointed out in his article very intuitively, there is no absolute correct degree of integration for any business environment because each organization has its own needs for future automation. It is, however, easy to see that the lower it is on the scale of integration of Nolan's stages, the more expensive it is to operate in the long run. This is because unintegrated environments waste expensive resources, cause duplication of effort, incur redundancy in maintenance, and aggravate problems in the synchronization of data content.

Keen and Scott-Morton

It was into this arena that Peter G. W. Keen and Michael S. Scott-Morton (1978) developed some concepts of business decision classification and decision support strategies for use in reporting and projective analysis. Theirs was the first comprehensive look at the business need to provide intelligence on the processing of the data for monitoring and control purposes. In their work on decision support they identified three classes of decisions: structured decisions, semistructured decisions, and unstructured decisions.

Prior to current-day efforts, structured decisions were generally made by operating management because they were regarded as needing certain expertise to be accomplished. We know now that these decisions are easily automated and generally choose to computerize them.

Semistructured decisions are less easily automated because they rely on judgment, intuition, and experience of management. The data that are needed for these semistructured decisions usually lies in the detail data of the business processes and can be retrieved for interpretation.

Unstructured decisions are decisions that rely completely on human intuition and analysis. The data needed for these must be formulated and structured for the purpose of presentation for evaluation, analysis, and assessment.

It is easy to see that what they were referring to in the structured decision classification was that set of data currently used for transaction processing systems. The set of data that is applicable for semistructured decisions is what is considered as reporting system data. And finally, the set of data associated with the classification of unstructured decisions is regarded as ad hoc query data.

Their work relied heavily on the tenet that decisions made by an organization must reflect the reality of that organization. The data structures then must be developed in accordance with that reality in order to solve the problems within it. Their work affirmed that all businesses were primarily controlled by discrete sectors of management and that a knowledge base existed in that management level that could exercise decisions based on the analysis of the intelligence in the data. Unfortunately, their assumptions were premature to the growth of the industry and their concepts and tenets which could have been the bedrock of business decision making became merely an acknowledged technique. They did not get the credit they deserved.

Decision Discussion

Over time it has become increasingly obvious that the knowledge of the data has been pushed downward in the organization and that the true understanding of the business processes as they operate on the data is in middle or lower management. In the words of Peter Drucker (1993), these "knowledge workers," then, are the set of individuals who utilize the information gleaned from the data being processed in order to translate this into something more understandable to the senior management as well as to maintain the monitoring and feedback processes to the overall function of the business. It is from this group that the requirements for decision support were born. These decision support requirements (foretold by Keen and Scott-Morton) needed to view data from a different perspective that allows the data to be detached from the processes that used it. Moreover, it also showed that there are different levels of abstraction of the data and that these levels of abstraction had different forms and structures of their own.

Components of Decisions

A decision consists of three parts: 1) What is the question that is trying to be answered? 2) What are the data or information needed to make the decision? 3) What action is taken based on the decision?

The first part can be broken down as: what question(s) are captured by analysis of the business process? What is being done (is this a monitoring question?) in the process? Is the question designed to help us follow the progress of a process? Is it a control mechanism that will help to slow or stop the business process? Is it a feedback mechanism that will allow information from the process to be used as input to subsequent iterations of the same business process or perhaps a different one?

The second part refers to the data or information required to supply the raw material for the answer to the question. Where are the data? What form is it in? How accurate are the data? How recent are the data? Are the data complete, or do the data depend on other pieces of data? What is the likelihood that the data for the decision I am making will persist long enough to be evaluated as either a good source or a bad source? The overall integrity of the data being used for the decision will affect the quality of the decision that is being made.

Lastly, the third part refers to what action will be taken based on the needs of the decision? This refers to both internal and external action. By *internal action*, I am referring to what actual processing is required to format, restructure, or transform the data into an array that will be sympathetic to the question being answered. External action in the last phase is what action is taken on the data as a result of the decision. Are partial products of calculations kept? Are summaries kept? Are the data time bounded? Are the internal actions transitional and have no lasting effect on the data or does the internal action become an external action? What is the presentation format? All of these affect the data as a result of the decision process being performed.

Responsibility

Information technology, or the IT area, as it was called, inherited the mantle of the analytical work that translates the decisions into structures that support or allow translation of processing arrayed data to information source. The people that needed to make decisions needed the data in their hands in the format that they desired it to be. This is a tall order for an organization whose sole purpose was to pass data as quickly and as efficiently as possible. An additional problem was that all the DBMSs to this point were designed to maximize the efficiency of the I/O process, since the data needed to be read, staged, brought into memory, evaluated and acted upon, and potentially restored. I/O was a limiting factor in many situations for many applications. The retrieval engines could be made to work only so fast. Vendors of the DBMSs were slow in responding to the need for more decision support retrieval engines but eventually began to address this issue.

In addition to this, there was the problem of who would gather the questions and who would consolidate the structural plan for the needed data. These problems fell on barren ground in some parts of the industry; in others the analysis was relegated as part of the modeling process along with logical and physical modeling. These requirements had to be gathered and assembled from the business areas to ensure that the true data requirement for the questions being asked was present and could be made to provide the answer.

The data administration data analyst became responsible for the research and interviews that comprise this activity. It was important that the data being defined or captured provide the raw material for the question to be asked. It is also important that the questions themselves be captured, not only for posterity but also as a foundation for future analysis.

In order to provide the best solution for decision support problems, the major specific area to be defined is, "What is the data requirement?" The specific areas may be associated with type of retrieval need or in other cases the structure and format of the data. While spoken of in generic terms, these specific areas and the requirements that support their consideration have evolved only in specification since the early days of decision support. These will provide the basic premises of the data warehouse concept. To that end let us consider the fundamentals first and consider the following: Restructuring and/or reorganization requirements for data allow the data to be arranged to better facilitate access for those users that use the data in a different or non-standard manner. An example of this would be the reorganization of a table to be in a candidate key sequence rather than a primary key sequence.

Segmented or partitioned requirements for data usually have to do with the accomplishment of bringing the data closer to the user. They can also be used to physically separate different characteristics about the same data. In all cases the structure of the data store is unchanged, but the data contents of the partitions are different.

Summary requirements for data are present when there is a need to allow viewing of the data store at higher levels of abstraction. By looking at the higher-level view of the data store, trend analysis and problem identification can take place by management operating at this level of abstraction. Levels within summary allow the separation of some information into the subcategories.

These categories will translate into more familiar modern-day objects and concepts that are developed in this chapter. It is then to the point where different options of data arrangement are considered to facilitate the reporting and querying aspect of information management. Decision support databases that provide report outputs and online query outputs have been the result of this need. Reporting databases were often kept apart from query databases in the early days to facilitate the type of activity being performed. Reports tended to deal with larger volumes of data viewed serially, whereas queries were much more specific. It is into this arena that the report writers and query engines began to compete.

Report Writers and Query Engines

While there were many different tools in the marketplace, the ones that survived had some common characteristics. These characteristics were that they upheld the basic tenets of decision support, they were flexible and responsive to the using industry pressures, and they allowed the drivers of the evolutionary processes of tool development to be the worker groups that had to use the data.

Many of these tools were or are based on some form of data dictionary or lexicon of the available data attributes that facilitates the queries being formulated. Others functioned on embedded code structures or associated data layout definitions within the tools that allowed parameterization to be utilized in selecting data from the database. Behavior rules associated with the data attributes were defined or made explicit in the dictionary meaning of the attribute or data layouts and thereby allowed the queries to be engineered with some level of efficiency. To optimize the interface, the structures and arrays of the data were arranged in such a way as to facilitate the utilization of these lexicons, dictionaries, and layouts. Thus, reporting and query databases were created. They survive today because they address a consistent need within the business to monitor and control ongoing business processes. They did not address that rapidly evolving portion of decision support known as trend analysis or projective analysis.

During this period of time, business management as a whole was becoming aware of the abundance of its own product types in the marketplace. It was also becoming aware of how fast it would be required to bring new products to the marketplace to ensure market share. It needed data to address this area in order to compete successfully and the current reporting data structures were too limited or inflexible to provide.

Warehouses versus Reporting Databases

Warehouses are the evolved concept of decision reporting that allow the data to be placed in an open area. The attractive perception of the warehouse is built on every person's concept of what a warehouse is: a no frills or glossy, large, open structure, with the sole purpose of storing everything in such a way that any given item or object in it can be accessed or retrieved in the minimum time possible.

Along with the good concept were bad concepts like, "If I don't want it, I'll toss it in the warehouse" or "I want to archive my data there" or "Dump all the corrupt (lacking integrity) data in there, and we'll get to it later."

Likewise there were concepts that there are very few rules governing how a warehouse works. Most of the concepts other than the initial everyman concept is wrong. Yes, they are large, open structures whose sole purpose is to store everything in such a way that any given item or object in it can be accessed or retrieved in the least time possible. But they have very specific rules of storage in them, since one type of material (acid) might affect the integrity of another type of material (silk). Also, they have an organization that is specifically keyed as to location (row and bin number). They are monitored for fullness and for environmental considerations like temperature and dryness.

Higher Level of Abstraction

Data warehouses are collections of data from many different levels of abstractions, where data in a reporting database is generally at one level of specificity or granularity. The different levels of abstraction allow the data warehouse to be used for multiple purposes and also allow the different levels of abstracted data to be used simultaneously. The result is that far more questions can be answered within a data warehouse than in a multitude of reports from reporting databases.

Based on Perceived Business Use

Although both are based on the perceived use of the data by the business community, the data warehouse is a more open structure and in time may supersede or obsolesce some reporting databases in the business environment. The key here, though, is that the business uses of the warehouse are multilevel and provide complex data results for evaluations, whereas the business use of the reporting databases is usually more run of the mill. In effect, reporting databases are used to monitor and control, and warehouses arc used to analyze, define, and project based on different types of data. Data warehouses are used for profitability analysis, pricing analysis, target market identification, risk analysis, fraud detection, and management cost projection. These are very different types of use, indeed.

Structure Evolution

Reporting databases generally are specific to the question they are being asked to answer. They are usually uncomplicated in nature and provide little in the way of analysis other than totals or specific breakdowns for known classifications. They do not change significantly over time other than some modifications that may add columns or new totals or classifications. On the other hand, data warehouses may start as merely an application-specific analysis basis that allows trend analyses and the like. As time passes and the application becomes more mature and is integrated with other applications and the inherent needs of the business, the data warehouse too must grow and evolve. Based on this simple premise, all warehouses should be designed as flexibly as possible while still answering the business questions.

Warehouse Components

The following is an overview of the data warehouse in brief terms. Figure 17.1 is a visual chart of the warehouse components. The data warehouse purposes are many, including the following:

- Profitability analysis
- Pricing
- Target marketing
- Risk analysis
- Customer retention
- Fraud detection
- Management costs

Why Can't OLTP Data Stores Be Used?

OLTP tables are, for the most part, normalized or denormalized for efficiency and performance. They will definitely not be in

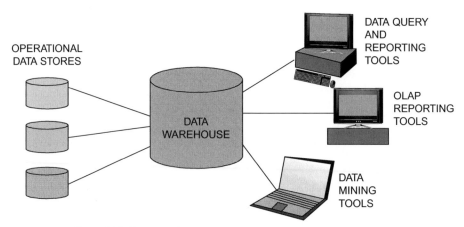

Figure 17.1 Data warehouse components.

a state that is usable for the warehouse. They also have eliminated redundant data that sometimes is desirable in the warehouse. Activity against the OLTP databases would entail complex joins of many tables in order to get the data they need. Additionally, since large volumes of data are needed, the retrieval from a relational database is not efficient.

DSS Requirements

In order to provide the data necessary for the decision support needs of the business, several factors about the data need to be considered. We will cover these separately. The first need is for trending data. Trending requires the retention of historical data; the more data retained the better. This retention allows time period comparisons such as month over month and year over year comparisons. A second requirement is nonvolatility of data. This is the characteristic that the data is not changed once it is loaded. If the data were changeable, then the comparisons and trends would be meaningless.

The performance of decision support activity requires the ability to handle high-volume input and high-volume extract output. And, lastly, the data should be separate and apart from the OLTP operational data stores to ensure noncontention.

Warehouse Characteristics

The data warehouse characteristics are that the data stored is subject area oriented. It is usually focused on customer, product, or business activity. It provides integrated data that has been gathered from many sources and has been standardized and formatted for the business user's retrieval. It is nonvolatile—that is, it is not subject to update. Data in the warehouse is time invariant. It is stable and remains so by being exempt from purges. In order to keep it stable and nonvolatile, the data is refreshed (reloaded or added to) and is exempt from update operations.

Warehouse Modeling

Modern businesses are faced with the problems of change. They are faced with change in their markets, changes in their products, changes in the legal arena in which they operate, and, unfortunately, in the data processing as well. On top of all this, businesses face increased competition for the same market share. The requirement today is to respond to the changes in such a way as to minimize impact and maximize speed of response. Structured techniques and methods are critical to achieve this goal. They aid in the production of higher-quality, more integrated systems in a more accelerated manner. Modeling is one such structured approach.

Warehouse Modeling Depends on Architectures

Data architecture is the transcription of the information owner's product requirements from the owner's perspective. Data architecture is dependent on the premise that data reside at the center of modern data processing. As discussed in previous chapters, data must be approached from the highest level of perspective, since it is perceived as the real-world objects it represents and exists as a function of normal business operation. The notion of enterprise data architecture delineates the data according to inherent structure rather than by use. In this manner it makes the data dependent on business objects, yet makes it independent of business processes. Processes that use data change far more frequently than the data itself. Data architectures, particularly the enterprise architecture, insulate a business from unnecessary data change.

The enterprise data architecture is essentially a strategic design model that becomes the environmental foundation for the development activities that ensue on owner approval of the plan. Many enterprise data models that are available for purchase today have been specifically tailored to the industry standards for that line of business. If you have no foundation architecture at the enterprise level, then this is a place to start. The following are some of the fundamental benefits of data architecture:

- Architectures provide global understanding of the business data needs, while still representing the corporate policies.
- Data architecture allows strategic development of flexible modular designs by insulating the data from the business as well as the technology process.
- Architectures provide a framework for communication between the customer and service agent so the customer understands the scope, options, and prices of the products/services.

Without architecture, decentralization of control would produce chaos.

Enterprise-Level Data Architecture

Enterprise-level data architectures ensure that disintegration of integrated data stores is minimized. This ensures that current activity is sustainable while new development can take place. Using the same template also ensures that a foundation exists for the implementation of new techniques and technologies. It places tools and methods in relation to one another by virtue of an engineered framework. It also provides a way of quantifying risks and costing for or against implementing a new component of the architecture. All of these points are critical in modeling and developing a stable data warehouse, enterprise or otherwise.

References

Drucker, P. F. (1993). *Managing for the future: The 1990s and beyond.* Plume, New York, NY.

Kimball, R., Reeves, L., Ross, M., & Thornthwaite, W. (1998). *The data warehouse lifecycle toolkit: Expert methods for designing, developing, and deploying data warehouses.* John Wiley and Sons. New York, NY.

Keen, P. G. W., & Scott-Morton, M. S. (1978). *Decision Support Systems: An Organizational Perspective.* Reading, MA: Addison-Wesley.

Scott-Morton, M. S. (1991). *The corporation of the 1990's: Information technology and organizational transformation.* New York: Oxford University Press.

Nolan, R. L. (1979). *Managing the crisis in data processing.* Cambridge, MA: Harvard University Press, March–April.

Suggested Reading

Berson, A., & Smith, S. J. (1997). *Data warehousing, data mining, & OLAP.* New York: McGraw-Hill.

Bischoff, J., & Alexander, T. (1997). *Data warehouse, practical advice from the experts.* Upper Saddle River, NJ: Prentice Hall.

Nolan, R. L., & Croson, D. C. (1989). *Creative destruction: A six-stage process for transforming the organization.* Cambridge, MA: Harvard Business School Press.

18

DATA WAREHOUSES II

Reprise

In brief summary of the previous chapter, the discussion has been the evolution of the data warehouse from its early beginnings in reporting through its maturing stages of decision support and into the realm of the true data warehouse. In that chapter Keen and Scott-Morton and their exploration of the decision process within companies was discussed. The components of a decision were discussed. The responsibility of informational sharing was discussed as being put squarely on Information Technology's shoulders. There was a recap of how the report writers and query engines drove the effort to design report databases. Also noted in the discussions were the differences between warehouses and reporting databases.

Background

There is often a significant discussion concerning whether a data warehouse should be relational or dimensional. While there is no discussion necessary on whether the logical model will be relational, the concern often rests in whether the physical model would be relational or dimensional. Properly addressing the matter of dimensional modeling versus relational modeling requires a number of definitions and some fundamental facts about the organization's data and how they use it.

The Many Types and Levels of Data

There are three levels of decision making within an organization: operational, tactical, and strategic. While some of these levels feed one another, they each serve distinct purposes and have their own set of data. Operational data deals with day-to-day operations. Tactical data deals with near-term decisions. Strategic data deals with long-term decisions.

Likewise, process for decision making changes as one goes from level to level. At the operational level, decisions are structured. At the tactical level, decisions are semistructured. Strategic decisions are unstructured. Within each level of organization, there are minimally four different kinds of data: internally owned, externally acquired, self-generated, and derived. External data, such as competitive data, are purchased from outside agencies. Derived data are data that are mathematically created. Strategic data are generally comprised of internally owned and external data, roll-up hierarchies, and derived data.

Management-oriented data, which can fall in all of the categories of decision data (but predominantly the last two), focuses on management metrics. It often uses different grains of data, such as transactions, periodic snapshots, and summaries, which roll up to different levels. Management also requires cross-functional information. External data are often used to supplement internal data for management reports.

Most data today that are used for management decision purposes reside in a data warehouse. As you might suspect, warehouse data are not used for transaction processing and maintenance but for reporting and different forms of analysis, such as data mining. The warehouse is read-only, and the environment it functions in needs to be able to support a wide range of query types, such as ad hoc and standardized. The warehouse can be queried directly or used to supply extracts or additional data sources called marts.

Proper analysis and reporting require data from multiple relevant sources. These can be internal, external, self-reported, and even simulated data sources. The data must be vetted to ensure its quality. This means that it must be cleansed to produce data of good quality before being integrated into the warehouse. In order for the warehouse to be created in the most efficient manner, it should be designed by a formal process called modeling.

Data Modeling: Definitions

An *ER model* is a logical and graphical representation of the information needs of an organization. The objects of interest are gathered into exclusive groupings called entities. These groupings are assigned characteristics that describe them, called attributes. The identifier or key attribute is the most important one. Finally, one grouping or entity can be associated with another via a connection called a relationship.

A *logical model* is an ER representation of a business problem, without regard to implementation, technology, and organizational structure. The purpose of a logical model is to represent the business requirement completely, correctly, and concisely. A constraint of this type of model is that all redundancy is removed in order to focus purely on the business requirements and rules. A logical model is not implemented; instead, it is converted to a physical model against which optimizations are performed, and this is implemented. A *physical model* is the specification of what is implemented. Physical models should be optimized, efficient, and robust.

Logical to Physical Transformation

The conversion of a logical model to a physical model depends on many factors, including the size and complexity of the data, the complexity of the queries, and the number of users. The conversion from logical to physical models can vary in complexity, depending on the requirements. As shown in Figure 18.1, a logical model undergoes transformations as it progresses from a purely logical model to a physically implemented model.

The three forms of optimizations or compromises are nonrisk, risk-involved, and technical choices. A compromise is the emphasis of one feature, which becomes an advantage, against another feature, which then becomes a disadvantage. Another word for compromise in this case is called denormalization. Nonrisk denormalizations do not introduce redundancy or any integrity compromises. They merely combine or split entities. Risk-involved denormalizations do compromise integrity and/or nonredundancy. For example, one could store derived data, including individual summaries and aggregate tables; add redundant data and relationships; or replace natural keys with

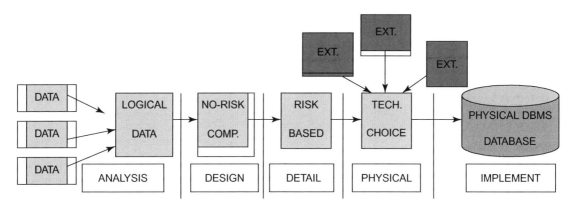

Figure 18.1 Progression from logical model to physically implemented model.

artificial/surrogate keys. Technical choices are DBMS-specific options, structures, or parameters. Most of these choices involve subtle compromises. For example, one could add indices, which can improve query performance but degrade load performance.

Entity Relational Models

Some practitioners from both the dimensional and corporate information factory camps use the term *ER model* incorrectly. They use it synonymously with a normalized model. For those who do so, there is a presumption that ER models are implemented directly as ER physical models, but in most situations they are not.

ER models are converted to physical models, and the physical models are implemented using denormalization techniques. An ER model can be used to represent any business problem domain. ER models can be logical or physical. Further, any logical model can be denormalized when it is implemented. The logical model represents the business information needs of the organization, independent of implementation. A physical model represents that which will be or is implemented, and is optimized.

Placement of Models

Figure 18.2 summarizes the placement of logical, physical, and dimensional data models in the overall spectrum of development. The logical (or ER) model and dimensional model do not cover the same development stage. The ER model is a logical model and represents the business. The dimensional model (offset in blue) is a predominantly physical model and must be an efficient design. A direct, judgmental comparison of the logical to dimensional is inappropriate, as would be that of apples and oranges.

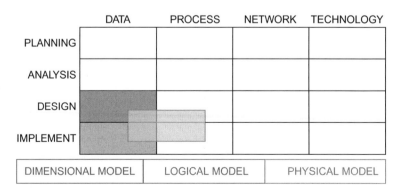

Figure 18.2 Placement of the dimensional, logical, and physical models.

Dimensional Modeling: Definitions

The purpose of a dimensional model is to improve performance by matching the data structure to the queries. The star schema concept arose out of the databases used to service query engines of the 1980s that required the data to be arrayed in such a manner as to facilitate expeditious processing, called the star schema. While it appears not to have any correspondence to the normal modeling concepts, it in fact does. These constructs have been highly denormalized and codified into the structure of the model such that it becomes a physicalized model that is designed for a specific set of questions to be answered.

It consists of a central fact table containing measures, surrounded by a perimeter of descriptor tables, called dimensions. In a star schema, if a dimension is complex or hierarchically leveled, it is compressed or flattened into a single dimension. This compression causes some redundancy, but does improve performance. An example of one is shown in Figure 18.3.

As noted before, star schema constructs include the following:

- Fact tables represent the set of facts (summable attributes, not descriptive attributes) at a specific level of granularity (detail) that the business area is concerned with.
- Dimension tables represent the implementation view of the access into the fact table. It often contains the keys and the descriptors of the data within the fact table as it pertains to the context of the dimension. Simply put, it is the embodiment of the access rules and path attribute values that allow specific perspective access to the fact table.
- Custom fact tables result when the granularity of a fact table is complex or of multiple levels and need to be separated from the original fact table.
- Custom dimension tables are the result of multiple specific conflicting business access views and result in the possible snowflake of dimensions.

Figure 18.3

Denormalization and the Dimensional Model

The process of systematic denormalization of models is reserved for physical models. The conclusion from this (and other discussions noted here) is that the star schema and snowflake schema are not logical models but physical models.

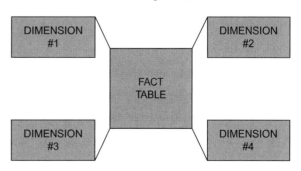

Dimensional Model Evaluation

Dimensional modeling has strengths and weaknesses, just as relational modeling does. In the reality of databases, there are three ways to improve performance: use better hardware, use better software, and optimize the data. Dimensional modeling uses the third method. The primary justification for dimensional modeling is to improve performance by structuring the data to compensate for the inefficiency of join processing

The secondary purpose is to provide a consistent base for analysis. Dimensional modeling does come with a price and with restrictions. There are times and places where dimensional modeling is appropriate and will work and other times and places where it is less appropriate and can actually interfere with the goals of a warehouse.

Data Evolution

The world makes up its own patterns, driven by dynamic forces generated from within and without. As a result, questions we may have now may or may not be stable. It is in this frame of reference that we enter to consider dimensional versus relational.

The dimensional model is based on the principle that information the user wants can be accessed best by structurally associating dimensions with facts. The premise for this is that most fundamental business questions are based on real business processes and thus are reasonably determinable and stable. It is also based on the belief that dimensionalized data allows better performance and is more user-friendly.

The relational model is based on the principle of fully expanded hierarchies, normalizing all business relevant data and eliminating redundancy. The premise for this is that if all data are defined, then business processes (currently known or otherwise) can be mapped against it. A second premise in the relational model is if the model is normalized, it can be denormalized to any degree necessary to get better performance.

What Are the Choices?

Oversimplifying it, it can be said that dimensional modeling requires all business processes to be known and driving the data from there and relational modeling requires all business data to be known and then defining the processes that use it. Chapter 20 discusses the enterprise data warehouse model. However, the following graphical depictions will help resolve any confusion and be more definitive than some of the more abstracted descriptions in that chapter.

Applicability of the Dimensional and Relational and Hybrid Models

We will cover all three types of the conceptual architecture in turn. The first is the relational.

Relational

It is often called the top-down approach, since it starts at the highest level of abstraction and goes downward with the increasing levels of complexity. I advocate it at a logical level but have reservations at lower, implementation levels. We will examine it from a data content level to see the impact of its implementation on business intelligence and analytics reporting.

Advantages associated with the relational architecture are as follows:

- It presents the entire enterprise's future data complement in one place at the atomic level, thereby eliminating data silos, including legacy data.
- It identifies business issues at the outset and provides a strategic view of data needed by the business across all functions.
- It allows identification of a broad scope of change across the enterprise, as well as providing a good foundation for risk assessment when business change or evolution is occurring.
- It provides, by artifact in the ETL, the entire source data inventory from all source systems and identifies decommission and life support candidates.

As you can see in Figure 18.4, the data from the source systems are extracted from the source systems or operational data stores and are ETL-ed (extract, translate, and loaded) into the staging area, where it is formatted, scrubbed, integrated, and loaded into the relational data warehouse. The data are loaded at the atomic level so operands can be executed against it to create higher levels of summary data for use in the data marts if required. The data are ETL-ed by subject area into subject area marts, where it can be queried and reported on. While Figure 18.4 assumes subject area orientation to the marts, it is not necessary to have them so. The marts or persistent view data repositories can be built to user specifications based on their business view requirements of the integrated data.

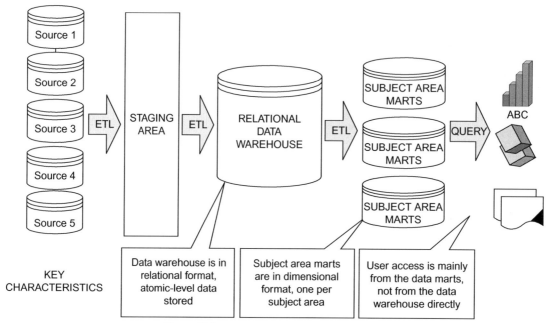

Figure 18.4

Some of the problems associated with the relational model from a business reporting perspective are as follows:

- It takes more time to build the entire structure before the user can experience the full benefit.
- The atomic-level data warehouse has to be built and then the data marts derived and populated from it.
- Cross-functional reporting is not possible until all the subject area data marts are developed.
- The modeling effort is duplicated. There is one effort to model the entire warehouse and then a second modeling effort to develop each of the subject area marts.
- There is a higher cost to develop the relational and it is larger and less agile. There are more physical objects and programs, and more databases, models, and ETL to build and maintain.
- There is a higher risk due to the long development cycle. The long delivery cycle creates problems due to not addressing natural business evolution and future business changes.
- In the relational scenario, governance means oversight of the architecture definition.
- The data collection process delays the introduction of data governance.
- The process requires enterprise-level data skills and business reengineering skills.

Dimensional Architecture

The second conceptual architectural model type is the dimensional architecture. It is often called the bottom-up approach, since it starts at the lowest level of detail and goes upward with the increasing levels of integration. This author advocates it at a physical level but has reservations at higher, more abstract levels. We will examine it from a data content level to see the impact of its implementation on business intelligence and analytics reporting.

Advantages of the dimensional model are as follows:

- There is a shorter delivery time for the warehouse. The analytical platform can be built sooner and provide value sooner.
- Cross-functional reporting is possible within the data warehouse once it is developed.
- The data modeling effort is done once. Additional modeling is not necessary unless the aggregates are desired.
- There are less complexity and fewer components. There are fewer databases objects and ETL streams to build and maintain.
- There is one single focal point for data governance.
- Prioritization is simple, since it addresses the business's pain points first.

As one can see, much like the relational architecture, the source system data is ETL-ed into a staging area, where it undergoes the scrubbing, cleansing, and validation necessary (Figure 18.5). It is stored at the atomic level as well. Where it differs from the relational architecture is that from the staging area it is *dimensionalized*—that is, it is separated into the data facts (the summable, aggregatable attributes) and the data dimensions (the perspective for viewing the data). Aggregations and specialized persistent data marts can be created from these facts and dimensions, but it is not necessary, since these can be done "on-the-fly." As you can see, there is one fewer ETL step in this architecture.

Some of the problems associated with the dimensional approach are as follows:

- The focused origination of the effort hampers efforts to expand scope. Once the initial projects are developed within a dimensional architecture, future influences of upcoming projects are sometimes thwarted for political and cultural reasons—and the effort can become stalled or stopped.
- The formalized dimensional approach is often perceived as a gating or policing action requiring standard conventions, thereby putting data governance at a disadvantage. This perception can be an additional reason that can hamper IT community buy-in and future attempts at expanded scope.

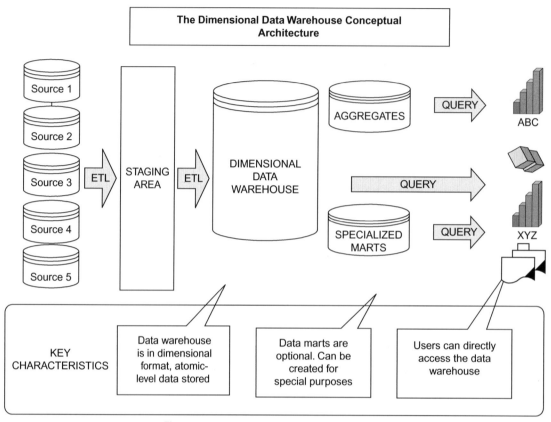

Figure 18.5

- Some business areas in need of improvement must wait or are overlooked. Some dimensional architects overlook potentially reusable efforts due to the lack of an integration architecture as they pursue their dimensional architecture.

Where Is the Relational Data Warehouse Best Suited?

- Where there is a lot of data scrubbing/massaging done on legacy source data
- When source systems have many data quality issues in existence
- Where business processes are not distinct and are overlapping
- Where the key purpose of the warehouse is operational reporting
- Where there is little transformation from relational source

- Where performance is not an issue
- Where analytical requirements are minimal—for example, drill down, aggregation, and so on

Where Is the Dimensional Best Suited?

- Where the data warehouse is needed to provide integrated data and thus support reporting and analytics
- Where persistent data repositories (data marts) are optional structures, required only for specialized reasons
- Where certain types of flexibility are needed
- Where the data warehouse needs to be developed from defined business processes, not specific reports
- Where the user is not required to know the reporting needs, only the grain and the facts involved in their business process

Hybrid ER-Dimensional

Hybrid ER-dimensional schema can be implemented for enterprise data warehouses. However, some fundamentals need to be discussed. First, these approaches must use an architecturally driven approach. Therefore, they will have a foundation within the corporate architectures and corporate data and process models. This foundation itself allows an enterprise to be more responsive to business needs as the enterprise expands to meet the competitive needs in the marketplace. Second, because it has a foundation in the corporate data model and process model, the key structures of the enterprise data warehouse are sympathetic to the operational data stores that are tapped to supply the data to the warehouse. Thus, it goes a long way in limiting data translation and data conflict resolution issues between business owners. And last, because it is linked to the corporate architecture, it will be driven by the same set of business drivers that the enterprise is facing. This minimizes the turnaround time of development, since the skeleton of the structure is known. This gives decision support data to the enterprise for rapid analysis when it needs it.

This author proposes a hybrid approach that chooses portions from each approach and modifying and merging them according to the specific needs of the organization. The hybrid structure will do the following:

- Provide a strategic data plan to define what is converted to dimensional, what remains legacy life support, and what is to be decommissioned. This is done by setting a broad scope at the beginning of the project and accomplishing a full inventory of the current default architecture.

- Specify and document with the business what issues need to be addressed at the enterprise level, thereby addressing the business's plan points first.
- Provide an integration architecture that sequences and prioritizes relational as well as dimensional efforts within the hybrid warehouse.
- Have immediate short-term impact and successes with implementation of dimensional structures.
- Support those areas that are not ready to be reengineered with a relational implementation (but will be considered in the future).
- Build enterprise-level scope and complexity gradually by integration every step of the way. It also allows the knowledge base to expand as each area is converted and integrated.

As you can see in Figure 18.6, the data are extracted from the source system and ETL-ed into a staging area. Some of the data are dimensionalized and are ET-ed into the dimensional data warehouse fact and dimension tables. Other data not yet

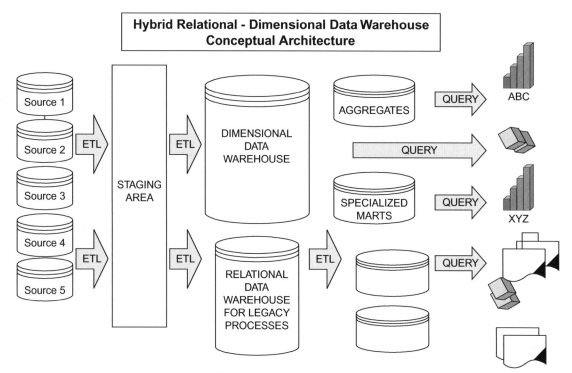

Figure 18.6

destined for conversion to dimensional are ETL-ed and stored in an atomic-level relational data warehouse for continued access under legacy conditions. As future projects for business intelligence and reporting are dimensionalized for the business user, the data will be ETL-ed into and integrated with the dimensional data warehouse. Reusability is ensured by the use of conformed dimensions. They are eliminated from the relational warehouse at this time and ETLs repointed to the original data source.

Problems Associated with the Hybrid Approach

The problems associated with the hybrid approach are few in nature but must be addressed:
- The primary objection is the establishment of the target enterprise data architecture to ensure integration.
- The secondary objection is that the current inventory needs to be established.
- There is no standard language to be utilized for mapping the current to future architecture.

All of these objections can be resolved with the utilization of commercially available solutions. I will address each of these in turn.

Target Enterprise Architecture

While there is no argument that an enterprise data architecture needs to exist for this and many other reasons, the development of an enterprise data architecture may be a long and costly exercise. One way of solving the dilemma is to purchase an industry standard model (as defined in the TOGAF enterprise architecture methodology) that has been tailored to our respective industry. Justifying it needs to be done to answer the question "Buy or build?"

Building an Enterprise Data Model

In order to justify the expense of purchasing an enterprise data model, there is a need to consider the cost justification logic for the "buy or build" decision for the enterprise data model. Here is some background information for that decision:
- Figures from Gartner and other similar research organizations regularly report that many enterprise modeling projects either

fail to deliver or only partially deliver due to business pressures. Starting with a prebuilt industry standard model greatly reduces risk of failure.

It is important to note that if the design of the enterprise data model is done internally, the following facts should be noted:

- According to firms like Gartner, most large companies building a large-scale enterprise or DW model find that it takes a team of several people 12 to 18 months to design a comprehensive enterprise data model. From a time perspective this makes a "buy" scenario more than justified. By simple calculations we can see what it would cost.

- Summary of possible build costs:
  This projects a build cost of [3 people $\times$ 375 person days $\times$ \$1,200/day (rough estimate for three enterprise data architects) = \$1,350,000].
  [This cost does not account for the cost of the business SME's time that is required to gather data and vett the model once developed, which would further lengthen the development time.]

- Internal enterprise modeling projects typically get bogged down in negotiations over definitions of entities and attributes, which often lead to data quality issues and (expensive) erroneous conclusions due to misinterpretation.

- An industry standard model provides unambiguous business definitions for all entities and attributes. This helps nontechnical businesspeople clearly understand the model and derive benefit from it. (More and more companies exploit the high-quality metadata further by flowing an enterprise data model through to their ETL and business intelligence tools so their staff can benefit from the clear and detailed definitions in the data sourcing and reporting environments when making decisions.)
  Additionally, it leverages any enterprise data governance effort that is being conducted by providing a model dictionary and metadata repository of all enterprise entities and attributes.

- Internally conducted enterprise data modeling projects will usually not incorporate outside experiences at other companies and risk continued propagation of existing information structures, which led to the requirement for the project in the first place. External models contain different industry perspectives.

- Purchased models can be used immediately, whereas an enterprise data model based upon internal designs typically must wait 12 to 18 months for design completion before it can be used.
  Most companies cannot afford the wait; just the cost of not being able to make better business decisions and plans for an extra 18 or more months dramatically outweighs the cost of the purchasable models.

There are over 50 commercial enterprise architecture packages available for review. Many of them are tailored for specific industries. Most of them avail themselves and integrate fully with the equally available ERP data models, such as those from SAP. Significant research has been made in this area by Jean-Paul Van Belle (2007) of the University of Cape Town, South Africa.

Current Data Inventory

In order to ensure that the enterprise model being developed or purchased meets the current and future needs of the organization, a current inventory of the models and processes that are being replaced needs to be documented. Admittedly, this would be done as a part of the build solution if that was chosen, but it would still take the same amount of time. A faster and easier way exists.

There are a significant amount of data design and modeling tools that allow reverse engineering of current data stores. Many of them have internal mapping tools that allow generation of relationships based on names and characteristics. While this is not a slam dunk solution, it will make short work of defining an entire data processing enterprise versus spending the 6 to 10 months of analytical work to produce a current application inventory down at the detail attribute level.

Some of the tools associated with this capability are ERwin, Embarcadero ER Studio, and Power Designer Data Architect, just to name a few. All will allow the tables and other physical objects to be reverse-translated to a logical model. Manual processes and spreadsheet data still need capture, and this has to be done the old-fashioned way.

Standard or Corporate Business Language

On the integration project, like master data management or data lineage definition or application and data consolidation, it is necessary to know what data you have, where it is located, and how it is related between different application systems. Software products exist today to move, profile, and cleanse the data. There are also products that address discovery and the debugging of business rules and transformation logic that mean they are different systems from one another.

If this is done manually, the data discovery process will require months of human involvement to discover cross-system data relationships, derive transformation logic, assess data consistency, and identify exceptions.

The data discovery products like Exeros and Sypherlink Harvester are software products that can mine both databases and applications to capture the data and metadata to define the core of a common business language and store it for actionable activity. It would take very little effort to turn the result into a corporate dictionary.

It is critical after the compilation that the accumulated result be opened up to all enterprise businesses to resolve and define data conflicts and definitional issues. Even this can be done expeditiously with the use of a Wikipedia-type tool that allows clarifications to be done in an open forum. This both accomplishes the standardization of the language and resolves issues, while educating the corporation as a whole.

Conclusion of Hybrid Approach

As noted, all of the exceptions to the hybrid approach can be addressed using automated tools. The goal is to provide a common enterprise integration model, a common business language, a relational enterprise warehouse for legacy application data awaiting transformation projects, and finally a dimensional reporting warehouse for those business applications identified as the most critical to be measured, monitored, and used for critical decision purposes.

References

Kimball, R., Reeves, L., Ross, M., & Thornthwaite, W. (1998). *The data warehouse lifecycle toolkit: Expert methods for designing, developing, and deploying data warehouses.* San Francisco, CA: John Wiley and Sons.

Van Belle, J. P. (2007). Evaluation of enterprise reference models. In: P. Fettke & P. Loos (Eds.), *Reference modeling for business systems analysis.* Herschey/London: Idea Publishing.

Suggested Reading

Berson, A., & Smith, S. J. (1997). *Data warehousing, data mining, & OLAP.* New York: McGraw-Hill.

Bischoff, J., & Alexander, T. (1997). *Data warehouse, practical advice from the experts.* Upper Saddle River, NJ: Prentice Hall.

19

DIMENSIONAL WAREHOUSES FROM ENTERPRISE MODELS

Dimensional Databases from Enterprise Data Models

Data warehousing is currently one of the most important applications of database technology and practice. A significant proportion of IT budgets in most organizations may be devoted to data warehousing applications. Although there is a high failure rate, high levels of user satisfaction and ROI have been reported about such applications. One of the most important issues in data warehouse is how to design appropriate database structures to support end-user queries.

Existing approaches to data warehousing design advocate an axiomatic approach where the structure of the data warehouse is derived directly from user query requirements. This chapter discusses a method for developing dimensional data warehouses based on an enterprise data model represented in entity relationship form. This is a more structured approach to data warehousing design and ensures the structure of the warehouse reflects the underlying structure of the data. It also leads to more flexible warehouse design, which makes it more responsive to change. And it is a surety that change will inevitably happen.

Warehouse Architecture

A data warehouse is a database that provides a single, consistent source of management information for reporting and analysis across the organization (Inmon, 1996; Love, 1994). Data warehousing forces a change in the working relationship between IT departments and users because it offers a self-service for the business model rather than the traditional report-driven model. In a data warehousing environment, end users access data directly using user-friendly query tools rather than relying on reports generally generated by IT specialists. This reduces user dependence on IT staff to satisfy information needs.

A generic architecture for a data warehouse consists of the following components:

- Operational application systems. These are systems that record the details of business transactions. This is the source of the data required for the decision-support needs of the business.
- External sources. Data warehouses often incorporate data from external sources to support analysis (purchased statistical data, raw market statistics data).
- ETL. These processes extract, translate, and load the data warehouse with data on a regular basis. Data extracted from different sources are consolidated, standardized, and reconciled with data in a common, consistent format.
- Enterprise data warehouse. This is the central source of decision-support data across the enterprise. The enterprise data warehouse is usually implemented using a traditional relational DBMS.
- User interface layer. This GUI layer provides a common access method against the enterprise data warehouse. Commonly this is where business intelligence tools are found.
- Persistent dimensionalized data repositories (data marts or, conversely, cubes). These represent the specialized outlets of the enterprise data warehouse, which provide data in usable form for analysis by end users. Data marts are usually persistent views tailored to the needs of a specific group of users or decision-making tasks. Data marts may be implemented using traditional relational DBMS or OLAP tools. Cubes are multiple-dimensional arrays that support the same type of analytical queries as data marts.
- Users. Users write queries and analyze data stored in data marts using user-friendly query tools.

Dimensional Modeling

From Ralph Kimball's (1996) perspective, the data warehousing environment is profoundly different from the operational one. Methods and techniques used to design operational databases are inappropriate for designing data warehouses. For this reason, Kimball proposed a new technique for data modeling specifically for designing data warehouses, which he called "dimensional modeling" (we touched on this in the previous chapter). The method was developed based on observations of practice and by vendors who were in the business of providing data in a user-friendly form to their customers.

Dimensional modeling, although not based on any specific scientific formula or statistical data occurrence theory, has obviously been very successful in practice. Dimensional modeling has been adopted as the predominant method for designing data warehouses and data marts in practice and, as such, represents an important contribution to the discipline of data modeling and database design.

In early works Kimball posited that modeling in a data warehousing environment is radically different from modeling in an operational environment and that one should forget all previous knowledge about entity relationship models:

> *Entity relation models are a disaster for querying because they cannot be understood by users and cannot be navigated usefully by DBMS software. Entity relation models cannot be used as the basis for enterprise data warehouses.*

It can be countered that the rigor in relational modeling is equally applicable to the warehouse context as it is in the operational context and provides a useful basis for designing both dimensional data warehouses and relational data warehouses.

Dimensional Model Concepts

There are two major differences between operational databases and data warehouses. The first is end-user access. In a data warehousing environment, users write queries directly against the database structure, whereas an operational environment makes users generally access the database from an application system front end. In a traditional application system, the structure of the database is unknown to the user.

The second is that the warehouse is read-only. Data warehouses are effectively read-only databases from which users can retrieve and analyze data. Data stored in a data warehouse is updated via batch load processes. The problem with using traditional database design methods in the data warehousing environment is that it results in complex database structures that are not easy for end users to understand and use. A typical operational database consists of hundreds of tables linked by a complex network of relationships.

Even quite simple queries require multitable joins, which are error prone and beyond the capabilities of nontechnical users. This is not a problem in OLTP systems because the complexity of the database structure is hidden from the user. Another major reason for the complexity of operational databases is the use of normalization.

Normalization tends to multiply the number of tables required, since it requires putting out functionally dependent attributes into separate tables. The objectives of normalization are to minimize data redundancy (Edgar Codd, circa 1970). This maximizes update efficiency because a change can be made in a single place. It also maximizes insert efficiency because there is only one place for the insert to be done. It does, however, penalize retrieval. Redundancy is less of an issue in a data warehousing environment because data are generally entered by batch loading, and this precludes trying to find the records for update.

The primary objective of dimensional modeling is to produce database structures that are easy for end users to understand and execute queries against. The secondary objective is to maximize the efficiency of the queries. It achieves these objectives by minimizing the number of tables and relationships between them. This reduces the complexity of the databases and minimizes the number of joins that require end-user query.

Review of Basic Components of Dimensional Models

Fact tables. In data warehousing, a fact table consists of the measurements, metrics, or data facts involved in a business process. It is often located at the center of a star schema surrounded by dimension tables. Fact tables provide the summarizable values that dimensional attributes are used to analyze. Fact tables are often defined by their granularity of detail or *grain*. The grain of a fact table represents the most basic level by which the facts may be defined and summarized.

A fact table typically has two types of columns: those that contain facts and those that are foreign keys to dimension tables. The primary key of a fact table is usually a composite key that is made up of all of its foreign keys. Fact tables contain the content of the data warehouse. Fact tables store different types of measures like additive, nonadditive, and semiadditive measures.

Dimension tables can be additive, nonadditive, or partially additive.

- Additive: measures that can be added across all dimensions
- Nonadditive: measures that cannot be added across all dimensions
- Partially additive: measures that can be added across some dimensions and not with others

A fact table might contain either detail-level facts or facts that have been aggregated. Fact tables that contain aggregated facts are called summary tables.

Differences between Dimension and Fact Tables

The question is often asked: What is the difference between a dimension table and a fact table? It is easiest to begin with an understanding of normalized data. Based on a relational system, we structured data for transactional systems (operational databases). Normalized data are held in a very simple structure. The data are stored in tables; each table has a key and contains certain data relating to another table. A normalized data table contains only data about the subject of the table.

When we need to make connections between the entities (tables), we use the keys to connect the two tables. We use a foreign key in one table to point to the primary key in the other table, and vice versa. One advantage of having data normalized is there is very little redundancy; each piece of data is stored once and only once.

In a dimensional model system, many of these rules go by the wayside. The fact tables contain the numerical measures whose attributes can be calculated or summed, and the dimension table contains the information about the ways in which we want to capture or view the data.

Dimension tables in particular are highly denormalized, so there is often massive data duplication. This is because we want to ensure that the users can get what they want from that particular table with the minimal amount of joins.

Dimension tables spell out the analysis that the users want to perform. Fact tables, on the other hand, contain numerical measures the users want to analyze. They are often called measure tables. In reality they are more than measures. Fact tables contain the context within which the measures are placed. A measure is a simple numerical value with a context applied to the data fact.

Star Schemas

The most basic building block used in dimensional models is the star schema. A star schema consists of one large central table called the fact table and a number of smaller tables called dimension tables that radiate from the central table. The fact table forms the center of the star and the dimension tables forms the points of the star. A star schema may have any number of dimensions:

- The fact table contains measurements that may be aggregated in various ways.
- The dimension table provides the basis for aggregating the measurements in the fact table.

Figure 19.1 A star schema.

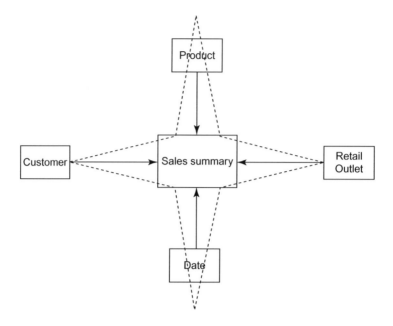

- The fact table is linked to the dimension tables by one-to-many relationships.
- The primary key of the fact table is the concatenation of the primary keys of all of the dimension tables.

A more concrete sample of a star schema is shown in Figure 19.1. In the example, sales data may be analyzed by product customer retail outlet.

Dimension tables are often highly denormalized tables and generally consist of embedded hierarchies. The advantage of using star schemas is that it reduces the number of tables in the database and the number of relationships between them, so the number of joins required in user queries is minimized. Ralph Kimball (1996) stated that the use of star schemas to design data warehouses results in 80 percent of queries being single-table browses. Star schemas may be implemented either in specialized tools or using a traditional DBMSs.

Star Schema Design Approach

The Kimball approach is an axiomatic approach that is based on the analysis of business process requirements. It begins by identifying business process, identifying the grain of the data, defining the relevant facts that need to be aggregated, defining the dimensional attributes to aggregate by, and then forming a star schema based on these. It results in the data warehouse design that is a set of discrete star schemas. However, there are some practical problems with this approach:

- User analysis requirements are unpredictable and subject to change over time, which provides an unstable basis for design.
- Sole use of business processes can lead to incorrect design because an unskilled designer may not understand the underlying relationships in the data.
- It may result in loss of information through aggregation, which limits the ways in which data can be analyzed.
- The approach is often represented by examples rather than via abstracted design principles.

The method reviewed here addresses these issues by using an enterprise data model as the basis for the warehouse. This uses the relationships in the data that have been documented and provides a much more structured approach to developing data warehouse design.

Enterprise Data Warehouse Design

This represents the foundation level of the data warehouse, which is used to supply data marts with the data. The most important requirement of the enterprise data warehouse is that it provides a consistent, integrated, and flexible source of data.

Most in the industry feel that traditional data modeling techniques (entity relationship modeling and normalization) are appropriate at this level. Normalized database design ensures maximum consistency and integrity of the data. It also provides the most flexible data structure. For example, new data can be easily added to the warehouse in a modular way, and database structure will support any analyst's analytical requirements. Aggregation or denormalization at this stage will lose information and restrict the kind of an analysis that can be carried out. An enterprise data model should be used as the basis for structuring the enterprise data warehouse.

Structure Design

Star and star-like schemas often represent the detail level of the data warehouse, where the data are accessed directly by end users. Data are extracted from the enterprise data warehouse and placed in these schemas to support particular analysis requirements. The most important requirement at this level is that the data are structured in a way that is easy for users to understand and use.

For this reason, dimensional modeling techniques are most appropriate at this level. This ensures the data structures are as simple as possible in order to simplify user queries. The following section describes a technique for developing dimensional models from an enterprise data model.

Categorize the Entities

The first step in producing a dimensional model from an entity relational model is to categorize the entity entities into three classes:

- Kernel or core entities. Kernel or core entities document details about particular events that occur in the business—for example, orders, insurance claims, salaries, payments, and hotel bookings. It is these events that decision makers want to understand and analyze. The key characteristics of kernel or core entities are that:
  - They describe an event that happens at a point in time.
  - They contain measurements or quantities that may be summarized (hours, pounds, gallons).
- For an example, a dental insurance claim records a particular business event and the amount claimed.
- Kernel or core entities are the most critical entities in a data warehouse and form the basis for creating fact tables and star schemas. Not all kernel or core entities will be of interest for decision support, so user input will be required in identifying which entities of this type are important.
- Detail entities. A detail entity is one which is directly related to a kernel or core entities via a one-to-many relationship. Detail entities define the specifics of each business transaction. Detail entities answer the who, what, when, where, how, and why of the business event. For example, a sales transaction may be defined by a number of specific detail entities:
  - Customer: who made the purchase
  - Product: what was sold
  - Location: where was it sold
  - Time frame: when was it sold
- An important detail of any transaction is time. Historical analysis is an important part of any data warehouse. Detail entities form the basis for constructing dimension tables in the star schema.
- Dependent entities. Dependent entities are entities that are related to detail entities by a chain of one-to-many relationships. That is, they are functionally dependent on a detail

entity either directly or in a transitive manner. Dependent entities represent dependency chain (hierarchy) participants within the data model, which may be collapsed into detail entities to form dimension tables in a star schema.

When there are situations where entities fit into multiple categories, there is an ordered set rules for resolving the confusion. The ordered set of rules are:

- Categorize the entity as kernel or core entity first. If not kernel, then
- Categorize the entity as a dependent entity. If not dependent, then
- Categorize the entity as a detail entity.

For example, if an entity can be classified as either a dependent or a detail entity, it should be classified as a dependent entity. Always categorize at the highest level available.

In practice, some entities will not fit into any of these categories. If this is the case, these entities are not consequential to the hierarchical structure of the dimensional model and should not be included in star schemas. Taking the resulting model, perform the following step.

Identify Dependency Chains

Dependence chains are an extremely important concept in dimensional modeling and form the primary basis for deriving dimensional tables from the entity relationship model. As discussed previously, most dimensional tables in star schemas contain embedded dependency chains. A dependency chain in an entity relationship model is any sequence of entities joined together by one-to-many relationships aligned in the same direction. For example, Figure 19.2 is a dependency chain: state is a parent entity, region is a child of state, sales location is a child of region, and so on. Normally we would see this vertically, but it is truly omnidirectional if read by the relationships.

- State is a parent entity.
- Region is a child of state.
- Sale location is a child of region.
- Sale is a child of sale location.
- Sale item is a child of sale.

An entity is called a terminal entity if it is at the end of a dependency chain and an originating entity if it is at the start of one. Terminal entities can easily be identified, since they are the entities with no one-to-many relationships. Originating entities are entities with no many-to-one relationships (or root entities).

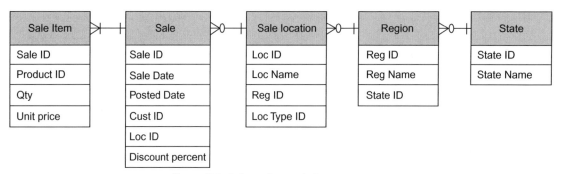

Figure 19.2 A dependency chain.

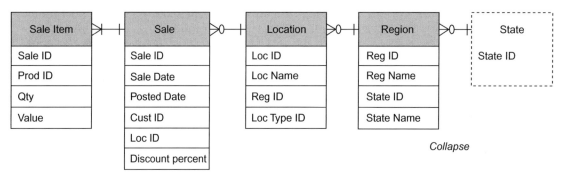

Figure 19.3 Collapsing a state entity.

Produce Dimensional Models

We use two separate operations to produce dimensional models from entity relationship models:

- Operation one: Collapse data dependency chains. Parent-level entities can be collapsed into child-level entities within a dependency chain. Figure 19.3 shows a state entity being collapsed into the region entity. The region entity contains its original attributes plus the attributes of the collapsed table. This introduces redundancy in the form of transitive dependency, which violates Codd's third normal form. Collapsing a dependency chain is therefore for a form of denormalization.

  Figure 19.4 shows a region being collapsed into a location. We can continue doing this until we reach the last kernel entity of the dependency chain and end up with two tables—in this case sale and sale item. An argument could be made for collapsing up sale item into sale, but the volume of sale item might preclude it by introducing too much redundancy.

- Operation two: aggregation. The aggregation operation can be applied to a terminal or originating entity to create a new

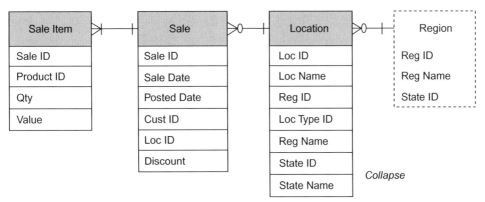

Figure 19.4 Region entity "collapsed" into a location.

entity containing summarized data. A subset of attributes is chosen from the source entity to aggregate (aggregation attributes) and another subset of attributes chosen to aggregate by (grouping attributes).

Aggregation attributes must be numerical quantities. For example, we could apply the aggregation operation to the sale item entity to create a new entity called product sold summary. This aggregated entity shows for each product: total sales amount [quantity × price], the average quantity per order, and the average price per item on a daily basis. The aggregation attributes are quantity and price, while the grouping attributes are product ID and date. The key of this entity is the combination of the attributes used to aggregate by (grouping attributes). It must be clearly understood that the aggregation process loses information. We cannot reconstruct the details of the individual sale items from the product sold summary entry.

Options for Dimensional Design

There are several options for producing dimensional models from entity relationship models that have been created thus far:

- Creation of a flat table schema
- Creation of a stepped table schema
- Creation of a simple star schema
- Creation of a snowflake schema
- Cluster existing star schemas

Each of these options represent different trade-offs between complexity and redundancy. Here we discuss how the collapsing dependency chains and aggregation operators previously defined may be used to produce different dimensional model.

The Flat Table Schema

A flat table schema is the simplest scheme possible without losing information. This is created by collapsing all entities in the data model down to into the terminal entities. This minimizes the number of tables in the database and therefore minimizes the possibility that joins will be needed in end-user queries. In a flat schema we end up with one table for each terminal entity in the original data model. Such a schema is analogous to the flat files used when using statistical packages such as SAS. The structure does not lose any information from the original data model. Unfortunately, it contains massive redundancy in the form of transitive and partially dependent dependencies but does not involve any aggregation.

One problem with the flat table schema is that it leads to aggregation errors when there are dependency relationships between kernel entities. When we collapse a numerical amount from higher-level kernel entities into another, they will be repeated in the sample data model if a sale is comprised of three sale items. The discount amount will be stored in three different rows in the sale item table. Adding the discount amounts together as we summarize results in triple counting.

Another problem with flat schemas is that they tend to result in tables with large numbers of attributes increasing the row length. While the number of tables is minimized, the complexity of each table is increased. This is not the best solution, but it can be made to work in certain situations.

The Stepped Table Schema

A stepped table schema is formed by collapsing entities down the dependency chain, stopping when they reach a kernel entity. This results in a single table for each kernel entity in the data model. Figure 19.5 shows a stepped table schema resulting from the sample data model. The stepped table schema is commonly used to create reporting databases. This option does not confuse an inexperienced user because a separation between the levels of kernel entities is explicitly shown.

Simple Star Schemas

A star schema can easily be derived from an entity relationship model. Each star schema is formed in the following way:
- A fact table is formed for each kernel entity. The key of the table is the combination of the keys of its associated detail entities.

Figure 19.5 A stepped table schema.

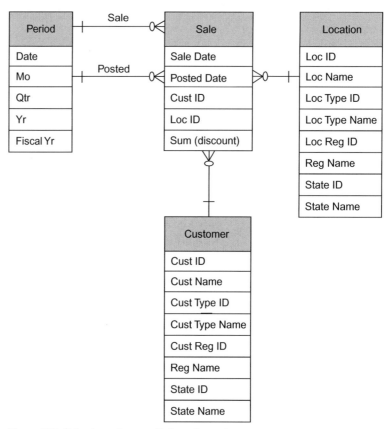

Figure 19.6 Sale star schema with four dimensions.

- A dimension table is formed for each detail entity by collapsing related dependent entities into it.
- Where dependent relationships exist between kernel entities, the child entity inherits all of the dimensions (and key attributes) from the parent entity.
- Numerical attributes within kernel or core entities should be aggregated by key attributes.

Figure 19.6 shows a star schema that results from the sales kernel or core entity. This star schema has four dimensions, each of which contains embedded dependency chains. The aggregated fact is discount amount.

Figure 19.7 shows the star schema that results from the sale item kernel entity. This star schema has five dimensions: four dimensions from its parent kernel entity (sale) and one of its own (product). The aggregated facts are quantity and item cost (quantity × price).

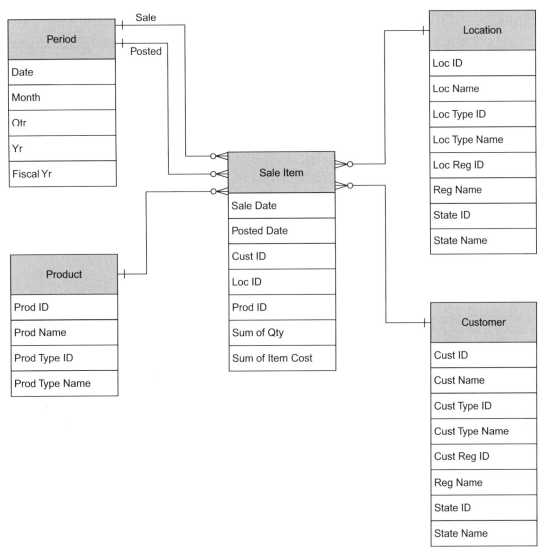

Figure 19.7 Star schema from sale item kernel entity.

A separate star schema is produced for each kernel table in the original model. The multiple star schemas that result can be related by keyed relationships between the kernel entities following the normal key propagation rules defined in ER modeling (i.e., the primary key of the originating kernel is propagated as a foreign key to the dependent kernel). It also can be related to existing or external data marts in the same way. While there is no official name for this, it can be considered a special type of extended star schema, since it represents a connected lattice of star schemas.

Snowflake Schemas

In a star schema, dependency chains in the original data model are collapsed or denormalized to form dimension tables. Each dimension table may contain multiple independent dependency chains. A snowflake schema is a star schema with all dependencies explicitly shown. A snowflake schema can be formed from a star schema by expanding out (normalizing) the dependencies in each dimension. Alternatively, a snowflake schema can be produced directly from the entity relationship model by the following procedure:

- Form a fact table for each kernel entity. The key of the table is a combination of the keys of the associated detail entities.
- Form a dimension table from each detail entity.
- Where dependency chain relationships exist between kernel entities, the child entity inherits all relationships into the detail entities (and key attributes) from the parent entity.
- Numerical attributes within the kernel entity should be aggregated by the key attributes. The attributes and functions used depend on the application.

Star Schema Clusters

My opinion is that neither pure star schema (which are fully collapsed dependency chains) nor the pure snowflake schema (fully expanded dependency chains) is the best solution. As in many design problems, the optimal solution is a compromise between the two options.

The problem with fully collapsing dependency chains is that it can lead to redundancy between dimensions when they are collapsed if there are shared dimensions. This can result in confusion for users, increased complexity in ETL processes, and inconsistent results from queries.

In the interest of clarity on this subject, shared dimensions can be identified by splits within dependency chains. A split occurs when an entity acts as a parent in two different dimensional dependency chains. This results in the entity and all of its ancestors being collapsed into two separate dimension tables. Split entities can be identified as dependent entities with multiple one-to-many relationships. On occasion they converge again lower down. This author refers to them as propagated dependency chains.

In the sample data model shown in Figure 19.8, a split occurs at the region entity. Region is the parent of both Location and Customer, which are both detail entities of the sale entity. In the star schema representation, State and Region would be included in both the location and customer dimensions when the hierarchies are collapsed. The result is an overlap or sharing between dimensions.

This author defines a star schema cluster as one which has the smallest number of tables while avoiding overlap between

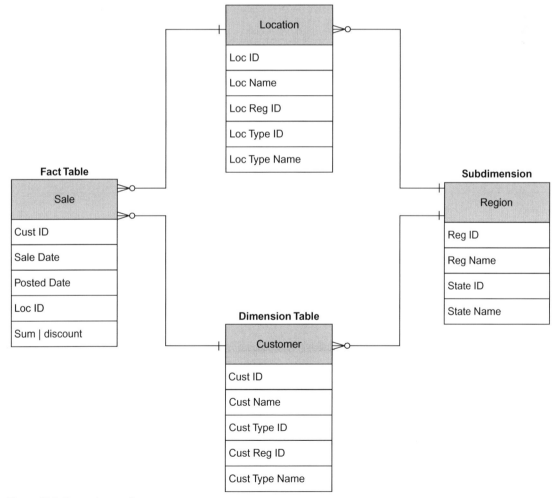

Figure 19.8 Star schema cluster.

dimensions. It is a star schema that is selectively snowflaked to separate out dependency chains or subdimensions that are shared between different dimensions. These subdimensions represent a shared bridge between dimensions.

I define a star schema cluster may be produced from an entity relationship model by using the following procedure. Each star schema cluster is formed by the following steps:

- Form a fact table for each kernel entity. The key of the table is a combination of the keys of the associated detail entities.
- Collapse dependent entities down their dependency chains until they reach a split entity or detail entity. If a split entity is reached, then a subdimension or shared dimension table should be formed. Collapsing should begin again after the split entity. When a detail entity is reached, a full dimension table should be formed.
- Where dependent relationships exist between kernel entities, the child entity inherits all dimensions (and key attributes) from the parent entity.
- Numerical attributes within a kernel entity should be aggregated by the key attributes (dimensions).

Iterate to Refine the Design

In practice, dimensional modeling is a cyclic process. The star clustering procedure described in step three is useful for producing an initial design but will need to be refined to produce the final design. Most of these refinements have to do with further simplifying the model. Some basic forms for refinement are as follows:

- Combine fact tables. Fact tables with the same primary keys (i.e., the same dimensions) should be combined. This reduces the number of star schemas and facilitates comparison activity between related facts.
  - Combine dimension tables. Creating dimension tables for each detail entity often results in a large number of dimension tables. In order to simplify the structure, related dimensions can be consolidated together into a single dimension table.
  - Resolve many-to-many relationships. Most of the complexities that arise in converting a traditional entity relationship model to a dimensional model result from many-to-many relationships or intersection entities. Many-to-many relationships cause problems in dimension modeling because they represent a break in the dependency chain and cannot be collapsed.
  - Two options exist for dealing with many-to-many relationships: (1) ignore the intersection entity, or (2) convert the

many-to-many relationship to a one-to-many relationship by defining a predominant relationship.

- Handling subtypes. Super type–subtype relationships can be converted to a hierarchical structure or by moving the subtypes and creating a dependent entity to distinguish between subtypes. This can then be converted to a dimensional model in a straightforward manner.

Review of the Process

The preceding method is useful for developing a dimensional data warehouse design from an enterprise data model. These are the basic steps:

- Develop or purchase an enterprise data model.
- Design an enterprise data warehouse. This will be closely based on enterprise data model but will be a subset of the model, which is relevant for decision-support purposes. A staged, accretive (project subject area by project subject area) approach is recommended for implementing the enterprise data warehouse, starting with the most important subject areas.
- Classify entities: classify all entities in the enterprise data model as either kernel, detail, or dependent entity.
- Identify dependency chains: identify the dependency chains that exist in the enterprise data model.
- Design a data warehouse: develop star schemas or clustered star schemas for each kernel entity in the enterprise data model. Each clustered star schema will consist of a fact table and a number of dimension and subdimension tables. This minimizes the number of tables while avoiding overlap between dimensions.

Review of Design Options

In summary there are a range of options for developing dimensional data warehouse models to support end-user queries from an enterprise data model. These options represent different trade-offs between the number of tables (complexity) and redundancy of data. The advantages of this approach to model translation are as follows:

- It ensures that data in the enterprise data warehouse reflect the underlying relationships in the data.
- It develops data warehouse designs based on a common enterprise data model and simplifies the ETL processes.
- An existing enterprise data model provides a useful basis for identifying information requirements in a top-down manner based on what data exists in the enterprise. This can usually

be combined with the bottom-up dimensional analysis to provide a hybrid approach.

- An enterprise data model provides a more stable basis for design and user queries which may be unpredictable and subject to frequent change. This approach also ensures flexibility in the enterprise data warehouse to support the widest span of analytical requirements by storing data at the most appropriate level.
- It maximizes the integrity of data stored in an enterprise data warehouse.

This one method, although not simple, can provide some guidance to designers of data warehouses when working from a defined enterprise data architecture.

Detail analysis by the architect or designer is still required to identify the entities in the enterprise data model that are relevant for decision making and the classification of them. However, once this has been completed, the development of the dimensional model can take place.

Using an entity relationship model of the data provides a better starting point for developing dimensional models than starting from a purely dimensional analytical modeling approach based on the identified business process.

References

Inmon, W. (1996). *Building the data warehouse* (2nd ed.). New York: John Wiley & Sons.

Kimball, R. (1996). *The data warehouse toolkit*. New York: John Wiley and Sons.

Kimball, R. (1997, August). *A Dimensional Manifesto*. New York: John Wiley and Sons.

Love, B. (1994). *Enterprise information technologies*. New York: Van Nordstrom Reinhold.

Suggested Reading

Chen, P. P. (1976, March). The entity relationship model: Towards an integrated view of data. *ACM Transactions on Database Systems, 1*(1), 9–36.

Codd, E. F. (1970, June). A relational model of data for large shared data banks. *Communications of the ACM, 13*(6), 377–387.

Devlin, B. (1997). *Data warehouse: From architecture to implementation*. Reading, MA: Addison-Wesley.

Halpin, T. (1995). *Conceptual schema and relational database design: A fact oriented approach*. Sydney: Prentice Hall.

20

THE ENTERPRISE DATA WAREHOUSE

As we've said before, 20 years ago, a new field was created that came to be known as *enterprise architecture*. The goal initially was to address two problems: application complexity (organizations were spending more and more money building IT applications) and poor business alignment (organizations were finding it more and more difficult to keep increasingly expensive IT systems aligned with the business needs). From the business perspective, it was more cost, less value.

The problems that were recognized two decades ago have today reached a crisis point. The cost and complexity of IT systems have exponentially increased, while the ability of deriving real value from those systems has decreased. Today's bottom line to the business is even more cost, even less value. Large organizations can no longer afford to ignore these issues. The field of enterprise architecture that 20 years ago seemed to be an abstract research exercise has become a critical necessity.

Over the last decade, IT management visionaries have interceded to bring order to the chaos that ensued as businesses became more competitive and data became the primary business driver. Their first step was reestablishing the control of a central IT management organization over computing resources. Their second step was the dedication of one or more staff to a formal architecture program.

Enterprise Data Warehouses

In order to stay competitive, an enterprise must continue to meet and exceed both the internal and external customers' needs. The enterprise needs to increase its competitive agility, and in order to do so, the CIO of the enterprise must respond by dropping the traditional role of simply managing the business-technology interface.

Today's CIO, as well as most of the IT organizations in the enterprise, should see themselves evolving into the new role of improving corporate performance. To achieve business objectives that will meet and exceed the need, the CIO must work side by side with business executives to rethink and reinvent how the company can innovatively anticipate and respond to changes in the market.

It is an ongoing effort (or a program, if you will) to measure, analyze, innovate, and implement. Then do it again, applying what you learned from the last cycle. Then do it again, and again, and so on. During this cyclical effort, the CIO and IT must leverage the company's data assets for the betterment of the entire enterprise. Applications may come and go, but data are here to stay, and data are the drivers of every modern business. It all boils down to a single, complex question: "Do we have the data that will tell us what has occurred in the past, what is happening now, and what is likely to happen in the future to our enterprise?"

Information technology is responsible for providing the data basis for key metrics and indicators such as revenue growth, margin improvement, and asset efficiency at both the enterprise and division levels. Simply put, data are the foundation for operating a business. It must be available from a secure source, at the right time, and in the right format. A repository like this is called an enterprise data warehouse. The key requirements for this enterprise data foundation include the following:

- Data that are relevant across the enterprise
- Trusted, accurate data that produce consistent answers
- Cross-functional enterprise analytical capability

When an enterprise data warehouse is proposed as a solution to the business needs that are present, the responses are already forethought, and I am sure we have all heard them before. For example, some typical responses are, "We tried this before and failed." "We are already spending too much for resources on IT. Why spend more?" "Nothing is broken, so there is nothing to fix." "What will [the enterprise warehouse] give me that I don't have or can get now?"

All of these responses can be addressed by ensuring that:

- Business sponsors understand the role that data play in their business and that their partnership with IT is essential to the future success of the enterprise.
- An enterprise architect presents a solid plan as to how EDW fits into the company's overall IT environment and architecture.
- Tactical data warehousing and data integration projects are implemented in sequence, with the focus being integration. This builds the overall EDW infrastructure, thereby providing value to the business while the enterprise warehouse is under development.

Why Would You Want an Enterprise Data Warehouse?

An enterprise data warehouse is a strategic repository that provides analytical information about the core operations of an enterprise. It is distinct from traditional data warehouses and marts, which are usually limited to departmental or divisional business intelligence. An enterprise data warehouse (EDW) supports enterprise-wide business needs and at the same time is critical to helping IT evolve and innovate while still adhering to the corporate directive to "provide more functionality with less investment."

Organizations that implement enterprise data warehouse initiatives can expect the following benefits:

- It provides a strategic weapon against the competition. The data that are needed to beat the competition to market are universally accessible in the structure needed to make agile business decisions.
- It addresses data governance and data-quality issues that profoundly limit the operational and strategic use of the cross-functional data. It also eliminates redundant purchasing of data.
- It addresses compliance requirements by validating and certifying the accuracy of the company's financial data under Sarbanes-Oxley and other compliance requirements.
- It improves alignment between IT and their business partners by enabling IT to deliver multiple initiatives, including data warehousing, data integration and synchronization, and master data management. These are all developed from the same data, and all of it can be propagated and reused for other purposes.
- It ensures cross-functional and cross-enterprise collaboration by guaranteeing that data are provided with relevant business context and meaning. A definitive meaning is ascribed for each context (i.e., there may be multiple defined "market baskets," but each will be identified clearly by name and use).
- It increases business productivity by leveraging integrated data for business decision queries and reports, thereby reducing delivery costs and time.

Enterprise Data Warehouse Defined

An enterprise data warehouse is a common data foundation that provides any and all data for business needs across applications and divisions. Enterprise data warehousing is the program that consists of designing, building, and managing an EDW to meet the requirements of the consuming applications.

What Are the Important EDW Driving Forces?

- Presence of business-relevant data across the enterprise. An EDW allows organizations to access, discover, and integrate data from virtually any business system, in any format.
- Universal data access by the business. Studies have shown that significant amounts of project time and effort are spent on gaining access to appropriate data. Operational and application reporting data are housed in a multitude of applications and storage media. Universal data access to data in one place provides one-stop shopping for the business.
- Data services mechanism for neutral access. To enable flexible reuse of data assets, a data services front end is a logical abstraction layer between data sources and consuming applications. This absence of fixed connection frees the EDW to serve multiple downstream applications. It also allows flexibility and adaptation should requirements change or new consumers emerge.
- Metadata management for business consistency. Data flows, data relationships, and the business context and definitions for data are often poorly documented. Attempts to integrate data without a foundation for governance create rework or manual analysis and coding. Metadata management can provide visibility to enterprise data and relationships across all types of applications and systems.
- Presence of trusted, accurate data. An EDW equips organizations to manage data quality in a programmatic manner. Maintaining data integrity and security across extended groups throughout the data life cycle is required to meet the governance and compliance objectives.
- Data quality. An EDW improves data quality. The presence of poor data quality is a costly issue. Findings from a recent survey found that over 65 percent of those surveyed reported significant problems as a result of defective data:
  - More than 50 percent had incurred extra costs as a result of the need for internal reconciliations.
  - Thirty-three percent had been forced to delay or scrap new systems. Data quality must be approached as a program. Integrated data quality, including data profiling, scrubbing/matching, and remediation, is critical to enhancing the accuracy and value of data assets.
- Data lineage. An EDW enables an enterprise to predict, assess, and manage the impact of change to enterprise data with a map of data dependencies.

To see what can potentially happen with the implementation of a data warehouse, I have provided a parable. It is a combination of many case studies that obscures the origin of each organization.

Case Study: An Enterprise Data Warehouse Practical Parable

A hypothetical telecommunication service provider went through profound growth as a result of mergers and acquisitions (let's say 30 of them in 7 years). The result was a patchwork of silo-type applications cobbled together across the many merged entities.

The company was unable to provide near real-time operational data consistently. The "daily reporting" often took more than a day, and changing reports often required significant analysis and development, sometimes months. Access to new information from other operating entities of the merged organizations was nearly impossible without coding new interface applications. Data quality was a major issue. There were no consistent governance and data standards. Furthermore, because of the lack of reuse and standardization, each application was addressed in a one-off manner.

Solution

After acquiring an Industry Standard model they enriched it with their unique specifications that varied from the Industry Standard Enterprise Model. From this Enterprise Model, they developed an enterprise data warehouse to address these problems they had been faced with. The company consolidated the silos and created a common framework for managing the data. Their vision was to move toward a single Source (emphatically not a "version") of truth and to provide relevant business reporting across the enterprise in a timely manner. They consolidated multiple reporting warehouses and data marts. They also used metadata at the core of their EDW to standardize common business terminologies, to ensure reuse of data and logic, and to deliver a common view of data.

Their results were remarkable. The EDW enabled the company to analyze all aspects of business by tracking key metrics and performance indicators. As a result of the first phase of EDW deployment, the company improved service levels in daily reporting from days to hours or less, and reduced the small project delivery time from several months to several weeks.

In addition, with the EDW, the company enhanced enterprise data access to the point where they could forecast revenues and staffing for all divisions. Executive officers, compliance management, and internal audit now had access to data-quality dashboards that tracked data-quality indicators against targets.

The EDW improved data integrity by enforcing robust security. Enterprise-wide data standards and a common, reusable technology infrastructure enabled faster application development, testing, and roll-out. With the EDW, the company increased visibility across numerous operational entities and now had the agility to respond to new business requirements and opportunities as they arose.

Some parts of this parable will ring true with each and every enterprise out there that does not have an established enterprise data architecture and enterprise data warehouse. Examine a sample of case studies, and this will be verified by them.

The Best Practices for EDW Implementation

To establish information as a shared asset across the enterprise, IT needs to follow best practices in implementing their enterprise data warehouse:

- Analyze the volatility and the commonality of data to determine data reusability. Certain types of data are used by specific applications and should not be considered enterprise data. Other types of data, such as customer data, are relevant across the business and should be treated as master data. Similarly, most transactional data attributes have no use beyond the context of the specific transaction, whereas master data or reference data need to persist and be controlled over time.
- Utilize a staged, incremental approach that shows business returns at each step. It is important to demonstrate the flexibility of the architecture by targeting specific areas and taking a least disruptive implementation approach. A good start is to restructure and reuse legacy data in the new environment. The use of metadata and standard practices ensures that the complete solution can be built by accretion, without compromising architectural integrity and flexibility.
- Approach data modeling and business process analysis from an enterprise perspective. Enterprise data warehouses require newer methods such as business process modeling to enable businesses to leverage the warehouse data in better and more powerful ways.
- Establish enterprise standards and data governance. The business agility, reuse of data, or business logic is worthless or, at best, rapidly obsolescent if IT does not adhere to governance and standards. In addition, IT has to put in place competency

centers to make sure that the various business divisions and IT groups working with an enterprise data warehouse follow a common set of procedures and techniques, ensuring consistency and manageability of the overall environment.

Enterprise Data Architecture Implementation Methods

For any organization, what will happen after the decision to build an enterprise data architecture depends on the approach taken. From the architectural point of view, a bottom-up approach involves setting the infrastructure standards and introducing governance processes to ensure adherence to those standards, while a top-down approach involves a formal analysis of the current state with respect to business process, application programs, data, and technology components.

Both approaches require senior management commitment and mark the first step of a journey toward changing how IT communicates, makes decisions, and engages in planning. Both approaches also promise an improved relationship with the business as technological planning is integrated with business planning. While there is no argument that an EA needs to exist, following are some of the benefits and drawbacks of each method.

The Top-Down Approach

The most positive aspects of the top-down approach, in order of importance, are that it does the following:

- Establishes a clear view of the existing environment in the beginning. The initial data collection activity enables a consensus regarding the current state environment, which is a critical component for defining the target solution.
- Emphasizes business issues at the outset. The top-down approach explicitly concerns improving the business. Technology plays a supportive role as the enabler of the business.
- Establishes a broad scope at the outset. There is a broad scope in the top-down approach. With the appropriate management support, all areas in need of improvement become subject to the EA program's efforts. Negative aspects of the top-down approach are that:
  - Top-down methods can be overly abstracted and not be impactful. The formal approach and broad scope require upfront training, process definition, and communication

efforts to launch the program. Conceptual frameworks and broad-based models for enterprise-wide involvement must be created. The team then must engage in the time-consuming data collection process to establish the current state. This can result in high expectations for enterprise-wide impact. In fact, there probably will be little impact in the first year of the program's existence. It is very difficult to maintain organizational focus and commitment over a long time.

- The data collection and mapping process delays the implementation of governance. In the top-down approach, governance means oversight of the architecture. Many top-down EA programs delay the introduction of governance processes that could influence design and technology selection, resulting in missed opportunities.

- The formal methodology requires a knowledge base to get started. Few organizations currently have the internal staff that understand the formal approach to EA. Training is required, both for the EA group and for the business and IT community that participate in the processes.

- The methodology requires business process reengineering skills. The creation of a business process inventory and the focus of eliminating redundancy and reengineering the current state require that the EA team have the expertise to draw important conclusions from the analysis of the current architecture data.

The Bottom-Up Approach

Positive aspects of the bottom-up approach are as follows:

- The method can have significant impact immediately. Given the appropriate authority by the CIO and integrating the technology architecture in a straightforward manner, sufficiently motivated organizations can implement a solution in 6 to 12 months. This can translate to millions in cost savings and cost avoidance.

- Early successes build credibility rapidly. Early wins start the EA effort off on the right foot and build credibility for the more politically complex efforts that follow.

- Problems are undertaken in priority sequence. The potentially overwhelming scope of an EA effort is simplified in a bottom-up approach. The biggest problem is attacked first, then the next, then the next, and so on. This can lead to significant early successes.

- Scope and complexity of the architecture and model build gradually. Bottom-up allows technologists and managers to learn as they go. Success is more likely when the problems are encountered in small size rather than trying to manage a large, complex scope from the beginning.
- A large central EA team is not needed to start. Creating a base architecture usually involves a central project manager and the borrowed expertise of internal SMEs. There is no need for funding additions to staff to create the EA group until the project has garnered credibility.
- The technology-oriented starting point can facilitate the effort. Many organizations can implement technology standardization efforts without reading EA textbooks, becoming familiar with abstract EA concepts, or even calling the project EA. Technology standardization often saves significant dollars.
- Standardization savings can help justify governance processes. Governance processes are often politically difficult to implement. When technology standardization and consolidation have yielded significant savings, management can be persuaded to review and participate in other technology choices and projects.

Negative aspects of the bottom-up approach are as follows:

- The IT infrastructure origination of the effort often impedes efforts to expand scope. Once the infrastructure-based EA group has cleaned up technology standards and attempts to broaden its scope, it is often blocked from influencing other development staff for political and cultural reasons.
- A standards-based approach emplaces governance as a policing activity. The most typical introduction of governance is via a board that reviews projects and designs and rejects nonstandard approaches. This makes architects the villains and can hamper business community buy-in and future attempts at expanded scope.
- The technology orientation appears to ignore business issues. Governance processes introduced to prevent the introduction of nonstandard technology don't please application developers or business project sponsors.
- Some areas that are in need of much improvement must wait. Bottom-up architects often perceive more clearly the problems that remain rather than the positive accomplishments they have made. The business can get frustrated watching the next technology problem being created because of the lack of an overall application or integration architecture as the technical architecture is being pursued.

Your Choices

Based on these review points, if you need to:
- Standardize your infrastructure technology architecture
- Standardize your application architecture
- Develop a technology road map
- Control project technology choices
- Show results within 12 months from an EA program
- Control scope and resource commitments carefully
- Avoid formal, abstract methodologies
  you should choose bottom up,

Alternatively, based on these review points, if you need to:
- Focus on information and data in the enterprise
- Establish a broad scope at the beginning of the EA program
- Satisfy management's project funding requirements
- Evaluate your business architecture
- Analyze the relationships between business processes, applications, and technology
  you should choose top-down.

Preliminary Conclusion

In conclusion, we can look at the preceding two methods completely and realize that sometimes *neither* works. What if there is a muddled mixture of legacy and planned efforts? What if you have an enterprise architecture but want to implement key areas first? How do you ensure integration and consistency over time?

In such cases, a Hybrid or Side-In (as opposed to top-down or bottom-up) approach may be an alternative. It selects the best characteristics of each implementation method and minimizes the negative aspects of each.

The Hybrid Approach

The following is a brief description of the Hybrid or Side-In approach to enterprise data architecture implementation.

Purchase an enterprise-level model. The Hybrid or Side-In implementation approach involves the purchasing of an industry standard model and implementing it and adjusting it to the business subject area need. Based on the implementation, a data governance process and any enterprise efforts such as an enterprise data warehouse can be sourced from this. Subsequently, as projects are identified and implemented, they are brought into line with data governance policies and integrated into the emerging enterprise data architecture.

Positive aspects of the hybrid approach are a combination of the best features of top-down and bottom-up processes with minimization of the negatives of both. These are restated here in that context:

- The approach begins by establishing a clear view of the existing environment. The initial data discussion activity enables consensus regarding the current state environment, which is a critical element for effective planning.
- Business issues are emphasized from the beginning. The hybrid approach ensures priority for improving the business. Technology plays a support role as the enabler of the business.
- It establishes a broad scope at the outset. The hybrid approach embraces the broad scope, much as the top-down approach did. Thus, with the appropriate management support, all areas in need of improvement become subject to the EA program's efforts.
- The program can have significant impact immediately. Given the appropriate authority by the CIO and sufficiently motivating organizations, it can be accomplished in 6 to 12 months. This can translate to millions in cost savings and cost avoidance.
- Early successes build credibility rapidly. Early wins start the EA effort off on the right foot and build much-needed credibility for the more politically complex efforts that follow.
- It attacks problems in priority sequence. The potentially overwhelming scope of an EA effort is simplified in a priority and sequence approach: This can lead to significant early successes.
- Scope and complexity build gradually. The hybrid approach allows technologists and managers to learn as they go. Success is more likely when the problems are encountered in bite-size chunks.
- It does not need a large central EA team at the outset. Creating a technical architecture usually involves a central project manager and the borrowed expertise of internal SMEs. There is no need to obtain funding for additions to staff to create the EA group.

Implementation Summary

For many enterprises, none of these approaches will therefore be a complete solution. For some organizations that are new or unsure, the alternative, hybrid approach is recommended. Since it is a blended approach, it consists of choosing pieces from each approach and modifying and merging them according to the specific needs of the organization.

But even a blended or hybrid approach will only be as good as the organization's commitment to making changes. This commitment must be driven by the highest level of the organization. With a commitment to change and a tailored methodology for guiding that change, the promise of enterprise architecture is within reach. With a solid enterprise data architecture seeding a solid enterprise data warehouse, the journey to enterprise redefinition can commence.

References

Date, C. (1998). *Relational database writings (1994–1998)*. Boston: Addison-Wesley.
Date, C., & Darwen, H. (2000). *The third manifesto*. Boston: Addison-Wesley.

21

OBJECT AND OBJECT/
RELATIONAL DATABASES

Object Oriented Data Architecture

In order to cover the subject of object and object/relational databases, there must be a thorough understanding of the concepts involved in object oriented architecture. Then some of the components of the extended entity relationship diagramming method can be examined. This fosters and includes concepts that will support both the object model and the relational model and their respective design processes. In this chapter the overall design of the object database will not be discussed, but some of the concepts that go into the design and development of the models will be. Object oriented architecture is based on the principle of recursive design. That is, it can be addressed by the following set of design constraints within a given enterprise:

1. Everything in the enterprise is an object. It is something that can be viewed and examined unto itself. It is an independent thing that can be specifically defined and that has characteristics.
2. Objects perform computation and process by making requests of one another through the passing of messages. This allows the data to be worked on by the process in place. As noted in other chapters, by the different layers of interaction and mapping, the objects can be kept from being embedded in a matrix that needs constant changing.
3. Every object has its own memory, which consists of other objects that are replications of its image. This is the history of the object that allows information to persist as objects after the process is complete.
4. Every object is an instantiation or instance of a class. A class groups, collects, or encompasses similar objects.
5. The class is also the repository for behavior or process actions associated with an object. These can be broken down into subclasses and superclasses.

6. Classes are most often organized into singly rooted tree structures, called inheritance hierarchies. Sometimes in complex systems, the classes have developed multiple inheritances, in which case the inheritance hierarchy really becomes a cross-reference hierarchy or lattice hierarchy.

The problem with the object data architecture is that it is so different from the traditional approach that there is often a need to give examples in order to prove the concepts. In the traditional approach it is far easier to understand the top-down or side-in approach to integration. The principles involved can be easily illustrated by considering how one would go about solving a real-life problem.

Sample Object Oriented Design Concept: Wiring Money

To illustrate the concepts of OOD in an easily understood design framework, consider the problem of sending money to a friend who lives in a different city. You can't deliver the money yourself, so you would have to use the local money-wiring agency. We'll call it Eastern Union.

The clerk at Eastern Union, Honey, has to be notified of the address for the target of the money transmission, how much money is to be sent, and the type of currency being sent. Honey contacts a clerk, Bunny, at the Eastern Union office in our friend's city, who accomplishes the transaction, then contacts a delivery person, who delivers the money. This all sounds very simple, but let's examine the complete process more.

When reviewed, it is obvious that there are other people involved in this transaction. These include the participating bank and anyone at the bank involved in the transaction—perhaps somebody in charge of arrangements and the wiring money process. The delivery person may be a handling agency for a bunch of independent bonded delivery people. Solving the money-sending problem requires the interaction of an entire community of individuals. Figure 21.1 shows where people exist in a hierarchy.

Figure 21.1 A hierarchy.

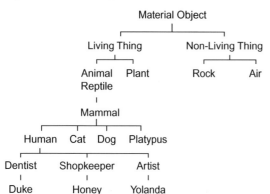

Concept 1: Everything is an object

Actions in OOD are performed by agents, called *instances* or *objects*. There are many agents working together in our scenario. We have ourselves, the target friend, the Eastern Union clerk, the Eastern Union clerk in our friend's city, the delivery driver, the participating bank's arranger, and the bank itself. Each agent or agency has a part to play, and the result is produced when all work together to solve a problem. The capacity of each object to interact is defined. In our case it is captured in the roles they play and the responsibilities they have had defined for them.

Concept 2: Messages

Objects perform computations by making requests of one another through the passing of messages. Actions in OOD are produced in response to requests for actions, called *messages*. An instance may accept a message and in return will perform an action and return a value. To begin the process of wiring the money, Honey is given a message. She in turn gives a message to Bunny in our friend's city, who gives another message to the driver, and so on. Each message contains information necessary for the object receiving it to act on.

How Information Hiding Facilitates Messages

Notice that the user of a service being provided by an object needs only to know the name of the messages that the object will accept. It is not necessary to know all of the messages it can accept or the object's internal structure. There is no need to have any idea of how the actions performed will be carried out in response to the request. It is unimportant. The important thing is that the message will be acted upon.

Having accepted a message, an object is responsible for carrying it out. Messages differ from traditional function calls in two very important respects:
- In a message there is a designated *receiver* that accepts the message.
- The interpretation of the message may be different, depending on the receiver.

Examples of Different Actions

Subjects involved:
    Roberto: Money wirer
    Yolanda: Roberto's wife
    Duke: Dentist

Process:
Beginning
   Roberto.sendmoneyTo(myFriend); { this will work }
   Yolanda.sendmoneyTo(myFriend); { this will also work }
   Duke.sendmoneyTo(myFriend); { This will probably not work }
End

Behavior and Interpretation

Although different objects may accept the same message, the actions (behavior) the object will perform will likely be different. For example, Duke will not be sending money unless he knows my friend or unless he and I reach an agreement beforehand. The fact that the same name can mean two entirely different operations is one form of polymorphism, a topic that will be discussed at length in subsequent paragraphs.

Concept 3: Recursive Design

Every object has its own memory, which consists of other objects. Each object is like a miniature machine—a specialized processor performing a specific task. These tasks follow a principle of noninterference—that is, they do not interfere with one another in their processes.

Concept 4: Classes

Every object is an instance of a class. A class groups objects that have similar characteristics and attributes. We will cover this in more detail in subsequent paragraphs.

Concept 5: Classes

The class is also the repository for behavior associated with an object. The behavior expected from Honey is determined from a general idea concerning the behavior of the money-wiring clerks. Honey is an *instance* of the *class* "money wire clerk." The behavior expected from Bunny (the receiver) is determined from a general idea concerning the behavior of money-receiving clerks (which may or may not be another instance of "money wire clerk").

Behavior is associated with classes, not with individual instances. All objects that are instances of a class use the same method in response to similar messages.

How Hierarchies of Categories Affect Classes

But there is more that we now know about Honey than just that she is a money wire clerk. When going up the levels of the abstraction of all things, it is obvious that she is an office clerk and a human and a mammal and a material object, and so on.

At each level of abstraction, there is information recorded. That information is applicable to all lower (more specialized) levels. This leads us to concept 6.

Concept 6: Inheritance

Classes are organized into a singly rooted tree structure, called an inheritance hierarchy. Information (data and/or behavior) associated with one level of abstraction in a class hierarchy is automatically applicable to lower levels of the hierarchy. If the classes within an area are complex and interact in a complex manner as objects, then the inheritance hierarchy is not single but compound. This is referred to as a shared or lattice hierarchy. This shared or lattice hierarchy illustrates a complex kind of inheritance known as multiple inheritance. This will be covered in subsequent paragraphs.

Elements of Object Oriented Design: Overriding

Subclasses can alter or *override* information inherited from parent classes. For example, all mammals give birth to their young in a living state, but a platypus is an egg-laying mammal. In order to properly execute the structure, it must be subclassed and overridden. (Actually, there are at least two different schools of thought on the issue of how classes go about overriding behavior inherited from their parent classes.)

Analogy and Problem Solving

Because the OOD view is similar to the way in which people go about solving problems in real life, intuition, ideas, and understanding from everyday experiences can be brought to bear on computing. On the other hand, common sense and everyday life experiences are seldom useful when computers are viewed in the traditional process-state model, since few people solve the enormous activity volumes every day that the traditional architecture was designed to do. Common-sense logic was too specific and unadaptable for such wide variance and volume. Some of the solutions that the traditional approach developed to deal with the common-sense problems dealt with the following issues, which are more easily handled with object design.

Coping with Complexity

Another way to understand object oriented architecture and design is to try and place it in a historical perspective. People have always tried to use computers to solve problems that were just a little more difficult than they knew how to solve. Perhaps they were ever so slightly larger than the brains trying to understand them. Software crises came about after people realized the major problems in software development were made more complex by oral and written communication difficulties and the management of interaction complexity.

Examining the history of mechanisms used to solve the problem of managing complexity can lead to a better understanding of the role of OOD.

Interconnections: The Perpetrator of Complexity

Many software systems are complex not because they are large but because they have many interactions. These interactions make it difficult to understand pieces in isolation or to carry them from one design stage to the next, or to the next design, for that matter. The inability to cleanly separate out components makes it difficult to divide tasks. Complexity can only be managed by means of abstraction, by generalizing the information that the user of the design needs to know. Object design accomplishes this in the simplest way.

Assembler Languages

Assembler languages and linkers were perhaps the first tools used to abstract features of the raw machine. Within them addresses could be represented symbolically, not as a number. The names for operations could be given symbolic names or mnemonics. Linking of names and locations could then be performed automatically. These were devised as the first level of abstraction, one step away from the actual machine language. Further levels of process abstraction took place in other generalized process oriented languages. Unfortunately, these led further and further away from the data as it existed in the raw state and forced a static view to be captured and held in order to allow the abstractions to work. But this was a digression that took place by choice. Object and its tenets were not mature at the time.

Procedures and Functions

Libraries of procedures and functions provided the first hints of information hiding. As mentioned in the chapter on Information Engineering, *information hiding* is what allows us to operate on just that set of information that needed. They permit the designer to think about operations in high-level terms, concentrating on *what* is being done, not *how* it is being performed. Traditional design processes took advantage of this to simplify their complex programs. Object accomplishes this handily by the objectification of the data and the processes associated with it.

Modules

Modules are small macro-like pieces of code that process one function for a particular piece of data. They function by way of parameter passing. Modules basically provide collections of procedures and data with import and export statements in the parameters passed. This solves the problem of encapsulation (the separation of data and processes associated with it from other data and processes), but what if the programming task requires two or more processes to interact? Object oriented design can do this because the process is captured at the data level, not in a fixed hierarchical data structure with a process bias.

Parameter Passing

Traditional design utilized a method of parameter passing to accomplish the movement of control information between modules. It acted similar to messaging in object design but was far more complex and only followed chosen process paths within a program segment. This was because of the hierarchical fixed nature of the traditional modularly designed programs. The use of objects allows freedom of "communication" between all objects as defined by their messaging capabilities.

Abstract Data Types

An abstract data type (ADT) is a user-defined data type that can be manipulated in a manner similar to system-provided data types. This data typing was discouraged by the traditional approach because it causes modification to the static structures they use. It is required and is a distinct advantage in the object oriented design world. These abstract data types must have the ability to instantiate many different copies of the data type and can be implemented using provided operations, without the knowledge of internal structure representation.

Objects with Parameter Passing

The following are some of the abstract data type characteristics of objects:

- *Encapsulation:* This is one of the main concepts that make object oriented differ from traditional designed databases. It is also related to the concept of information hiding in programming languages. In traditional databases the entire structure of the database was visible to the user and the programs using it.

  - In the object oriented world, the concept of information hiding and abstract data types take the form of defining the behavior of a type of object based on the external operations that can be applied to it. The internal structure of the object is not known; the user only knows the interface with the object. The implementation of the operation is also hidden from the users. In the OO world the interface part of the operation is called a *signature,* and the implementation side is called a *method.* The means of invoking a method is by simply sending a message to execute the method.

  - For some database applications, it is too constraining to require complete encapsulation. In these cases the designer/programmer can decide what attributes of the object are to be hidden and which are to be visible. Thus, hidden attributes are regarded as being completely encapsulated and addressable via the methods route and the visible attributes regarded as externally viewable to high-level query languages.

- *Classification and classes:* Classes are a way of organizing things that permits sharing and reuse. The act of classification is the systematic assignment of similar objects to object classes. Often a group of objects share the same attributes and by classifying objects it simplifies the data discovery process for that and other objects. This also applies to subclasses that experience inheritance.

- *Instantiation:* Instantiation is the inverse of classification. That is, it is the generation and specific examination of distinct objects within a class. It is an example of or a single selection of an object. An object instance is related to its object class by the relationship *is an instance of.*

- *Identification:* Identification is simply the mechanism of defining an identifier for an object or class. It does, however, exist at two levels. The first level is the identification to distinguish database objects and classes. This first-level identification is exemplified by the internal object ID contained and maintained within the system. The second identifies the database objects and relates them to their real-world counterparts. For example, there may be an occurrence of Tupper, C.D., in the Person object and 010-38-1369 in the Employee object, but they both may refer to the same external real-world object.
- *Aggregation and association:* By nature of its name, aggregation is the grouping and compaction of some things to make another thing. In object oriented, aggregation is the concept of building up composite objects from their component objects. The relationship between the component objects and the new aggregate object is an *is a part of* relationship. These structures are ideal when dealing with a group of things to make some common changes.
  - An association is the concept of grouping several independent classes together for process purposes. This relationship between the components and the association is called an *is associated with* relationship. The difference between the aggregation and association is that the association can be made up of dissimilar components. Both of these constructs allow us to take advantage of inheritance.
- *Messages:* These are a dynamic binding of procedure names to specific behaviors, which we will define further into its detail in the following paragraphs.

Object Oriented Architectures Summary

Object oriented design is not simply features added to support a programming language or even an application. Rather, it is a new way of *thinking.* Object oriented design views the enterprise as a community of agents, termed *objects.* Each object is responsible for a specific task.

An object is an encapsulation of *state* (data values) and *behavior* (operations). The behavior of objects is dictated by the rules and principles associated with its object *class.* An object will exhibit its behavior by invoking a method (similar to executing a procedure) in response to a message. Objects and classes extend the concept of abstract data types by adding the notion of *inheritance.*

Enhanced Entity Relationship Concepts

An enhanced entity relationship (EER) diagram includes all of the concepts and constructs that exist in an entity relationship diagram, with the addition of the following concepts: subclasses and superclasses, specialization and generalization, categories, and inheritance. There isn't a standardized language for this area (although critically good work is occurring and has been published by Chris Date and Hugh Darwen in their book). Their work based on the exploration and clarification of the original relational model dovetails neatly with the work done on the EER. For clarity, the most common terms available will be used, and when pressed, these will be clarified.

Subclasses and Superclasses

Entities, which are discussed in Chapter 11, often have additional subgroupings that are of critical interest because of their significance to the business area. For example, if a human resource application is reviewed, there will be an entity called employee. Within that entity there are different classifications of employees, such as manager, director, vice president, technician, and engineer. The set of occurrences in each of these groupings is a member of the grouping but in the larger sense a member of the employee group. Each of these subgroups is called a subclass, and the overall employee group is called the superclass.

A critical concept here is that an occurrence of the subclass is also an occurrence of the superclass. It is merely fulfilling a different specific role. It has to exist as a member of both classes. For example, in the preceding group, a salaried engineer who is also a manager belongs in two subclasses: the engineer subclass and the manager subclass. Another critical concept is that all entity occurrences don't have to be defined at the subclass level; sometimes there is no subclass, only the superclass.

Attribute Inheritance

An important concept associated with the superclass/subclass is the concept of attribute inheritance. One of the definitions of *inheritance* is "the derivation of a quality or characteristic from a predecessor or progenitor." Simply put, the child or subclass contains qualities or characteristics of the superclass (parent or grandparent). Because an entity in a subclass represents membership in the superclass as well, it should "inherit" *all* of the properties and attributes of the superclass entity. The subclass entity will also inherit all relationship instances that the superclass participates in.

Specialization

Specialization is the process of defining the subclasses of a superclass. The set of subclasses that form a specialization are defined on some distinguishing criteria of the different subclass entities in the superclass. The specialization characteristic for our previous example of employee (manager, director, vice president, technician, and engineer) is the "job title" attribute. There can be several specializations of an entity type that are based on other identifying or specialization characteristics. An example of this would be the subclasses of hourly paid and weekly paid as defined by the specialization characteristic "pay method."

If all members of the subclass have the same attribute value on the same attribute in the superclass, then the specialization is called an attribute-defined specialization. An example of this is the "job title" example we just saw. If there is a conditional to the value of an attribute that defines whether the subclass occurrence is a member of the subclass, then it is called a predicate-defined specialization. An example of this would be a constraint that the value in the "job title" field would have to be "engineer" for the occurrence to have membership in the engineer subclass. Depending on the value of the attribute "job title," an occurrence will be in one subclass or another.

If the subclass has a specialization and it is neither of the preceding, it is called a user-defined specialization. This can take whatever form is necessary for the application.

Generalization

The opposite of specialization is generalization. It is the suppression of individualizing attributes to allow the grouping of the subclasses into a superclass. For example, dogs, cats, bears, and moose all are subclasses of quadrupeds (four-legged animals). Notice that the generalization can be viewed as the inverse of the specialization. The generalization in the first example was the "employee," and in the second example it was "quadrupeds."

Generalization Hierarchies

A generalization hierarchy is the view of the structure from the bottom up, which leads us to a more generalized or abstracted view of the higher classes. A specialization hierarchy is one where the view is from the top down, where each level leads to more defined levels of specification. It is simply the top-down view or the bottom-up approach and view that make the difference.

Multiple Inheritance

A subclass with more than one superclass is regarded as a shared subclass. For example, an engineering manager is a salaried employee, an engineer, and a manager—three superclasses. This leads to something called multiple inheritance, which is simply that it inherits characteristics from all of the superclasses with which it is associated.

Physical Data Design Considerations

Polymorphism: Polymorphism (or operator overloading) is a manner in which OO systems allow the same operator name or symbol to be used for multiple operations. That is, it allows the operator symbol or name to be bound to more than one implementation of the operator. A simple example of this is the "+" sign.

In an application where the operands are of the type *integer*, this plus sign means integer addition. In applications where the operands are of the type *set*, then this means it represents a union. From this you can see that an operator symbol or name can have two different effects while being the same and not changing its original characteristics.

Persistence: In most OO databases, there is a distinction made between persistent classes and objects and the transient classes and objects. Persistent objects and classes are just that. They persist after the operation and existence is stored permanently. Persistence is one of the most difficult problems to address in object, and it may or may not be completely worked out as yet.

Persistent objects represent the historical aspect of the database. Transient objects, on the other hand, exist solely during the execution of the process and are released when the operation is complete.

Type hierarchies and class hierarchies: In most database applications there are a lot of objects of the same type. Therefore, most OO systems have a method for classifying objects based on their type. But it goes to the extent that the system permits the definition of new types based on other predefined types, which leads to a type hierarchy. A type hierarchy is typically defined by assigning a name and a number of attributes and a method for the type. These together are often referred to as a function. An example of a type function would be:

> PERSON: Name, Address, Age, and Social Security Number (where the format was TYPE_NAME: Function, Function, Function).

A class hierarchy, on the other hand, is a collection of objects that are important to the application. In most databases the collection of objects in the same class has the same type. As previously covered, the class hierarchy is usually the set of superclasses and all subordinate subclasses in a top-down hierarchy.

Messaging

This is the operational heart of object oriented processing and operational activity, which can be best described in the words of one of the gurus in the field. The topic is the design of Smalltalk, one of the first object languages and databases developed.

To quote Daniel Ingalls, August 1981, issue, Byte magazine in *Design Principles Behind Smalltalk:*

> In most computer systems the compiler figures out what kind of number it is and generates code to add 5 to it. This is not good enough for an object oriented system because the exact kind of number something is cannot be determined by the compiler…. Smalltalk provides a much cleaner solution. It sends the name of the desired operation along with any arguments, as a message to the number, with the understanding that the receiver knows best how to carry out the desired operation. **Instead of a bit-grinding processor raping and plundering data structures, we have a universe of well-behaved objects that courteously ask each other to carry out their various desires.**

Object Identity

An object database must provide a unique identity to each independent object stored in the database. This unique identifier is typically implemented by means of a systems-generated identifier. This object ID (OID) is not visible to the outside world but is kept internally for the system to use when creating, activating, and using interobject references and operations. It is also immutable. That is, the OID can never change for an object. If the object it was assigned to is removed, then the OID should not be reused, since this would have an impact on the historical ability of the database and on the persistency of the data within it. The purpose of the systems generation is that the two main traditional methods of identification (use of attribute values and physical addresses) leave the identifiers at the mercy of physical reorganizations and attribute value changes.

Type "Generators" and Type Constructors

Complex objects within the database must be constructed of other objects found within the database. Type constructors are the mechanism for this purpose. The simplest constructors are base or atomic, tuple, and set. For instance, if we view an object as a three-term definition, we could have the object ID as the first term, the second term would be the constructor type, and the third and last would be the value we are establishing for it. In illustration some of these would be:

object1 = OID1, set, {I1,I2,i3}
object2 = OID2, atomic, 5
object3 = OID3, tuple, (DeptName, DeptNumber, DepMgr)

With these types of constructors, one can establish the new object, get its object ID, and give it a value. This definitional process may vary between different implementations, but the principle is the same.

The support of these constructors requires the working presence of type "generators." (I am using Chris Date's term here to separate these from the constructor types that are used to create new physical objects in the database.) These "generator" constructors—set, list, array, and bag—are collection types or bulk types. This helps to set them apart from the simpler type of constructors. A *set* is a group of like things. A *list* is similar to a set, only it is specifically ordered. Because we know the sequence, we can refer to it by position, such as the *n*th object in a list. A *bag* is also similar to a set except that it allows duplicates to exist within the set captured in the complex object. As we know, an *array* is similar to a list, with a third dimension added that we can also address by positional reference.

Summary

In this chapter we discussed the concepts and important principles in the object approach to databases. We discussed object identity, type constructors, encapsulation, type hierarchies, inheritance, polymorphism and operator overloading.

While it is not a complete picture, it will familiarize managers with the concepts they need to investigate and research further with the appropriate detail texts. Further reading on object/relational databases is recommended, since this appears to be the next developmental stage in the evolution of data processing. It will merge the benefits of the object design process with the efficiency of relational data structures.

References

Date, C. (1998). Relational database writings. (1994–1998): Boston, MA: Addison-Wesley.

Date, C., & Darwen, H. (2000). Foundation for Object/Relational Databases. *The third manifesto*. Boston, MA: Addison-Wesley.

Ingalls, D. H. H. (1981, August). Design principles behind smalltalk. *BYTE Magazine*. Reproduced with permission. © The McGraw-Hill Companies, Inc., New York, NY. All rights reserved.

22

DISTRIBUTED DATABASES

In order to describe how distributed databases are structured, we need to understand fully how centralized databases are formed and what some of their characteristics are. In a centralized database all the components exist on a single computer or computer site. The components of this centralized site or computer consist of the data itself, the DBMS, and any other storage media necessary to provide an orderly operation. Access to the data stored in the centralized site has been provided by the use of intelligent workstations and remote access terminals that utilized directed communication links. In recent years a trend has developed that allows the data and process to be disseminated to a large geographic area and linked together via a communication network. These networks are intelligent communications computers and communication mechanisms of their own.

Some Distributed Concepts

First, let us state that a distributed database is a store of data that should be logically housed together, but for one reason or another it has been spread over a large geographic area. As stated before, in today's corporate world, business is not only country-wide but often global in its reach. It is a fact we have to live with. These geophysically distributed sites or locations are connected (as we said before) by a communication network that breaks down or all but eliminates those geographical limitations that have been imposed upon it.

We will discuss some of the characteristics and concepts about distributed databases (DDBS) and distributed database management systems (DDBMS) in this chapter and cover some of the concerns.

The Distributed Model

Let us take a look at a distributed architecture model. If we look at it closely, we will see the familiar three levels of design

Data Architecture.

covered in previous chapters: the user view layer, the conceptual or model layer, and the physical layer. Let us look at each of these familiar layers and see how they differ in the distributed model.

In the typical distributed model we can see that the user view layer looks very much the same as the traditional database design. As you remember, it was this layer that allows us the logical view of the database and permits us to design without the constraints brought about by the physical world. It contains that set of criteria that permits an intercommunication between the top two layers. Since the look downward can also be a feed upward, it must be taken into consideration.

The conceptual layer is similar as well. Since the user is depending on being insulated from the physical world, he or she is expecting that there is a coherent view of what data content is available in the database. And it is so.

As the users look down into the database, what they see is the view of one combined, or centralized database. When they are expecting a retrieval of information, they expect it back in the structure that their view has accustomed them to. The conceptual layer also contains the necessary mappings and translators that allow it to talk upward to the user layer as well as downward to the physical layer. This is still similar to the traditional model, but there are some dissimilarities that we will cover later.

It is at the physical level that things differ significantly. The physical layer is fragmented and distributed over many sites, and possibly many different machines at those sites. Each site may or may not be in the same format or data structure that is sympathetic to the client site. One key principle to the distributed design is to strategically place the data structures so as to discourage or minimize distributed joins from being accomplished due to the overhead they place on the system. Depending on what type of database it is (read-only versus transactional), it may be more prudent to replicate data than fragment it.

How Does It Work?

The user layer manages the user interface. That is, by utilization of the conceptual layer mappings, it knows how to format and translate all the interfacing activity to be applied to the appropriate entity in the conceptual layer. It takes results being returned and routes them to the appropriate device in the user's world.

The conceptual layer manages the translation of the downward view into the physical world by way of a global schema, which identifies all the components in the distributed environment. This is in turn connected to and associated with a global catalog that maintains data mapping strategies and access paths. Also, as part of the conceptual layer is a transaction monitor that works with the global catalog to ensure it can "farm out" the work and coordinate the response to the work unit correctly for presentation back to the user. All of these things are bidirectional and allow the data to flow upward as well as downward.

Distributed Data Design Concepts

The following are some concepts and techniques for disaggregating the database into component structures that can then be distributed. As has been pointed out before, it is best to develop from a conceptual model that does not have any physical environment bias. There are two main concepts that we can cover here. The first one is *fragmentation* and the second is called *data replication*. When we are examining data replication, we will cover fragment allocation that will allow us to replicate pieces of data to different areas. All of this information on the fragmentation and replication will have to be handled within the DDBMS'S global system catalog.

Fragmentation

It is a basic assumption that all conceptual models that we are starting with will be in a relational format. This allows the various relations or tables to be placed in the locations where they are needed. Obviously, the full table is the most common and complete form of the fragmentation. An example of this could be where a company has a particular department that operates strictly out of one location and none other or is compartmentalized so some functions only occur at specific sites. However, there are possible situations where the tables could be broken down and distributed to different locations, such as when a company's personnel files are allocated to the location where the employees work.

There are two ways to break down the tables for distribution of this type. The first is by horizontal fragment, which is the selection of a subset of the rows of a table that when distributed become the table definition and content at the distributed location. This type of fragmentation is often controlled and/or guided by key attribute values. For example, if employees with employee IDs between 100 and 1,000 are at location A, and those between 1,001 and 2,000 were at location B, then the subset of records for location A could be kept at A, and those for B could be kept at B.

In this case the employee ID was used as the controlling/locating attribute. Horizontal fragments don't have to be limited to a specific entity such as employee. A particular site may have all of the horizontal fragments of all of the entities involved in the company's business at that site. It is in effect a microcosm of the company built on the company's lines and structures.

The second type of fragmentation is vertical fragmentation. This type of fragmentation splits tables into multiple tables with the same key. Let us look at the employee's table again. We can take the same employee table and separate all columns that reference personal information (such as marital status, home address, birth date, and sex) and keep them in one table. We can then take the remaining columns that have to do with business (skills, payroll, title, hiring information, and current rating) in another table. This allows two separate processes in two separate places to access and control the two subsets of data.

The drawback to this type of fragmentation is that in order to facilitate the complete reuniting of the information, a complete copy of the original primary key must be attached to each one of the tuples in each of the tables, making it longer. Surrogate keys are a possible solution, but it must be evaluated carefully before implementation.

Replication

Replication is the creation of redundancy that will allow the processes needing to access information to proceed smoothly and effectively. It maximizes the availability but has its drawbacks. At its very worst it is complete redundancy at every distributed location. This is the worst because the data has to be freshened at each of the sites in order to keep it accurate. Very careful evaluation should be done before entering the replication game unless it is for slowly changing reference data that can be updated on a weekly basis or if you have the interval of time and overhead capacity to keep the data referentially intact.

The process of analyzing and selecting the best approach of distributing the data for replication is called distributed data allocation. Allocation is simply the process of defining what data will be replicated on what site.

Homogeneous Distributed Model

When a distributed data model refers to data that are fragmented on similar devices in its geographic distribution, it is

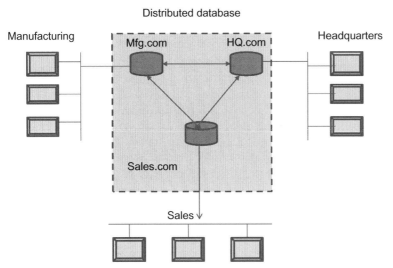

Figure 22.1 A homogeneous model.

called a homogeneous model. That is, all components of this model are consistent as to platform, protocol, and communications interface. Homogeneous distributed designs are much easier to implement than others because everything is consistent and has no need for translation or reformatting.

Figure 22.1 shows an example of a common homogeneous distributed model. Within this new homogeneous distributed model we have but two concerns. The first is to ensure that we have analyzed and fragmented the overall schema to build detail schemas for the local databases so they service the local work need. The data needs of the local users will take priority over the centralized users if we want to maintain the autonomy that is so highly prized.

The second consideration is that we have to fill the global schema with all of the information from the local database schemas so all the transaction activity can be directed appropriately. This ensures that the centralized users get what they need without victimizing the local sites for either control or performance.

Federated or Heterogeneous Distributed Model

When the concept of the federated/heterogeneous model was first introduced, it seemed impossible to use without sophisticated software to accommodate and otherwise enable the distributed process. With the advent of many different platforms, all providing useful data, it becomes critical to address this problem.

The problem with the federated/heterogeneous model, if you remember, is the diverse distribution of data among many different software products and data structures. It is not uncommon, for example, to have relational, hierarchical, and network models all being part of a federated/heterogeneous model and each of these being implanted on different vendors' DBMSs. Nor is it uncommon for us to see a conglomerate of client-server and centralized applications. How do we make them all work in today's marketplace?

As you will remember, the communication network is the key to a distributed architecture. Into this need came the evolution of the Internet and the Intranet (a corporate private form of the Internet). With the communication links in place, let us examine the federated/heterogeneous distributed model.

Looking at Figure 22.2, we can see the different front ends that are present. They include user views, local servers, schemata, and local databases. This can be categorized by the distributed or centralized in viewpoint. It looks like all the other distributed models, but there are additional components.

The new components of the federated/heterogeneous architecture are the import schema, the export schema, and the

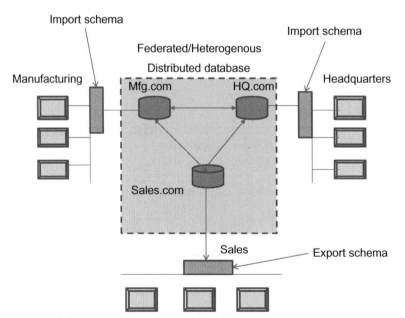

Figure 22.2 A federated (heterogeneous) model.

federated interface. The import and export schemas are to define what data are to be imported into and out of the federation. In other words, what accessibility do we want to give to the outside world to the data, and what data do we want to access in the outside world?

These represent a layer in the security architecture. It is the first layer and can be as specific as down to the column level. The second level of this security architecture is the federated/heterogeneous interface.

Within the federated/heterogeneous interface is something called the protocol manager or contract manager. This is responsible for partnering with the import and export schemas to ensure that the only data that are viewed are specified in the protocol manager or import/export contract. By examining the messages coming in and going out of the federated/heterogeneous server and adhering to all the import and export rules, all members of the federated/heterogeneous database can have the access to the data they need for the time they need it.

This discussion on distributed models has been simply stated in order to facilitate understanding the concepts. It is, however, not nearly so simply implemented. We are only trying to discuss the concepts involved, not the actual implementation, which may have many different forms and involve many different products.

Distributed DBMSs

Why did distributed DBMS develop? What are some of the advantages of distributed over centralized DBMSs? These are good questions, and we answer them in the next few paragraphs.

Many applications are distributed by nature. A container shipping company can have multiple locations or branches in the same or different countries. How do companies handle this? Most companies of any size have this problem (or advantage) and handle it by distributed data processing. Imagine if you can an application that services this Acme Container shipping company. The local application users can do their local work on their local data structures at the local sites. The global or parent users of the application can have access to the local data for summary or control functions like locating shipments.

One characteristic of the local database in this company is that most of the users and data sources and processes are located at the local site. This permits autonomous or semiautonomous activity. That is, it allows the local site control over its own data without shipping its shipping data anywhere. This autonomy allows separation of function to take place and local control over local data. When the parent company needs the local data for problem resolution or tracking, it can easily get to it using the interconnections of the network.

Reliability and Availability

The distributed concept allows more reliability and availability. *Reliability* is defined as the probability that the application will be up and connected at any given time. *Availability*, on the other hand, can be defined as the probability that the system will be continuously available during a period of time. Reliability and availability at a local level provide process independence should the central location go down or lose connectivity, which was a major flaw with the centralized structure. When further reliability and availability and independence are needed, it can be ensured by the replication of data at other sites so the process could be done at the other site if the primary site is down.

Controlled Data Sharing

One of the major obstacles that had to be overcome was the need for the ability to share certain data. In most cases it is a class of data that we often refer to as reference data or domain constraint data. This is data that are common for validation and translation throughout the distributed database. By having access to and sharing common reference data, it adds business integrity to the overall distributed application. When this common reference data are shared throughout the application, then there is no need to reconcile between sites or to the centralized site. Of course, there are reasons for sharing nonreference data on a read-only basis, as well as having distributed update and insert activity take place. It just has to be planned for and controlled through either the application code or the vendor software.

Certain vendors' distributed DBMSs allow for the sharing of data from site to site while still allowing autonomous control to the local site. This allows local control and processing but also allows a limited form of control by a centralized or parent site. By setting and defining options within the environment correctly, the amount of data sharing and remote access to shared data can be controlled to prevent unbalanced or poorly distributed access loads to occur on any local site machine.

The limited control of data sharing can also be set to allow distribution of DDBMS software changes to the remote sites in a central push to local pull scenario. The software could be pushed out of the central location and pulled and applied at the local level. This allows for smoother distribution of software and the consistency of protocol to make everything run smoothly.

Performance

Another advantage that fostered the growth of distributed databases is improved performance. When a large database is distributed, it becomes (in effect) a bunch of smaller ones. Each smaller database, while retaining the overall characteristics and structure of the other components, runs in its own environment and on its own hardware, software, and transaction load. This will result in the local databases having much better performance for queries and accesses run on the local database than if they were in a large database. In addition, transactions that involve access to more than one site can take advantage and run the process streams in parallel, thus shortening the throughput time of the transaction. The separate results are then recombined to give the final answer.

The use of a distributed database also offers local tuning ability. When a distributed database is designed properly, it provides for performance independence. For example, if for some reason one particular distributed site had a hardware, software, or even data volume problem, it can be analyzed, corrected, tested, and implemented without impacting the performance of the application of any of the other sites and users.

Qualities Required in a DDBMS

Distribution as a whole causes problems, but these are complicated even further when it comes to the DBMSs that have to handle the distributed process. One of the complexities that is involved in the DBMS side of it is the need to handle certain additional functionalities over and above those normally handled by the centralized DBMS. Let us examine each of these additional functions:

1. The distributed DBMS needs to be able to access remote sites and transmit queries and data among the various sites by way of a communications network. This means splitting the activity apart but keeping information on how to recombine it.

2. The distributed DBMS must be able to keep track of the data distribution and replication within a DBMS catalog.

3. It needs to have the ability to devise execution strategies for transaction activity that accesses more than one site.
4. It must have the ability to decide which copy of the replicated data is the book of record data to ensure the proper control over the update process.
5. It must have the ability to maintain consistency between all the replicated copies of data.
6. Finally, it must have the ability to recover from individual site crashes and new failures, such as communication failures.

All of these issues need to be dealt with by the distributed DBMSs, and, indeed, most of the successful products in the marketplace have addressed these to some degree or another. Additional levels of complexity may arise when the location of the data and the physical network topology are brought into play.

Other Factors

The design of the databases may have a profound effect on the load that the DBMS must handle. An analysis of what data are needed where, and where and how replication, segmentation, or separation will be handled, is a necessary part of the design. Critical importance must be considered when developing recovery scenarios and backup plans.

The physical topology of the network that is connecting the sites is also problematic. An example of this might be that sites 1 and 2 are directly linked by land lines (phone lines as opposed to microwave or satellite), and sites 2 and 3 are also linked by land lines. But there are no direct links between 1 and 3. This can cause a problem. Because of this topology, all activity going from 1 to 3 must go through 2. This builds a certain dependence on site 2, which profoundly affects performance management, distributed query management, and backup/recovery scenarios. Site 2 becomes the limiting factor in the process. To resolve this, it becomes critical that the limiting or gating site be the most optimally tuned, the best hardware equipped (speedwise), and the best backed up and most secure. Above all in a distributed environment, protect the investment.

An Overview of Client Server

Let us look at a bit of history before moving on. It might help us understand the driving forces behind distributed processing. Client-server architecture was developed to deal with the new computer environments in which we exist. There were many computers and data files and peripheral equipment that needed to be linked together for efficiency purposes. The idea was to bundle things together to allow economy of processing. Specifically, the idea was to define servers (high-speed computers that exist to serve some capacity) to respond to the various functionalities that might be needed for the everyday processes.

Following this line of thinking, we would have file servers, which would contain all of the files needed by the group of users that the network connecting them served. A specialized form of this, the database server, would handle the group of users' data resource needs. A print server would store, queue, and print the group of users' hard-copy outputs. It is through this process that specific electronic resources can be used for common functions by many different clients. This idea was carried over to software, where specialized software tools such as Microsoft products and DBMSs could be installed on a common server and used by the client group.

This client-server architecture has been used to facilitate the growth and has been incorporated in the distributed DBMS packages as they moved closer and closer to the full support of a distributed environment. The technique that is being used most commonly today is to divide the DBMS software into two components to eliminate some of the complexities that we have mentioned in the preceding paragraphs. Some sites may run the client software only. Other sites may be dedicated server machines of some type. Still others might have both in their configuration.

Functionality within Client Server

Being able to divide the functionality between the client and server environment has not been standardized. Different strategies have been posited. One approach is to include the functionality of the centralized DBMS at a lower level. Several products have taken this approach with their DBMSs. In these products a SQL server is provided to the clients. SQL is a standard among all relational DBMSs, and various servers, even those that are provided by different software vendors, can often be made to talk to one another via SQL. Modules exist in these products that break down global queries into local queries that can be handled at each site. Interaction between the sites would loosely follow the following protocol.

1. The client-server software parses a user query into a number of independent subqueries. Each subquery is then sent to a different site to be handled.

2. Each server processes its own subquery and sends the result back to the sending client server.
3. The client-server software at the originating site then recombines the result of the subqueries to come up with the complete answer.

In this scenario the SQL server is called a database processor or database server. It is also called the back end server. The client-server machine, on the other hand, is called the front end processor or machine. The interaction between these two machines can be defined explicitly by the user, or in other implementations it may be done automatically by the software.

In another scenario, the software of the DDBMS is separated between the client and the server in a more integrated way. In this case the server may contain the part of the DDBMS that handles storage, concurrency, replication, and retrieval. Conversely, on the client side, the user interface, data dictionary, and code used to interact with programming languages, query optimization functions, buffering, and the like are retained to ensure the best functionality. This client-server interaction is often referred to as tightly coupled, as opposed to the previous proposal, which is regarded as loosely coupled.

A Typical DDBMS

In a typical DDBMS there are three generally recognized levels of software:
1. The server level. This software is responsible for maintaining local data management, much like a minicentralized DBMS.
2. The client software level. This software is responsible for distribution activities. It reads a DDBMS catalog and routes or directs all requests and queries to their appropriate destinations.
3. The communications level. This software enables the client to transmit commands and data among the various sites as needed.

Although this is not strictly part of the DDBMS, it does provide the necessary communication linkages and services.

Aside from the basic functions that we have mentioned, a possible function needed by the client side of the client-server interface is the ability to hide the details of the data distribution from the user. This, in effect, allows the user to write global queries and processes as if the database were centralized. Moreover, it does not require that the necessary site of processing be specifically noted. This is normally referred to as "distribution transparency."

Distribution Transparency

DDBMSs that have a high degree of distribution transparency make it much simpler for the using client to access the database, but it imparts a more complex operating environment and increases the burden on the software to do translation, location, and distribution within itself. Low-transparency systems, on the other hand, need to have a well-educated and skilled client and user community, since they are burdened with the specification of the translation, location, and distribution. This requires that the client software and users have more knowledge of the complexities and can actively construct the transaction distribution that is required.

Simply put, if the client sees a single integrated schema of all the data, then there is a high degree of integration or transparency. If on the other hand the client sees all the fragmentations, replication, and segmentation of the data, then there is no schema integration. In this second case the client needs to append the site name of the residence of his or her data to the reference in the query. As stated before, it is more complex, and the burden is on the client side in this type of DDBMS.

Types of DDBMSs

Distributed database management system is a loose term that covers many different types of DBMSs. The principal thing they all share is the fact that the data and the software are distributed over many sites and are connected by a network that allows communication and processes to be shipped and activated from site to site. In any discussion of the types we must consider some of the characteristics that differentiate these types. One factor that we have to consider is the homogeneity of the DDBMS software.

If all of the servers and all of the client computers and all of the software are identical throughout the DDBMS, then it is regarded as being homogeneous. If they are not, then it is regarded as heterogeneous.

Another factor to be considered is the degree of local autonomy. If the DDBMS has all access to the DDBMS through a client, then the system is said to have no local autonomy. If, however, there is direct access to the DDBMS by transactions and access is allowed to the server, then it is said to have some degree of local autonomy. The range of flexibility of autonomy is very wide. On the one hand, we can have a single view, which looks like a single centralized DDBMS and database and has access through a client. This provides no local autonomy and resembles a centralized system using distributed equipment for query and transaction purposes. On the opposite side of the range is the federated database, which is an amalgam of servers, each having its own independent DBMS, its own local transactions, and its own local users. This results in a high degree of autonomy because each system has to run independently, although they can be connected when necessary.

In a heterogeneous environment such as the federated database architecture, the needs of the other sites for access are handled by the use of export schemas that will allow the structure to be used and interpreted elsewhere. As you may have already surmised, the federated database is a hybrid of the distributed and centralized systems.

Problems in DDBMSs

There are numerous problems that occur in distributed environments that don't happen in the centralized ones. This is simply due to the complexity of one versus the other. The complexity is from both the physical components and the software components. There is also the network, which in fact has become part of the DDBMS. We can discuss some of the things here and then address each in a conceptual manner. The specific method needs to be addressed within and as part of the implementation of the vendor's DDBMS product.

One of the first problems is with the distributed information. Multiple copies of data such as reference data need to be kept in synchronicity with each other. A concurrency management mechanism needs to be in place that coordinates the consistency of these copies.

Individual Site Failure's Effect on Data Integrity

Failure of individual sites in the distributed network soon creates a situation where data has become nonsynchronous. Not only does the transaction activity to the site have to be rerouted or returned, it has to carry a message to resubmit or, better yet, automatically resubmit the transaction after the recovery is complete. It is for this reason that the recovery mechanism has to be tied to the concurrency manager to ensure that when the site does come up, it is immediately brought up to date so it can pick up where everyone else is at that point and subsequently open the door to transaction activity.

Individual Site Failure's Effect on Traffic Flow

Individual site failure can also have a profound effect on transaction flow. Based on the topology of the distributed environment, key sites may severely affect transaction routing and load balancing. While this is normally taken into consideration in the distributed database design, it also affects the dissemination and placement of the software that will accomplish the rerouting of activity should something go awry.

Communication Failure

Another problem associated with DDBMSs is the failure of the communication links. Complete dependency of the entire distributed environment is in the hands of the network. A mechanism must be part of the DDBMS that will ensure that the overall majority of the DDBMS and the applications that run on it can continue running autonomously until the communication failure has been corrected. One way to compartmentalize and limit failure is to partition the network into failure segments that will allow the DDBMS to do precisely that. Unfortunately, network partitioning increases the amount of complexity that has to be dealt with in both application access and backup and recovery.

Distributed Commitment

Distributed commitment for data integrity is another problem for DDBMSs. Commit strategies are developed to ensure that the integrity of the work is finalized or "committed" when the unit of work is completed. When the unit of work involves data from many sites, the "commit" cannot be done until all of the individual sites have completed their units of work. When a failure occurs, data must all be "rolled back" to what it was before any activity took place so a resubmission of a process will start with a fresh slate. A two-phase commit protocol has been developed that will address this by ensuring that there is an appropriate handshake made before the sites commit. Most DDBMSs have the capacity to handle two-phase commits.

Distributed Deadlocks

A deadlock or "deadly embrace" is defined as two different resources that require the same resource at the same time.

Normally, most DBMSs have a prioritization and sequencing scheme set up so no two processes are at the same point at the same time. It does occasionally happen, and when it does, there needs to be a mechanism in place that will choose one of the deadlocked partners as the victim and terminate it. Without this logic in place, a deadlock can cascade and build up additional locking to the point where the DBMS will fail and come down.

Within the distributed environment, deadlocks are more prevalent because the objects of access are distributed. Therefore, when Application A needs resources 1, 2, 3, 4, and 7 and Application B needs 3, 4, 5, 6, and 7, Application A takes what it needs and Application B takes what it needs. Whoever gets to 3 and 4 first will be the temporary owner of these until they are done with them. All this is fine until they both need 7. At this point, Application A has grabbed, say, 1, 2, and 7, and B has taken 3, 4, 5, and 6. What begins now is a deadly dance while each waits for the other to release its use of the conflicted resource. And each continually checks for the release by the other. Without the system choosing a victim, the machine would back up and come down.

Summary

This is a very broad subject area, and we have only touched on the salient points and concepts. If distributed databases hold promise for the company's business, then they should be investigated further. Remember the simple caveat: if you break it apart, remember two things: first, how many pieces there were, and second, how they all fit together.

Reference

Elmasri, Ramez, & Navathe, Shamkant B. (1999, August). *Fundamentals of database systems*. Reading, MA: Addison-Wesley.

INDEX

Printed and bound by CPI Group (UK) Ltd, Croydon, CR0 4YY

09/10/2024

01042666-0001